The Impact of
Devolution
in Wales

The Impact of
Devolution
in Wales

Social Democracy
with a Welsh Stripe?

Edited by

**Jane Williams
& Aled Eirug**

UNIVERSITY OF WALES PRESS
2022

www.uwp.co.uk

British Library Cataloguing-in-Publication Data
A catalogue record for this book is available from the British Library.

ISBN 978-1-78683-886-5
eISBN 978-1-78683-887-2

MIX
Paper from
responsible sources
FSC® C013604

Typeset by Marie Doherty
Printed by CPI Antony Rowe, Melksham, United Kingdom

Dedicated to the memory of
Mike Sullivan and Rhodri Morgan

CONTENTS

Tables and Illustrations   ix
About the Contributors   xi
Preface and Acknowledgements   xv
Foreword *by Prys Morgan*   xvii
Abbreviations   xxi
Chronology of Welsh Devolution   xxiii

Editors' Introduction   xxv
Aled Eirug and Jane Williams

Chapter 1:   The Sullivan Dialogues   1
             Aled Eirug

Chapter 2:   Iechyd Da? Devolution and Healthcare   35
             Ceri J. Phillips

Chapter 3:   Education in Wales since Devolution   61
             David Egan

Chapter 4:   Economic Development in Wales: Evolution   95
             and Revolution
             Gareth Davies

Chapter 5:   Welsh Devolution and the Quest for Sustainable   119
             Development: Into a New Era
             Terry Marsden

Chapter 6:   Civil Society, Equalities and Inclusion   151
             Elin Royles and Paul Chaney

Chapter 7:   Threads in Policy on Children and Young People: 179
             Rights and Well-being
             Jane Williams

Chapter 8: Towards a Million Speakers? Welsh Language   205
            Policy Post-devolution
            Huw Lewis and Elin Royles

Chapter 9: Wales and the World   235
            Geraint Talfan Davies

Index   265

TABLES AND ILLUSTRATIONS

2.1   Comparison of Welsh health surveys, 2003 and 2015   51

4.1   Gross Value added by UK nation, 1997–2017   102

6.1   Constitutional preferences in Wales, 1997–2011   167

6.2   Constitutional preferences in Wales, 2014–20   167

8.1   Summary of strategic themes, targets and aims included in *Cymraeg 2050*   212

8.2   The main actors involved in Welsh language revitalisation governance   222

9.1   Welsh exports 2013–2018   259

ABOUT THE CONTRIBUTORS

Paul Chaney is co-director of Wales Institute of Social and Economic Research, Data and Methods (WISERD), and professor of policy and politics at Cardiff University School of Social Sciences. He has served on various government advisory bodies including the UK Government steering group on the Equality and Human Rights Commission. He has authored or contributed to ten books and written over sixty papers in leading peer-reviewed journals. His research and teaching interests include territorial politics, public policy-making, civil society, and equality and human rights.

Gareth Davies is a professor in Swansea University's School of Management, specialising in innovation management and regional economic development. He worked on the Welsh Government's Knowledge Economy Nexus review of academic-industrial links and on projects around the world to develop science park and technology transfer models. He is experienced in supporting deployment of disruptive technologies for partners from micro-businesses to multinationals in multiple sectors and conducted appraisal work for the Swansea Bay City Region Deal. He is a member of the All-Wales Intensive Learning Academy for Innovation in Health and Social Care, and of a regional collaboration for health.

David Egan is emeritus professor of education at Cardiff Metropolitan University. In his early career he was a history teacher and researcher. From 1993 to 2000 he was head of the Cardiff School of Education at Cardiff Metropolitan University. From 2005 to 2008 he served as special adviser for education to the Welsh Government first minister and the Cabinet. In a further secondment to the Welsh government he is leading the development of a National Strategy for Educational Research and Enquiry. His research interests and publications range widely across the field of Welsh educational history, policy and practice.

Aled Eirug is a writer and broadcaster with over twenty-five years' experience as a journalist and broadcast executive. Formerly head of news and current affairs for BBC Wales and constitutional adviser to the National Assembly for Wales, he has served also as chair of the Welsh Refugee Council, member of the British Council board and member of Ofcom's content board. He has published two books, including one on opposition to the Great War. He was a founding member of the Morgan Academy, the policy think tank established by Professor Mike Sullivan in Rhodri Morgan's memory. He is a visiting research fellow at Cardiff University.

Huw Lewis is senior lecturer in politics at the Department of International Politics at Aberystwyth University. His research and teaching interests include language policy and planning, multiculturalism, nationalism and contemporary Welsh and UK politics. He coordinated the Revitalise research network, bringing together an international group of academics and practitioners to consider the implications of major instances of contemporary social change for our understanding on how language revitalisation efforts should be designed and implemented. He has authored multiple peer-reviewed publications on language policy and is co-author and co-editor of books on geographies of language and language revitalisation.

Ceri J. Phillips is emeritus professor of health economics at Swansea University, an honorary professor in Cardiff University School of Medicine and vice-chair of Cardiff and Vale University Health Board. He has been an independent board member of Health Education and Improvement Wales and Abertawe Bro Morgannwg University Health Board, head of the College of Human and Health Sciences at Swansea University, chair of the All Wales Medicines Strategy Group and member of the Bevan Commission. He has authored over 220 publications, advised Welsh and UK governments, and served on reviews, committees and evaluations for multiple organisations.

Terry Marsden is emeritus professor of environmental policy and planning at Cardiff University. He has served as head of the School of City and Regional Planning, director of the University Research Institute, Sustainable Places and as an external advisor on rural development, land management and agri-food policies to the Welsh Assembly, Senedd and Welsh Affairs UK parliamentary committee. He led the Marsden Report emerging from the Welsh Government's review of Welsh designated landscapes which he chaired. He is chair of the Alliance for Welsh Designated Landscapes, and writes on rural development and sustainable development issues.

Elin Royles is senior lecturer at the Department of International Politics, Aberystwyth University, and is a member of the Centre for Welsh Politics and Society. Her research and teaching are on territorial politics and sub-state governance. She has published on different areas of Welsh public policy post-devolution, particularly civil society, regional and minority language policy and planning, the international relations of sub-state governments and inter-governmental relations. She is involved in inter-disciplinary research grants on EU Horizon 2020-funded IMAJINE on Spatial Justice and Territorial Inequalities in Europe (EU Horizon 2020), and on Civil Stratification and Civil Repair (WISERD, ESRC).

Geraint Talfan Davies is a writer and broadcaster who has had a long involvement with public policy and the arts in Wales. He is chair of The Cyfarthfa Foundation, aiming to develop a national centre for industrial heritage at Merthyr Tydfil. He was controller of BBC Wales from 1990 until 2000. He is a co-founder of the Institute of Welsh Affairs and was its chairman from 1992 until 2014. He chaired Welsh National Opera, the Arts Council of Wales and Cardiff Bay Arts Trust, and was chair of Wales for Europe from 2016 until 2020. His memoir, *At Arm's Length*, was published in 2008.

Jane Williams is professor at Hillary Rodham Clinton School of Law, Swansea University. Formerly a practising barrister, UK and Welsh Government legal adviser and professional trainer, she was married to the late Professor Mike Sullivan and worked with him to produce the *Wales Journal of Law and Public Policy* (2001–6) and to advocate for legislation on the rights of the child in Wales. She is co-founder of the Observatory on Human Rights of Children, based at Swansea and Bangor universities. Her academic publications are in the fields of devolution, child law and children's rights.

PREFACE AND ACKNOWLEDGEMENTS

This volume's origin lies in a commitment made by the late Professor Mike Sullivan to write an academically grounded analysis to accompany Rhodri Morgan's personal memoir of his political life in Wales and Westminster. Rhodri's book was near completion at the time of his death in 2017 and the final editorial work was done by Mark Drakeford and Kevin Brennan, supported by the University of Wales Press.

Mike died the following year when work on his book remained at an early stage. This volume is not, of course, the book that Mike would have written. Instead, it contains a distillation from research he had conducted, together with contributions by scholars on the impact of Welsh devolved government in different policy fields, and reflections on present and future challenges and opportunities. In this way we have sought to honour Mike's dedication to better interaction between theory, practice, policy and research, especially in the context of the development of Wales post-devolution. His own academic work was always engaged with the question of how to make a positive difference through a process of social democracy. In a similar vein, in their different fields and in different ways, this volume's contributors each have contributed to the story of Welsh devolution.

As co-editors, we bring to the project personal as well as professional involvement with the lives and work of the two men to whom it is dedicated. Aled Eirug was head of news and current affairs for BBC Wales between 1992 and 2004, with a ring-side seat in the battle for devolution and its early manifestation. Between 2006 and 2011 he was constitutional adviser to the presiding officer of the National Assembly for Wales and, as such, involved in the process of separation of the parliamentary body of the Assembly from the Welsh Government. He witnessed Rhodri Morgan's ability to bridge political and cultural divides first-hand, and Mike Sullivan's success, when working on secondment as Rhodri's special adviser, in pursuing important policy improvements. Jane Williams, a former UK Government legal adviser, was assistant counsel general in the early months of the first National Assembly for Wales. She met and married Mike Sullivan after moving to Swansea University in 2000, and the two worked together on many aspects of devolved law and policy, most notably on the delivery of Rhodri Morgan's proposal for a Welsh law on children's rights.

We gratefully acknowledge the encouragement and support of the University of Wales Press in our endeavour, and the generosity of all the contributors who have engaged with us as we developed the project. Thanks are due to all the Dialogues participants who graciously agreed to our approach to deployment of their insights. Special thanks to Julie Morgan, Mark Drakeford, Jane Hutt and Helen Mary Jones for their encouragement and support. Finally, we wish to thank Professor Emeritus Prys Morgan, Rhodri's elder brother, for his uniquely insightful foreword to this volume. Responsibility for the content of this volume, for good or ill, lies with us as editors.

Aled Eirug and Jane Williams, May 2021

FOREWORD

Prys Morgan

I can see three important themes outlined by the editors of this book appearing in my brother's youth. One is the distinctive Welshness of his family background. Another is the urge for social reform arising from the inequalities of contiguous but contrasting areas of south Wales in the 1930s. A third is the growing importance of Welsh institutions in the 1950s and 1960s. I rarely heard Rhodri talk about political theories. So it was a surprise to me, when I was about to give the opening talk to the International Folk Song Conference in Cardiff in 2008, to hear Rhodri as First Minister come to inaugurate the conference, revealing something of his political principles. Explaining that his mother had been a devotee of Welsh folk songs, he said that he saw the conference uniting two of the important themes of his political life, his purpose as First Minister being to reconcile two different kinds of Wales, the UrWales – he pronounced this in German – of his family background, and the 'Cosmopolitan Wales' of the present day.

What did he mean by UrWales? He explained that his father was a Celtic scholar and academic, a Welsh author and literary critic, his mother also a Welsh writer, so he was brought up surrounded by Welsh books, with a network of family friends who met in cultural societies or in Eisteddfodau, to discuss things Welsh. He also meant that his background in Victorian Welsh radicalism associated with religious dissent. His great-grandfather had been evicted from his tenant farm for speaking on political platforms on Welsh land reform with Tom Ellis MP, and he in turn had had a grandfather who had been imprisoned (with his wife and family) for leading the Rebecca Riots near Swansea in 1843. He explained that he saw the new National Assembly as a meeting place for blending the traditional Wales with the larger world of modern urban secular Welsh society, in order to create a sense of unity, self-confidence and resourcefulness.

The second formative influence was Rhodri's upbringing in Radyr. The suburb we knew was a late Victorian creation of the Earls of Plymouth to house the managerial classes around its golf club, with a railway station for people in 'The Valleys' who could not find land to build or golf, or for those who were 'Something on the Docks'. One of my earliest childhood memories was of the morning parade of the nannies in their grey uniforms showing off their babies in Silver Cross prams. People often told our parents not to ruin our careers by talking Welsh to us, and whenever our neighbour could hear me calling Rhodri in the garden, would start to whistle 'There'll always be an England'. Our parents, when they rented a house there in 1955, were able to walk the few miles north to Gwaelod-y-garth to Welsh chapels there. This was the contrasting world of unemployed miners, with our friend Mrs G. J. Williams (whose husband had been one of the founders of Plaid Genedlaethol Cymru) teaching quilting to the miners' wives, so as to bring some income to the village. My mother, after completing her research degree under Saunders Lewis in Swansea, had found work in 1929 teaching Welsh in Rhymni at the top of the Gwent valleys, an area of total unemployment, where the children were so hungry that they slumbered all day until the weekly arrival of a train from Eastbourne brought clothes and food parcels in a kind of Oxfam rescue operation. Such stories created a haunting contrast to Radyr's political world, dominated by its Conservative MP Sir Lewis Lougher.

I recall standing with Rhodri in 1945 at the Cardiff end of Heol Isaf in Radyr listening to Lynn Ungoed-Thomas (Labour candidate for the Barry constituency) canvassing with a loudspeaker; by the elections of the 1950s, Rhodri, with his highly developed sense of politics, forced my mother and me to go with him to the church rooms for political meetings. Rhodri was furious with the way Dorothy Rees (Labour) was howled down and reduced to tears by the Radyr Tory mob. In 1955 he floored Raymond Gower (Conservative) with a question as to which of the three constitutions offered to Cyprus the candidate would recommend. Did he retain memory of it? When Rhodri entered the Commons in 1987 nobody could have been kinder or more welcoming than Raymond Gower.

Despite the dramatic contrast of valleys poverty and suburban prosperity to be found cheek-by-jowl between Gwaelod-y-garth and Radyr, there was a third element emerging in the Radyr of the 1950s, which rendered the picture more nuanced. We noticed that as several of the older capitalist families moved out of Radyr to places such as Llanblethian, their place was taken by civil servants or employees of corporations such as the BBC. T. J. Morgan himself had worked during the war as the secretary to the Wales Tribunal on National Service, and during the 1950s was registrar of the University of Wales; our closest friend in Radyr was A. B. Oldfield-Davies, 'Controller Wales' of the BBC; another neighbour, Bill Arnold, was the director of the Temple of Peace and the Welsh branch of the United Nations Association; another friend Iorwerth Peate was the creator of the Welsh Folk Museum at St Fagans; and yet another, William Thomas, was the under-secretary of the Ministry of Housing and Local Government, in the very building in Cathays Park where Rhodri later had his office as first minister. This was the world into which Rhodri would go as a young technocrat in the 1960s. This awareness of the potential of Cardiff as a real capital city came initially from his knowledge of the wider circle of friends of the family in the 1950s, powering the reasoning of Rhodri's book, *Cardiff: Half-and-half a Capital*.*

Just as Rhodri envisaged the new Assembly as a body that could unify his UrWales and cosmopolitan Wales, or could act to bring greater prosperity to poverty-stricken Wales, so he also saw that an Assembly could harness the know-how of Cardiff's jumble of national regional and local bodies to empower Wales. It would not be easy, and Rhodri told me that he did not expect to see the Assembly truly accepted for a generation. But I recall that in March 2011, when I was being nursed back to health by Rhodri and Julie in their home after a serious operation, how immensely gratified he was by the general approval of the Assembly shown by all parts of Wales in the second referendum. He said, 'I think I can retire a happy man.' I remonstrated, 'Surely Enoch Powell said the careers of all politicians end in disappointment?' He replied, 'In this as in so many things, Enoch was wrong.'

---

* Rhodri Morgan, *Cardiff: Half-and-half a Capital* (Llandysul: Gomer, 1994).

ABBREVIATIONS

ACW   Arts Council of Wales
IWA   Institute of Welsh Affairs
NAW   National Assembly for Wales
NGO   Non-governmental Organisation
WAG   Welsh Assembly Government
WDA   Welsh Development Agency
WAI   Wales Arts International
WG   Welsh Government

CHRONOLOGY OF WELSH DEVOLUTION

1979   Referendum
1997   White Paper and referendum
1998   Government of Wales Act
1999   Elections to first Assembly
2000   Rhodri Morgan becomes First Minister. Partnership
        agreement (Labour/Liberal Democrats coalition)
2003   Elections to second Assembly
2004   Report of the Richard Commission
2006   Government of Wales Act
2007   Elections to third Assembly and One Wales coalition
2010   Carwyn Jones becomes First Minister
2011   Second referendum and elections to fourth Assembly.
        Silk Commission set up
2013   First Silk Commission report
2014   Second Silk Commission report
2014   Wales Act
2016   Elections to fifth Assembly
2017   Wales Act
2018   Mark Drakeford becomes First Minister
2021   Elections to the Senedd

EDITORS' INTRODUCTION

Aled Eirug and Jane Williams

This book was inspired by two great friends, the late Professor Mike Sullivan and the late Rhodri Morgan. Mike had undertaken to write an analytical account of Rhodri's political legacy and its place in the context of distinctive themes in public policy that have developed within the exercise of devolved governmental powers. To that end, during 2018, Mike conducted interviews to gather the reflections of selected protagonists and observers of Rhodri's tenure as first minister. We have been able to draw upon these both in our chapter 'The Sullivan Dialogues' and in the task of curating the essays that follow it in this volume. Mike's epithet of 'social democracy with a Welsh stripe' has remained for us apt to describe a direction of travel enabled by Rhodri's political leadership and which seems likely to endure into a third decade of Welsh devolution. At the same time, the totality of the contributions to this volume paints a complex, multifaceted picture of the drivers of policy, of continuity from the pre-devolution era as well as change driven by factors beyond as well as within Wales.

For those who longed for greater recognition of Wales as a nation in the modern world, the referendum of 1997, which led to the establishment of the National Assembly for Wales, was the vindication of a long campaign that could be dated back to the 1890s. The creation of the National Assembly for Wales was the result of a compromise that delivered a single corporate body encompassing both executive and parliamentary functions. Constitutional progress followed, with the move to a more traditional separation of executive and legislative powers in 2007, followed by enhanced law-making competence and latterly independent tax-raising powers. At the time of writing, debate on further progression has shifted to embrace increasingly radical and wide-ranging constitutional reform in the context of a United Kingdom in which relations between the component nations must be re-thought following its exit from the European Union. In Wales it has been a remarkable journey from an unpromising, fragile beginning, to this point. A theme emerging strongly from the Sullivan Dialogues is Rhodri Morgan's pivotal role in achieving recognition and acceptance for Welsh devolution and its institutions.

Despite a continuing lack of coherence in the powers devolved to Wales, successive Welsh governments have managed to develop distinct policies in many fields. Labour has been the governing party since 1999 but not always with a working majority and never with a large majority of seats in the Assembly. Collaboration and compromise between and within political parties has been essential. Rhodri Morgan was, perhaps, uniquely able to unify the twin traditions of Labour and Welsh patriotism. Whether or not he embodied both the red of Labour and the green of Welsh nationalism, in which he saw no contradiction, Rhodri warned against Labour failing to place itself within its own distinctively Welsh political tradition and did much to create the 'masterstroke'* of 'Welsh Labour'.

Much has been written about the politics and constitutional development of Welsh devolution, and somewhat less about its impact in terms of policy, policy process and their ultimate consumers: the citizens of Wales. It is in this space that we hope this volume will contribute. A mixed picture emerges, featuring variously (and in various combinations of) boldness of ambition, distinctive ideological positioning, homegrown priority-setting, the frustrations of the devolution settlement and adverse, arguably unfair, international comparisons.

The largest part of the Welsh budget, at over 50 per cent, is spent on health. Ceri Phillips's assessment of the state of the nation's health concludes that hopeful devolutionists underestimated how difficult it was to reform the sector. Wales's health has improved but, he observes, fundamental economic and social inequalities persist. A broadly consistent, distinct 'Welsh way' in health care, pre- as well as post-devolution, has been frustrated in its implementation by complex factors including cross-border comparisons and issues of quality in service delivery. This is echoed by David Egan in his chapter on the second biggest spending field, education, although he points also to the utility of looking to comparisons with small nations outside the UK. Egan applauds Welsh

---

* Adam Price, quoted in Chapter 1 in this volume.

innovations in the foundation phase and national curriculum but finds overall a disappointing lack of boldness in Welsh governments' approach to educational reform.

Gareth Davies's chapter on economic development also shows a disappointing picture, with no real improvement in economic performance. He emphasises the lasting bond with the wider UK economy and the Welsh Government's (WG) lack of the necessary economic levers to effect economy recovery. There is no 'devolution dividend' as such, yet it is also difficult to gauge whether, in the context of austerity and economic crisis (2008–16), and the decline of foreign direct investment, the failure to narrow the economic gap with the rest of the UK was inevitable. Davies suggests that WG's shift in emphasis from attracting inward investment to developing indigenous companies may have longer-term impact.

Several of the essays point to devolution as an important accelerator to policy development. One of the most remarkable innovations, stitched into the Welsh devolution settlement from the start, was the principle of sustainable development as a guiding duty on the exercise of devolved governance. This, coupled with the shared vision of key political protagonists, including Morgan himself, enabled progression in policy and the enactment of the groundbreaking Well-being of Future Generations (Wales) Act 2015. Terry Marsden's chapter however reinforces the impact of 'events', specifically how the shock of Brexit undermined a 20-year political consensus and galvanised the onset of what he calls 'disruptive governance'. He links debates about the future of food and the environment with issues about participative and devolved forms of effective democratic governance.

Elin Royles and Paul Chaney emphasise the central role of 'civil society', 'equality' and 'inclusiveness' to both the structure and practice of devolution in Wales, and how this has shaped an approach to policy development and service delivery. They explore how devolution has institutionalised the promotion of equalities and the engagement of civil society, achieved through the investment of significant levels of political capital and instances of cross-party working. They point to a resultant devolution dividend for interest representation, at least for those groups sufficiently large or well-connected, as the locus of policy advocacy and negotiation has shifted to Welsh national institutions. This may have helped to grow a sense of Welsh national civic identity which, in turn, has helped to legitimise the devolution project itself.

Increased opportunity for civil society influence features also in Jane Williams's chapter on the Welsh children's rights legislation. She examines the resonances between the international law on the rights of the child, now drawn into the law of Wales, and an agenda for social justice, supporting the notion of 'social democracy with a Welsh stripe'. Common to Royles and Chaney's discussion of equalities and Williams's discussion of children's rights is the challenge of effective 'mainstreaming' following efforts to systematise 'due regard' to the desired objectives of, respectively, equality (whether of opportunity or outcome) and real-isation of children's human rights. In both arenas, these contributors conclude that devolution has enabled the construction of new citizen rights distinctive to Wales. In terms of hard outcomes for children, by conventional measures such as health, educational achievement and pov-erty eradication, Williams, in common with Phillips, Egan and Davies, notes as yet, little change.

Huw Lewis and Elin Royles emphasise the changing nature of Welsh language policy as one of continuity from the creation of the Welsh Language Board by the Conservative Government in 1993, through to the Welsh Language Act of 2011 and the creation of the role of the Welsh Language Commissioner. Lastly, Geraint Talfan Davies draws on his experience as an arts administrator to assess WG's record in the arts and in projecting Wales in the international context.

At the time of submission of our manuscript to the University of Wales Press, in May 2021, the elections for the first Senedd (and sixth term of devolved parliamentary government) have delivered a further period of continuity in Welsh Labour's dominance, with thirty of the sixty Senedd seats. The thread of 'social democracy with a Welsh stripe' discussed here both in relation to the legacy of Rhodri Morgan, and in relation to the areas of public policy that we have examined, might therefore be expected to continue to characterise the further evolution of practices and policies in Welsh devolution. As ever, only time will tell.

1

THE SULLIVAN DIALOGUES

Aled Eirug

This chapter is based on a series of interviews that the late Prof. Mike Sullivan conducted with nineteen of the key people in the development of Welsh devolution between 1997 and 2018.[1]

Whilst professor of social policy at Swansea University, Mike Sullivan chaired the very first exercise to identify and select Labour candidates for the inaugural National Assembly election in 1999. He served as a specialist policy adviser on health policy within the Welsh Government (WG) between 2007 and 2011 and was particularly influential in and around the formation of the One Wales administration, which created the coalition between Labour and Plaid Cymru. He was a key figure in shaping the children's rights agenda, and in ensuring that WG's legislation on children's rights was put in place. On his return to academic life after 2011, his experience of the One Wales coalition led him to join Plaid Cymru.

Mike Sullivan had given a commitment to Rhodri Morgan, the former First Minister (2000–9), and chancellor of Swansea University, that he would write the story of devolution from a more analytical and academic perspective than Morgan's engaging autobiography. He conducted nineteen interviews with key politicians that would pave the way for this companion book which attempts to provide a more sober analysis of the successes and failures of devolution. Inevitably, the interviews dwell on the years 2007–11, when both Mike Sullivan and Rhodri Morgan were part of government, but they also delve into the political crises of the early 2000s, when for many devotees of devolution, its prospects seemed bleak.

Rhodri Morgan's autobiography is revealing in its recognition of the precariousness of the early years of the National Assembly. Its editors, Mark Drakeford and Kevin Brennan, compared devolution to 'a delicate and fragile flower to be nurtured, grown organically, and never to be taken for granted. The fact that there was a future for devolution owed more to Rhodri than anyone else.'[2] The crucial contribution of Rhodri Morgan and the other factors that served to rescue this new political process are examined in this chapter.

Rhodri's personal background and character are key to an understanding of his politics and what lay behind his approach to devolution. His mother had been a supporter of Plaid Cymru and his father inclined towards the Labour Party, but generally had a low opinion of politicians. His brother, Dr Prys Morgan, dismisses the idea of him as a 'crypto-nationalist' and recalls him advising young Welshmen against joining Plaid Cymru in Oxford University in the late 1950s.[3]

After gaining a degree in philosophy, politics and economics at Oxford, Rhodri Morgan studied for a masters in government at Harvard University. On his return, he was employed by the Workers Educational Association, and joined the Labour Party a month later, in December 1963. The doyen of Welsh historians, Prof. K. O. Morgan got to know him in the USA and regarded him as less of a philosopher than a practical, pragmatic thinker. His political views were articulated even then:

> He was very strongly committed to the European Movement ... he saw Wales as part of its own evolution ... but tied in with developments in Europe too. He believed very much in a regional Europe. I saw Rhodri as a kind of Fabian really, a Fabian with a Welsh accent. He was a man who was sort of left of centre but not far left. I think a book that had quite an impact on him was Hilary Marquand's book *South Wales Needs a Plan*[4] which is really an appeal for a more distributive but active state policy with the central government in Westminster that would have to do it. The central government in Westminster had destroyed much in south Wales so its power should be used to rebuild in south Wales. That was the kind of thing which had quasi-nationalist overtones. It never struck me that Rhodri was any kind of nationalist ... but he certainly did see Wales as being different and distinct and needing separate government formations.[5]

Morgan went on to become a planning officer in South Glamorgan County Council, then the Welsh Office and the Department of Trade and Industry in Whitehall, before becoming the European Commission's regional officer for Wales in 1980. He became Member of Parliament for Cardiff West in 1987 and gained a reputation as a combative and aggressive deputy shadow spokesman on Wales in the House of Commons. He showed a willingness to take on the Welsh political establishment represented by unelected 'quangos' (quasi-autonomous non-governmental organisations), such as the Welsh Development Agency (WDA), led by the Conservative Government's appointees. But he was dropped unceremoniously by Tony Blair after the 1997 election and, as a backbencher for the following two years, became a respected and fearless chairman of the Select Committee on Public Administration before being elected to the National Assembly for Wales (NAW) in May 1999.

Creating Welsh Labour

During the 1990s, Rhodri Morgan played a key role in shaping Labour's devolution policy for Wales. He was shadow deputy Secretary of State to Ron Davies covering Welsh affairs, and his role in Westminster led him to expect to be a government minister after Labour's election win in May 1997.

His reputation in the period 1992–7 was that of an iconoclastic troublemaker against the Welsh political establishment, no more so in his unsuccessful opposition to the development of the Cardiff Bay Barrage, and his hounding of what he viewed as unaccountable and undemocratic quangos, such as the WDA. In doing so, he alienated the more traditionalist wing of the Labour Party in Wales.

Lawrence Conway had met him first of all when he worked as a civil servant in the Welsh Office and was later parliamentary clerk in its office in Whitehall. He worked on the Cardiff Barrage Bill which Rhodri Morgan opposed vehemently, whilst Alun Michael supported it enthusiastically:

> I was from Grangetown, and I resented the way in which the Nick Edwardses of this world and Inkins and everything else was being geared towards giving ABP this huge public sector gift in order for them to develop the whole Cardiff Bay area … His feeling was similar – it was a resentment of these people coming in to change what he would regard as his city, in the same way as I did. This is a key part of Rhodri's makeup, looking back at

it all. This iconoclasm – he should have been natural Plaid, but he wasn't because he had a strong sense of social justice, and he rejected the Saunders Lewis stuff.[6]

Both Andrew Davies and Edwina Hart, brought up in Swansea Labour politics, were shocked by the virulence of party politics in Cardiff and the hostility of the local Labour establishment towards Rhodri Morgan:

> they were frightened and fearful that he actually believed in devolution, that it wasn't going to be a cosmetic exercise to keep people happy, it was actually going to be real, and it was actually going to develop and evolve … they were frightened of him intellectually, he was bright. He was certainly a one-off, he was great company, and he personified the split there was in Cardiff Labour politics in the 80s and 90s between Alun (Michael) and Rhodri. Rhodri represented Cardiff West, and Alun Michael represented Cardiff South and Penarth. Alun was very much a machine politician, the creature of Lord Jack Brooks, who was Callaghan's agent. That split was a symbolic face-off between that long-standing and deep-seated culture, and continued into the Assembly in later life, because there was a group around Rhodri when he was First Minister. There was Mark Drakeford, Jane Hutt, Sue Essex, otherwise known as the 'Riverside Mafia' … and on the other side, you had Russell Goodway … I couldn't believe how poisonous politics was in Cardiff. Swansea politics was bad enough, but this was something else, really personal.[7]

This poison spread publicly when Goodway's reign as council leader was brought to an end after 2004's local election, and he accused Rhodri Morgan of having attempted to oust him.[8] Rhodri Morgan had already succeeded in preventing Goodway from being selected as the parliamentary candidate for a by-election in 2002 in the safe Labour seat of Ogmore.[9]

Rhodri was married to Julie in 1967 and their political and personal partnership guided him to understand how women should contribute to politics. He was 'very pro women'[10] and progressive, and he and Julie were driving forces behind the controversial adoption of 'twinning', that ensured that women Labour candidates were selected for at least half of the Labour nominations in the 1999 National Assembly election. Inevitably he allied with Julie's Labour council colleagues – the 'Riverside Mafia' – who were constant thorns in the side of Russell Goodway and Lord Jack Brooks, the patrician Labour establishment running the council. This group were close friends and counted Rhodri as one of their number, but his political experience was that of a civil servant. His intellectual hinterland was more pragmatic and technocratic, less ideological and tribal. Rhodri Morgan, according to Jane Hutt, 'was always seen as a great character, huge brain, wonderful memory, good socially, very well loved'.[11] One of his early tests as a Member of Parliament was the controversy over the Cardiff Bay Barrage scheme, in which Jane Hutt and Mark Drakeford opposed the project and were suspended by the party's council leadership. He eventually opposed the barrage, but as Hutt recalls, did not do so unquestioningly, but when he did so, 'he was formidable'.[12]

For his future adviser, Paul Griffiths, who came from a background of activism in local politics, Rhodri Morgan's reputation as a maverick was sparked by the fact that he was an 'outsider':

> He didn't fit the expectations of many mainstream politicians around him – he made relationships far and wide and was fascinated by everyone he met. But I'm not convinced that this maverick tendency converted to policy or ideological terms. I don't think Rhodri was hugely enthused himself by political ideas. He was enthused by people and by getting things done, keeping people on side.[13]

This view of Rhodri as an outsider is echoed in Mike Sullivan's memory of Rhodri Morgan relating his sense of detachment after a particularly difficult meeting of the Welsh Labour Party executive:

> The atmosphere was icy between the apparatchiks including Rhodri … They hate you, or at least they behave as if they do. 'Yeah', he said, 'that's probably pretty close to it.' I said, 'Why do you put up with it?' and he said, 'because I'm that unknown person who is in the tent pissing in.' So he obviously saw himself as in some way very deeply embedded within the movement but at the same time not of them at all.[14]

Rhodri Morgan, by his own admission, felt 'disrespected' by Blair's refusal to give him a ministerial post in the new Labour Government in 1997, even though he had been a shadow minister for Welsh affairs and energy for nine years.[15] In the absence of a commitment by Ron Davies to stand for the leadership in Wales, he threw his hat in the ring. But Davies finally decided to stand in July 1998, and Rhodri Morgan, partly handicapped by his lack of ministerial experience in government, but more fundamentally by Tony Blair's opposition, lost the subsequent election. Credited as the architect of devolution, Davies won the support of over 90 per cent of trade union and affiliated bodies, 60 per cent of MPs, MEPs and assembly candidates, and 52 per cent of the local parties. But within weeks, on 27 October 1998, Davies sensationally resigned, following his 'moment of madness' on Clapham Common, where he was mugged at knifepoint.[16]

Tony Blair made it abundantly clear to Rhodri Morgan that Alun Michael was now undoubtedly his preferred candidate for the Welsh Labour leadership, but Michael's burden was to then appear to be London Labour's candidate rather than Welsh Labour's choice. Whilst Rhodri Morgan had already been chosen for an Assembly seat, Alun Michael had to be shoehorned into the regional list for south-west Wales against local wishes, which did not necessarily guarantee him a seat, and which embarrassed him throughout his leadership campaign. The leadership developed into a battle over the nature of Blairism. Roy Hattersley, previously deputy leader of the party, accused Alun Michael of being Blair's 'poodle':

> Blair dictates that, in principle democracy must be extended at every level. But, in practice, that means only as long as Tony Blair can be guaranteed the result which he wants ... By its very nature, devolution means that sometimes Cardiff will disagree with London. If the Prime Minister is not prepared to risk the leader of the Welsh Assembly arguing for Wales, he is denying the purpose of the Assembly's existence.[17]

Paul Griffiths recalls that, during this period, he watched the way in which parts of the Labour Party set themselves against Rhodri and worked hard to prevent him becoming leader:

He just wasn't part of their gang, but having said that he never sought to set himself against Blair … [and before 1999] he desperately wanted to be a junior minister and he was genuinely disappointed and perplexed, didn't understand how it could be that he hadn't been selected.[18]

The Prime Minister's support for Michael proved to be key. He visited Wales three times to endorse his candidacy and on 20 February 1999, following a three-month campaign, Alun Michael's victory was announced. In spite of the Labour hierarchy ranged against Rhodri Morgan, he had won the vote amongst the membership, but failed to gain a majority of the trade union block votes and, not unexpectedly, the support of elected Members of Parliament and Assembly candidates. As defeated candidate, his ebullience was reflected in his loser's acceptance speech, 'I don't feel like a loser tonight. Runner-up, Yes! Loser, No!'[19]

Rhodri Morgan understood that devolution would change the nature of Welsh politics – and that devolution under Labour would fail if Wales was perceived as a branch office of Labour HQ. The leader had to be not only from Wales but to be made in Wales, and for Labour to succeed in the devolution era, he thought that the party needed to prevent space opening up between being Labour and being Welsh. He viewed the state of the Labour Party in Scotland as a dire warning to the party in Wales:

He thought the party in Scotland was absolutely awful, that they were arrogant and un-Scottish. Because of their Irish Catholic base in Glasgow, they didn't like Scottish Presbyterianism. The result is the Scottish Labour Party is hopeless at trying to pretend that it can fly the standard of Scottishness and therefore it's very vulnerable to a very Scottish Party. 'We mustn't let that happen in Wales … there are enough very Welshy people inside for us to fly the standard of Welshness and that is the way we will keep Plaid at bay.'[20]

The Prime Minister had tried to persuade him not to stand, citing Rhodri's ministerial inexperience, an ironic argument given that Tony Blair had only held ministerial office for a matter of months. Blair viewed Rhodri as a 'maverick':

He was very similar to Blair in many ways. He was from the same type of background as Tony Blair ... they'd been to the same college in Oxford and so on, so Rhodri couldn't be terribly impressed by Tony Blair.[21]

Blair's parents had lived in Radyr, and Rhodri believed that Tony Blair associated Wales with the tragedy of his mother's death there at the early age of 52. Prys Morgan recalls that in 1998–9:

Rhodri began to realise that Tony Blair disliked Wales, 'fucking Welsh' always and he could never talk about the Welsh without 'fucking Wales' and so on. Tony Blair introduced Rhodri, in 10 Downing Street at a seminar, and said 'I'm sure you're all looking forward to hearing what the First Minister has got to say, about this, so without any more ado. Rodney, you fire away Rodney,' he said. And Rhodri said 'Oh, thank you very much for those kind words of introduction, Toby, that really was kind of you Toby, and launched into his talk.'[22]

In his autobiography, Rhodri referred only fleetingly to Blair because he 'did not want to give reviewers or the public a chance to say that I'm dividing the Labour Party. In the end, Tony Blair did not stop devolution, which he could easily have done.'[23] Rhodri feared Blair's attitude towards Wales because he thought that he would go back on his word and cause endless difficulties in allowing Wales to establish and develop devolution. Tony Blair was the dog that didn't bark. In the end he did play along, so he didn't want to portray him negatively.[24]

May 1999 to May 2003

The NAW elections in 1999 proved a serious setback for Labour. The Labour Party lost heartland seats, including Neil Kinnock's old seat of Islwyn, the Rhondda, Llanelli, and won twenty-eight seats out of a total of sixty – twenty-seven of them constituency seats, and just one out of regional list seats. With no majority, Labour was therefore 'in office' but not 'in power'.[25] Helen Mary Jones was the winning Plaid Cymru candidate in Llanelli in May 1999, and recalled the reverberations of the election:

This was the 'dragons versus poodles'[26] period and the impact of Alun Michael being imposed as Labour leader ... from my perspective, undoubtedly contributed to how well Plaid Cymru did in that election, particularly in places like Llanelli, Islwyn and Rhondda. Ordinary long-standing Labour were really angry, they felt they had been forced to accept a leader they hadn't chosen ... I think people also knew they had a Welsh Westminster Labour Government with a strong overall majority so in a sense they could afford to kick against Labour.[27]

The early chaotic months of the National Assembly, before Rhodri's election as First Minister, had seen the new institution descend into 'rancorous contention and bitter partisan arguments'; by February 2000, its very existence sat on a knife-edge.[28] The wafer-thin vote for the Assembly, in September 1997, Labour's wrangling for the Welsh leadership and the limitations set by the difficulty of running an effective minority government contributed to a sense of drift. Whilst Alun Michael had defeated Rhodri Morgan to become leader of the Labour Party in Wales and First Secretary, in the Assembly he had failed to gain the trust of his political opponents, many of his group Assembly members and his loss of a no confidence motion – ostensibly on the subject of the government's failure to secure match-funding from the Treasury for European Objective One funding – triggered his ill-tempered resignation. He was succeeded by Rhodri Morgan, who won unanimous support from the Labour group.

Rhodri Morgan's unwavering belief in the importance of devolution and his own sense of personal destiny was reflected in his commitment to the project. His wife and political soulmate, Julie Morgan, saw Rhodri Morgan's innate self-confidence as his main asset in leading the minority government:

that confidence really ... in a way almost put him beyond party and he wanted everyone to be part of it. He was able to relate very well to people from all sorts of different beliefs and different sections of society, such as economic development and dealing with business people ... He was very determined to avoid the problem he could see emerging in Scotland where people were being taught that if you saw yourself as Scottish, that meant having to vote for the SNP. He was determined I think, that in

Wales, to vote Labour and to be Welsh would be as natural as you could imagine and that those two identities had to be right on top of another and he lived it out himself. It wasn't an act. It was how he was.[29]

The veteran Conservative member of the Senedd David Melding viewed the assembly's plight at the time as existential:

Rhodri was almost the metaphor for the political situation in Wales in terms of a very narrow result for the Assembly ... In Alun Michael, we had a leader that needed to form a stable government and project enthusiasm about the project and I'm afraid he struggled on both those counts, in that he decided to lead a minority government ... Alun Michael was a very House of Commons man and someone that I think wanted to be in the heart of the UK Government. Everyone looked at Rhodri and thought, 'Well he wants to do the job, and probably had an idea of what needed to be done quickly' and I think more or less that's what happened when he became First Minister.

It was a very strange time. An infant institution endorsed by the thinnest of margins in a referendum against this over-whelmingly large and mighty political tradition at the British level, to try and eke out its own little niche and personality. I think most of us felt that Alun Michael's tenure was not secure as Wales's political leader. I believe Rhodri believed in urgency, that the prize had been snatched away from him ... but then ... the wider Welsh political forces did exert themselves and that's when in an odd way this false start created a firmer foundation for the assembly to succeed.[30]

Mark Drakeford recalled the parlous state of the Assembly in its first year, under Alun Michael's leadership:

when I arrived in the Assembly in the beginning of May 2000, I thought this institution might not last. People are exhausted. They are the end of their tether. They are hand to mouth. Unless we manage to turn this around, we may all conclude in a short order that this was just a bad mistake and it couldn't be made to work. I always felt that the tide turned during that autumn. Primarily because we got the stability to be able to have a government that could make its writ run on the floor of the Assembly, but then a series of events happened. Foot-and-mouth, flooding, the fuel crisis, and suddenly there was a sense of when something went wrong in Wales, where do people look?[31]

In Rhodri Morgan's view, the turning point for public acceptance of the National Assembly was in the autumn of 2000, and formation of the partnership government with the Liberal Democrats, that gave much needed stability to the new institution. The Welsh public gained confidence from the way in which WG met the challenges of the crises that struck the United Kingdom from the autumn of 2000. The fuel tanker driver dispute in September 2000, in which tanker drivers and small hauliers opposed increases to fuel duty, triggered the first public test for the Blair government and, whilst not a devolved matter, also tested the National Assembly and WG. Further crises, such as the serious flooding in October 2000, and the decision by the Corus steel company to make 3,000 employees redundant across Wales, including closing the Ebbw Vale steelworks and Llanwern steelworks, made the National Assembly seem more responsive to the public mood than the UK Government. But the most momentous crisis of all was the foot-and-mouth outbreak, which dominated the work of the National Assembly until August 2001. This outbreak caused the 2001 General Election to be postponed for a month because of curbs on movement. Again, animal health policy at the time was not devolved, but the Welsh Agriculture Minister, Carwyn Jones, earned his political spurs in this crisis as an adroit and decisive minister.

Within days of arriving as First Minister, chief whip Andrew Davies and his special adviser, Kevin Brennan, were dispatched to talk to the Liberal Democrats 'as the most obvious fit' for coalition:

Once they were within government, he absolutely regarded them as ministers in the same way as anybody else ... and that was against a lot of backwash from the Labour Party ... He made a deal [with the Liberal Democrats] and he then went on the road ... I remember going to a meeting in Newport. It was a difficult and bitter meeting. Harry Jones, the leader of

Newport council, called him a traitor. We forget the strength of that feeling, and there were people in the Labour group whose own careers had to be moved to one side, often with good reason, to make way, and they never forgot this. The price of coalition was high, but it brought stability ... I think Rhodri believed that coalition governments brought a greater degree of internal challenge to decision making. He felt that it gave an intellectual edge.[32]

One of Rhodri Morgan's key qualities was his ability to strike the right balance between emphasising the developing autonomy of the new devolved Assembly, and working effectively with the UK Government in Westminster. But Rhodri also loved the House of Commons and Westminster, and enjoyed interacting with politicians at a UK level: 'to be so fully at home in two such different places was a rare quality, and it was to the advantage of devolution that, just at the point when it mattered the most, the project was in the hands of someone who was decidedly at home in both'.[33]

His leadership style was consensual and in sharp contrast to Alun Michael's micro-management, who took control over all ministerial decisions, whereas Rhodri had greater faith in his ministers: 'Rhodri knew how to work with other people, and he trusted people ... it worked because he saw the end game as being about embedding devolution moving forward.'[34] His continuing support for women in the assembly's Labour group was reflected in his appointment of women to most of the senior jobs in his administrations. When he carried out his first Cabinet reshuffle, in creating the partnership administration with the Liberal Democrats, he brought five women into ministerial office: Jenny Randerson from the Lib Dems, and Sue Essex, Edwina Hart, Jane Hutt and Jane Davidson from Labour. His 2000–3 Lab-Lib Democrat Cabinet had a majority of women, and when he stood down, women had been responsible for every Cabinet portfolio, other than economic development, and that was put right when Edwina Hart took on the job from May 2011 to May 2015.

Beyond ministerial appointments, his record was as strong. He supported and agitated for gender equality inside the Labour Party, and delivered a groundbreaking candidate selection process to ensure gender equality and equal opportunity principles, and the result was a Labour group in the second Assembly (2003–7) made of nineteen women and eleven men. He selected the first woman permanent secretary, Dame Gillian Morgan, in 2008, and later supported Rosemary Butler for the role of presiding officer in 2011.

The constitutional reformer

Rhodri Morgan was determined to resolve some of the critical issues facing the new institution, commissioning Lord Ivor Richard to conduct a review of the early period of devolution, which was to lead to the 2006 Government of Wales Act, and that changed the National Assembly from a corporate body (similar to the county council model) to a more appropriate parliamentary model, with a separation of powers between the legislature of the NAW and the executive of WG.

As a civil servant, Lawrence Conway believed that unless the original corporate body had been changed, devolution could not have lasted:

> I don't think it would survived it from the point of view of the constitutional arrangements, and secondly it would have led ineluctably to the capturing of the political agenda by the civil service at Cathays Park. Their position before the Assembly was one of a kind of undemocratic bureaucracy. You had absent Tory Secretaries of State, you had little meaningful political accountability, which created an atmosphere of lethargy almost, an intellectual 'us too-ism' approach to legislation. The corporate body would have led to strong bureaucracy and very weak parliamentary oversight.[35]

Rhodri's understanding of the weakness of the original devolution settlement is the key to an understanding of his impatience for constitutional change throughout his period as first minister. Edwina Hart, as a fellow Cabinet minister in this period, identifies his reforming vision:

> he would have liked to have a parliament first off … he didn't want us to be a super-duper council, he wanted us to be a proper assembly, a proper Parliament, and he wanted to see that element of self-government quite strong in Wales … he was far too nice to them across the border in Parliament in some ways,

understanding where their position was ... I think I might have
seen things perhaps in electoral spans ... I think he saw things
in half-centuries.[36]

Its original legislative powers were limited to secondary legislation, but
the growing pressure for formal legal separation and for legislative powers
led to the Government of Wales Act 2006. Gwenda Thomas recalls
Rhodri's clarity on this issue:

Rhodri saw accountability as important in leadership and also
saw that if you were going to grow into a Parliament in accord-
ance with the rights we were claiming from Westminster ...
there had to be that executive-parliament split. I think he did a
lot to make that acceptable within the party.[37]

The Government of Wales Act 1998 had termed members of the assembly executive 'Cabinet secretaries' but Rhodri started calling them
ministers. He also started the process by which the executive became
known as the Welsh Assembly Government (WAG).

The Richard Commission (2002) had recommended that the
National Assembly should have powers to legislate in certain areas of
domestic policy, whilst others would remain the preserve of Westminster.
Whilst much of the report of was rejected by the UK Government, it
did agree to create a more permissive law-making system for the assembly, based on the use of Parliamentary Orders in Council. The resulting
Government of Wales Act 2006 conferred on the Assembly legislative
powers similar to other devolved legislatures through legislative competency requests which were subject to the veto of the Secretary of State for
Wales, House of Commons or House of Lords. The Act finally killed the
assembly corporate body and established WG as a separate entity from,
but accountable to, the National Assembly, and enabled the Assembly to
legislate within its devolved fields. Although it represented a substantial
development from the original settlement, yet its dependence on the
goodwill of Parliament and Secretary of State for Wales made the process
cumbersome and opaque. Rhodri Morgan characterised it as a 'halfway
house' and compared it to the assembly government (as it was known at
the time), being given '"L" plates fixed clearly on the back bumper', in
order to initiate legislation.[38] According to Paul Griffiths, it was Rhodri

who succeeded in finding a fudge to support the legislation, even though the change to law-making powers was predicated on a future referendum: 'he was a pragmatist. He was an enthusiastic devolutionist. He wanted to press the boundaries all the time but to take people with him.'[39]

This system meant that those measures that Welsh Ministers were particularly keen to implement, such as a ban on smacking children as part of a broader children's rights measure, were blocked by indications from the Welsh Office that the proposal would not be supported.[40] This byzantine and opaque system infuriated not only Plaid AMs, but Labour ministers too. Plaid Cymru made a referendum on direct law-making powers one of the fundamental conditions for the 2007–11 coalition. Gwenda Thomas, as the deputy minister for social services, took legislation through the complexity of legislative competency orders in the period 2007 and voiced her frustration with the process:

> When Rhodri was First Minister and we had the first set of powers, I think there was real frustration because we were having to take policy decisions, having to catch the train to Westminster, and just sit there giving evidence to a committee up there, please can we do this is it all right with you if we do that? And I did that on various things and I think that kind of 'begging bowl' attitude towards Wales was completely intolerable and I think he showed that. So at that point devolution had to move on because something had to give. Those legislative powers, the 'LCO' [legislative consent order] system, couldn't sustain a nation that was to grow more independently in its power to serve the people.[41]

Coalitions

Rhodri Morgan's readiness to enter into coalition with progressive parties, initially with the Liberal Democrats in November 2000, and with Plaid Cymru in the summer of 2007, proved fundamental to the stability of the first and third Assemblies. Certainly, in the autumn of 2000, it proved the saving of the Assembly's reputation as a workable parliamentary institution. Brennan and Drakeford suggest that before Rhodri Morgan's leadership, the Labour Party in Wales was too often beset by increasingly arcane 'blinkered tribalism', and the failure of Alun

Michael's mode of operation illustrated the need to reach out to other political parties.[42]

David Melding explains Alun Michael's fall as a result of his failure to recognise the changed political landscape:

> the reason why [Alun Michael]'s government collapsed is that it was a minority government, he could have formed a coalition because the Liberal Democrats had made that very clear in all the political sign language that goes on ... Rhodri saw that and moved very quickly, he did run a minority government for a while until he agreed the coalition terms ... From our point of view, a stable government is what we want in many ways ... what we admired is that he realised that he had to form a coalition ... It survived a crisis of the whole issue of Mike German and the expenses matter – he was exonerated but it obviously was a very shaky time for them ... I think Rhodri was generous about who had the credit for any success. He was collegiate in that way, and it also showed in his ability to let ministers get on and do a job ... I think that made him a good coalition boss. That gave him the stable platform to project himself in representing the nation. He was comfortable in the role and had the personality for it.[43]

The Plaid leader between 2000 and 2011, Ieuan Wyn Jones, suggests that Rhodri Morgan was most comfortable in coalition with the Liberal Democrats in the first Assembly (1999–2003). During the second Assembly, the Labour administration was deprived of a majority by the defection of two members of its group, Peter Law (Blaenau Gwent) and John Marek (Wrexham), who became independent members. According to Ieuan Wyn Jones, the government's precarious position forced Rhodri Morgan to deal with the Liberal Democrats up to the 2003 election:

> the dynamic changed in about 2005, when the Peter Law row blew up and they lost John Marek. In a sense they were at the mercy of opposition parties. I think Rhodri was very uncomfortable at that point. He made no effort to reach out. In the period 2005–7, Plaid worked more closely with the Conservatives and

the Liberals … I had a very good relationship with Nick Bourne and Mike German and we worked together like a team. The first thing we did was to join forces on the budget. Because that was the first time that Rhodri felt vulnerable, because he knew that if he lost the budget he was out, he had to deal with us, and he didn't like that at all. Basically, it was a bit of guerrilla warfare then and we knew if we got Peter Law and John Marek on board we could just strike when we wanted to.[44]

Whilst WAG had succeeded in a number of policy initiatives – such as the creation of the foundation phase for nursery-age children, the lack of a clear majority after 2005 blocked much of Rhodri Morgan's political programme, amongst which he wished to transfer other quangos apart from the WDA, such as the Arts Council of Wales (ACW) and the Wales Tourist Board, into government. Whilst he succeeded with the WDA and the regional skills councils, he was unable to take this process further because of his lack of an Assembly majority. Ieuan Wyn Jones recalls that:

We used all the tactics that we could and of course they lost a lot of their [battles]. Rhodri wanted to abolish the Arts Council, the Welsh Language Board, a lot of the quangos and of course we said 'No, you're not going to do it'. And he could see there was no way he could get it through. So in the end they had to draw back and they couldn't abolish them because there was no majority in the assembly for it. Clearly, that period 2005–7 was uncomfortable for him.[45]

The 2007 election gave Labour only twenty-six seats out of sixty, and necessitated discussions with other parties for a workable coalition. But the other parties attempted to put together a 'rainbow coalition' to build on their alliance during the 2005–7 period. David Melding was of the view that a rainbow coalition between the Conservatives and Plaid or/ and Liberal Democrats was a real possibility:

Nick Bourne raised the possibility with David Cameron, who was persuaded that if the platform for government had enough that aligned with Conservative interests and advanced some significant ones and then the costs were not so great that there were things in it that we couldn't live with, so open negotiations proceeded. And he was true to his word, when we did get an agreement, he strongly backed it, and our Executive Committee met the same day as the Liberal Democrats, unanimously put it through. If David Cameron had withheld his consent, then I don't think we would have got it through the Executive Committee of the Welsh Party. It was part of New Conservative thinking. The rainbow coalition did produce an agreement and it stands to this day as a very reasonable alternative that could have worked.[46]

Ieuan Wyn Jones, in spite of some internal opposition, had also taken part in discussions to create the rainbow coalition:

I think the deal with Labour could only have been done because the rainbow had failed. We knew that the rainbow coalition was a realistic option … the discussions with the two other parties were on the basis of me leading the coalition as the leader of the largest party, so we set up a team to do the coalition agreement which became the All Wales Accord and was actually agreed between the three parties. The crux came when we then had a group meeting at which the All Wales Accord was put forward and a confidence and supply agreement with Labour as an alternative. A majority of the group, apart from Leanne [Wood] and Helen [Mary Jones] and others at that point, was to go with the All Wales Accord … we were ready to go with this, but Mike [German] couldn't get it through his executive.
    I've been told that one of the people who stood against the coalition was Kirsty Williams. There were people in the Liberal Democrats who were similarly minded, such as Alex Carlile and who were very much against working with us. So I went back to my party and said 'we can't really proceed with this because the Liberal Democrats could pull out at any time'. That's when Lawrence Conway realised what was happening and the request that the Assembly be reconvened to install Rhodri as First Minister, because it would be then more difficult for us to knock him out.[47]

Ieuan Wyn Jones recalls being called to a meeting with Rhodri Morgan in June 2007, having received a message that the Liberal Democrats had declined to enter into coalition with Labour:

> What Rhodri wanted was a coalition with the Liberal Democrats. I remember I went to a meeting with him and he was distressed, it was just him and me in a room, he was utterly distressed, and we were there to talk about this confidence and supply proposal, but all he wanted to talk about was the fact that the Liberal Democrats had decided they weren't going to speak to him. 'I can't understand it' he said it was almost he was using me as a confessional. I just went out and I was totally bewildered by it all. In a later meeting to discuss the coalition, we went round in circles a bit, but eventually we got around to the fact that what he was offering was a coalition. Prior to that Jane Hutt had given Jocelyn a piece of paper which stated said Labour would agree to a referendum on our law-making powers and legislation on the Welsh language as a basis for entering into discussions. The interesting part was the referendum because clearly that was something he was finding it difficult to sell to Westminster particularly I understood with Peter Hain. Because Peter Hain had apparently told all his Labour colleagues that there wouldn't be a referendum. But Rhodri knew there had to be one, or there wouldn't be a coalition.[48]

The 'One Wales' agreement was eventually made between Labour and Plaid Cymru in June 2007. The leaders for the talks were the two business managers, Jane Hutt and Jocelyn Davies, and as Rhodri attests in his autobiography, 'there was a bond of trust, and obviously no macho posturing. I couldn't have guaranteed no macho posturing if it had been me and Ieuan.'[49] The agreement included commitments to legislate on Welsh language rights and for a referendum that would provide the National Assembly with full legislative powers. In addition, Plaid Cymru was given three Cabinet posts, with Ieuan Wyn Jones as deputy first minister and responsible for economic development, Elin Jones as minister for agriculture and Rhodri Glyn Tomos as minister for culture. There was also a deputy minister post for Jocelyn Davies, responsible for housing policy.

The price of coalition

On the eve of the talks to flesh out the final One Wales agreement, Rhodri Morgan was taken gravely ill with a heart attack. His brother Prys recalls speaking to him before the momentous weekend in July, and the crucial Labour conference to vote on the coalition:[50]

> I've never had a phone call, a more unhappy phone call from Rhodri, than on the Friday before his heart attack. He phoned here on the Friday and I said to myself, 'Oh, my God, what is going to happen? He sounds exactly like someone who is going to have a heart attack.' He said 'You know, I mean, all these people are stabbing me in the back simply because I'm trying to get the Labour Party, the Labour Government to survive by having a coalition with Plaid. The Liberals are too flaky, but at least they're not going to form a rainbow coalition ... the way that people like Kinnock[51] are turning against me and saying how can I betray Labour by making government with Ieuan Wyn Jones and so on.

Rhodri Morgan was taken to hospital the following Sunday afternoon with a suspected heart attack and in his brother's view, the strain of bringing about this coalition 'cost him his life in the long term'. But he also had never seen Rhodri:

> look happier than when he had the One Wales Government ... I think he felt it was very easy and partly because he could see that the government that he was running was run by the twin spirits of my Labour father and Plaid mother.[52]

Lawrence Conway recalls the fractious process of achieving agreement within the Labour Party to enter into coalition with Plaid Cymru:

> the lowest point for me was the meeting a few days before the vital weekend of the special conference (of the Wales Labour Party) in the House of Lords tearoom. Neil Kinnock patronised Rhodri dreadfully from a position of ignorance in terms of the

realities of the Welsh political situation and the Assembly and so on – we were there – Mark Drakeford, Neil Kinnock, myself and Rhodri. Both of us were very angry – he went on to meet the Welsh Labour group. We formed the Cabinet in my house on the Sunday which is when he had his heart attack. I have no doubt that the stresses of the preceding weeks and quite possibly the venom that was involved, even on the Saturday, was enough to put his heart up the Richter scale.[53]

But Plaid's current leader, Adam Price – then a bystander from his vantage point as a Member of Parliament – considers the One Wales coalition to have been a lost opportunity to radicalise Welsh politics:

The Welsh Labour Government could have taken intellectual risks … in re-shaping the public services etcetera but that didn't happen, that's a great shame. I see a positive legacy in terms of the Labour Party's electoral position for the Labour Party, a negative legacy in terms of the culture and practice of the Welsh state and what it's ossified into is a form of conservatism and I think there is a worrying … what we do have in Wales is a kind of deep one-party state and increasingly the dividing line between politics and bureaucracy has become very, very blurred … People are unable to imagine an alternative and that has consequences for public life and there are throwbacks to an earlier period of Labour hegemony at local government and you end up in bad policy and bad decision making.[54]

Rhodri Morgan's remarkable achievement in the creation of both coalitions was to ensure that Labour remained in charge. It retained control of finance, and the biggest elements of the National Assembly budget by far, in health and education. It also retained the environment brief and developed the sustainable development agenda with Jane Davidson's later influence delivering the Well-being of Future Generations (Wales) Act 2015 in particular. Rhodri Morgan's generosity of spirit made these coalitions work, and his style of leadership was fundamental to its success and his readiness to trust his ministers and delegate authority made for more effective government. Jane Hutt describes his style as:

in a sense, presiding over it, because of his intellect, because of his brain, he could have ended up wanting to micro manage, and there were some things he did get very engaged with, the delivery of improvements to the health service, he was always passionate about education in terms of the foundation phase, and getting rid of the quangos … this Rhodri leadership was partly his vision and partly enabling others in his team to have the vision.[55]

'Clear red water' – a 'socialist of the Welsh stripe'

To what extent was Rhodri Morgan in the period 2000–9 developing a distinct and alternative agenda to that of the UK and Westminster-focused Labour Party? The New Labour philosophy encouraged greater choice in the provision of public services such as the provision of foundation hospitals, where institutions could opt out of government control and could raise their own finances, or in the case of school academies, allow pupil selection.

His key speech to Mike Sullivan's Centre for Public Policy in Swansea University in December 2002 marked 'clear red water' between the 'Welsh Assembly Government' and New Labour.[56] The speech signalled Rhodri Morgan's credo that, in Wales, the belief in universal services free at the point of delivery overrode New Labour's mantra of increased marketisation. This seminal speech was drafted by his special adviser, Mark Drakeford:

Mark is the key person … Rhodri agreed with Mark in so far as there needed to be something that gave the Labour Party in Wales a sense of its own identity and purpose … he was very dependent on Mark for his theoretical base and the red water speech … it would reflect Mark's sort of collectivist, universalist view about public service and so on … I don't think Mark realistically felt that the speech would drive some significant policy change through the Welsh Government and its administration, etc. What it was all about was trying to create an identity, and to some extent, it did create difficulties with the Labour Party elsewhere.[57]

As chair of the event, Mike Sullivan recollected how Rhodri Morgan developed the theme that Welsh Labour should follow a more left-wing trajectory than Labour in England:

> he talked about creating 'clear red water' between Labour in London and Labour in Wales … but he didn't say it … although the speech had been released to the media, the Western Mail and the UK nationals had 'clear red water' in big print in the headlines. He never got to that part of the speech. He went off script. Rightly or wrongly, he was seen as Welsh Labour and following a more left-wing trajectory than Labour in England.[58]

A reflection of this speech's significance was that it was only the second speech that he had ever delivered with a fully written script; that is, until he lost patience six pages from its end, explaining that he disliked wearing glasses, and omitted to include the key passage that had been trailed to the media beforehand. At the time, however, he explained that he had to leave early to see his ill mother.[59] Paul Griffiths considers that in spite of his protestations, Rhodri Morgan had not been completely comfortable with the phrase and that his explanation of why he did not utter the key words reflected his occasional tendency to obfuscate rather than clarify:

> If he'd wanted to say it, he would have said it. He wasn't attuned to the message. so it didn't come easily so it never came out, is my view. By the time he came to do his book it seemed to be important to him to say, 'I wanted to say it.' It just never happened.[60]

Mark Drakeford recalls how Rhodri approached the speech:

> Rhodri remained confidently and determinedly himself and was 'classic Labour'. He was in the Labour mainstream in his consistent belief in the shaping impact of economic opportunities on the lives of people. In his 'clear red water' speech, he amended the text as drafted to refer to himself as a 'socialist of the Welsh stripe', a reference to the industrial as well as the cultural heritage he brought to his politics.[61]

Edwina Hart emphasises that the term 'clear red water' did not adequately reflect the nuances of Rhodri Morgan's views in this period, although he ceased private finance initiatives (PFIs) in the health service, for example:

> Alun Michael was First Secretary ... they were still signing PFIs and they signed up for a PFI in Port Talbot, which I as a Finance Minister wouldn't sign. I did not support PFI and discussed my concerns with Rhodri, who was supportive ... he wanted to maintain the health service in the spirit of Nye Bevan in Wales, and that was when the division started to emerge with the politics of London, and especially as time went on when you saw the Labour Party starting a privatisation process in England. You could see that he [Rhodri] was very strong on that, because he wanted to remain true to his principles. But on other things Rhodri would want to compromise because it was the bigger [Labour] family that you didn't want to fall out with.
>
> Rhodri always wanted to keep up good relationships there, but he knew when he had to stand up ... he never went for rows that he couldn't win that would upset the broader family but kept very much in the politics of what we could deliver through devolution in Wales ... everybody says Rhodri was on the left ... he wasn't on the left in strategic terms within the politics of socialism at all. Rhodri was quite mainstream, left of centre yes, but not in the true terms of how you define the left, even within the party. Rhodri had integrity and an understanding of Wales as a nation very strongly from that. But it was a nation, not only to do with language ... but also about a sporting identity and everybody being involved.[62]

Edwina Hart sees Rhodri Morgan's strength in his intellect and delivery, as evidenced in his success in re-shaping devolution throughout his period in office, and his ability to navigate the occasionally fraught relationship with UK Government and maintaining the unity of the Labour Party.

Andrew Davies's experience of working with Rhodri Morgan led him to doubt whether Rhodri had an overarching coherent political philosophy, and that the nearest he got to an articulation of one was in the separation between Welsh Labour and UK Blairite Labour policy. He does not believe that Rhodri Morgan was a 'deep thinker' about these issues and that 'it was almost like sufficient to the day, if he hadn't had Mark [Drakeford] there'. Davies quotes a senior civil servant close to Rhodri Morgan, who said that it was almost 'by accident that we've arrived where we are' and that there was no clear agenda. Davies considered the concept of 'clear red water' to be ill-defined. That was partly because, in his view, Rhodri was essentially a civil servant, and 'temperamentally, he was an official'.[63] Certainly Prys Morgan attests that his brother was more interested in administration and governance rather than 'philosophising'.[64]

Rhodri's legacy

Rhodri's leadership style was presidential and chairman-like, rather than as the micro-manager. He was disarming and could be frustratingly discursive in Cabinet, but Edwina Hart's recollection of his Cabinet was of its pleasantness and tolerance, even when former political foes, such as the Liberal Democrats and Plaid shared the table:

> it was one of the nicest Cabinets I ever served in and I served in all of them until I finished. Rhodri knew how to work coalitions because if you were dedicated to Wales and what you wanted for Wales, he could deal with that.[65]

But it would be mistaken to confuse this tolerance for partners such as Plaid Cymru with agreement with their aims. Edwina Hart had no doubt of his antipathy to elements of nationalism:

> I think Rhodri because of where some nationalists stood on fascism was a clearly defining thing for him for why he was a socialist … he wasn't a closet nationalist, he believed in us as a nation. There is a difference because I'm the same. I used to identify myself as Welsh European, and that's the test, if you're Welsh British, it's different.[66]

This echoed the beliefs of Rhodri's father who actively campaigned against Saunders Lewis for the University of Wales seat in 1943. Rhodri

despised this right-wing tradition within Plaid Cymru, but his understanding of the Welsh character enabled him to project Labour as a
genuinely Welsh patriotic party. Adam Price, Plaid Cymru's leader in
the Senedd, but between 2001 and 2010 the Member of Parliament
for Carmarthen East and Dinefwr, believes that the creation of 'Welsh
Labour' was a master stroke:

> I think the reason for the success of the Labour Party is not to
> do with a re-invention of social democracy but because they
> completely stole Plaid's intellectual territory. 'One Wales' then
> allowed them actually to continue down that road, ironically,
> in many ways and Plaid hasn't fully been able to recover, re-
> position itself since then, so it was a very successful re-brand.
>
> I think the key to understanding Rhodri Morgan's success
> and his historic status is in his relationship to nationalism,
> national identity and the Labour Party's relationship with that,
> than it is to do with a kind of successful re-brand of social
> democracy ... it took the rug from beneath us and we haven't
> been able to respond.
>
> The Labour tradition in Wales is now in some sort of soft,
> nationalist mould ... They basically stole Plaid's intellectual ter-
> ritory. One Wales [the coalition agreement in 2007] allowed
> them actually to continue down that road and Plaid hasn't been
> able to recover, to reposition itself since then.[67]

His ability to be a man of the people, known by his first name, caused
even his political opponents to identify with him, but his avuncular
style masked a razor-sharp intelligence and encyclopaedic knowledge.
According to Adam Price, Rhodri Morgan succeeded in stealing Plaid's
clothes and left a political mark characterised by 'socialist managerialism':

> One of the most interesting things about the Welsh Labour
> Party is that almost uniquely in Western Europe now, it is almost
> the last man standing. I'm not sure if he ever had a fully worked
> out ideological framework. Progressive universalism was the best
> attempt to furnish some kind of heft and to create a Morganism.
> I'm not convinced he had anything like a fully worked out ideo-
> logical framework ... he was an enabler, and keen to encourage

others and others. He was quite receptive to new ideas ... and sometimes could be very perceptive and radical. What he said he most proud of was the foundation phase for children which, as he said, is probably the most radical of all policies that the Welsh Government, even to this day have embraced, because it is a compete break with 100 years of pedagogy by adopting this child-centred based education.[68]

In Andrew Davies's view, Rhodri saved devolution:

Rhodri's lasting legacy will be that the Assembly was going nowhere with Alun Michael ... It was a disaster. He lost the Rhondda, Llanelli, Islwyn, a whole raft of seats ... We had constant motions of no confidence in Christine Gwyther and it was uncertain – was the assembly going to thrive? Was it going to survive? ... When Rhodri took over, 'the next day, going up to the fifth floor [the government floor of the National Assembly's administrative offices], it was like the whole institution had a whole weight lifted off it. Everybody was smiling, the civil servants were smiling, journalists were smiling. Everybody could breathe. I like Alun but he was a disaster. He was a control freak, he is not somebody who can build bridges and alliances.[69]

Helen Mary Jones considers Rhodri Morgan's contribution to the increased acceptance of devolution by Welsh people as absolutely critical:

I don't think the people of Wales would be as solidly behind devolution as they are now if it hadn't been for the way Rhodri managed his own party and the appeal that he could have to the electorate, by being both Welsh enough and socialist enough but not too Welsh and not too socialist ...

... part of his legacy is the affection that the people of Wales have for devolution. Can you be a passionate devolutionist? Well of course you can't. Devolution is based on the presumption that the power belongs in the centre and that it can hand out as much or how little as it wants. I think you can argue that Rhodri could be passionate about taking the nation on its national journey within a timeframe that it could swallow. The downside of his legacy is that what you do when he's not there anymore. I don't think he was a crypto-nationalist ... he was carefully managing how he was perceived and he needed to do that.[70]

Mark Drakeford recalls how Rhodri Morgan grew his authority throughout his period as a Labour leader from 2000 onwards:

You had MPs who were very clearly the political aristocracy. You had Labour local government leaders who were powerful people and at one end of the fiefdom approach to Labour, and then there was the Assembly. By 2007 when Labour Party members were faced by a choice between [what] leading politicians at the Assembly are suggesting to them and what leading people in London are saying to them, they decide it is the Assembly's voice that they will listen to ... That's pretty remarkable isn't it? ... who else could have managed to pull it off?[71]

Rhodri Morgan's lasting political contribution, according to Paul Griffiths, was that Labour managed to hold on to power in the National Assembly in 2000 and 2007 during periods when other parties could have easily taken over:

In 2007, because of his illness, he wasn't on top form but he ensured that the coalition with Plaid happened. That is the reason why Welsh Labour has not gone the way of Scottish Labour. If it hadn't been Rhodri, it would have been anyone else in the Welsh Labour tribe. We'd have turned our backs on government as the Scots did. We would have lost that assumption of government which Scottish Labour lost. So the reason we are still in business is actually not because Rhodri was a nationalist but because Rhodri was a pluralist who was willing to go and make governments when he needed to.[72]

Paul Griffiths summarises the legacy of Rhodri Morgan in relation to the Labour tradition and to the government's adamant refusal to adopt Blairism:

Welsh politics is not a game of 'winner takes all'. It's not as tribal as it was expected to be and Carwyn has continued with that … He started off with a programme of government which was Labour, which was modern but did go in a significantly different direction to New Labour. It did not put itself in hock to the marketisation of public services which was at the core of the Blair agenda, and we didn't marketise schools, we didn't marketise health, we didn't go down the PFI route. History is proving us right … don't think many give us credit for it but it does mean in Wales, almost no government we could foresee would undo these things. Blairites refer to it as 'caveman politics'. Rhodri wasn't enamoured by controlling bureaucracies but his government and the people around him and himself set themselves against the marketisation of public services and that's a big achievement, not well understood or commented on outside.[73]

David Melding views Rhodri Morgan's lasting legacy as the leader who ensured the strengthening of Welsh democracy:

This is the legacy. I think Rhodri's main concern was to establish the Assembly as an institution that was going to endure and be part of the natural fabric of the British constitution and an incredibly important historical development for the Welsh nation. If you want a test of whether he made a difference, I think that's it, we went from an endorsement of devolution by 0.5 per cent [in 1997] to a nearly two-thirds endorsement of having effectively full parliamentary powers (the 2011 referendum) … in terms of nation-building, a central institution, the assembly and then the Welsh Government, firmly establishing those institutions in a way that just didn't need to be done in Scotland. We almost had a 10-year constitutional convention. The Scots had done it before devolution, we had to do it through devolution.

Melding disputes the label of 'maverick' for Rhodri Morgan, and identifies his confidence in his own political and personal character as one of his winning characteristics:

I suppose compared to the pattern-book of the Blair government, he stood out a mile. But of course, that was part of his charm and

I think he drew on a genuine Welshness and his deep reverence for the Welsh language and his family roots, which greatly helped him in being able to reach out to the whole of Wales. It made him a very powerful figure and a very necessary figure I think for the success of devolution from very fragile beginnings.[74]

Mark Drakeford points to the influence of women on Rhodri's political outlook:

Julie's influence on him was huge and unseen in many ways, and he would often say that she was a Labour Party person before him and he knew the Labour Party through Julie to begin with. She has always been more to the conventional left than Rhodri. The powerful people in his life around him were Julie and their two daughters, his mother Huana, and Julie's mother. Home was to be surrounded by women and in the Assembly the people who were closest to him were women – Jane Hutt, Sue Essex, and Edwina Hart in a different way … he always wanted to push Cabinet members to the front. I think he knew he cast a very long shadow and in the public mind, Assembly, Labour, Rhodri were the same thing.[75]

His special adviser Paul Griffiths, noted his endearing warmth and open personality that made him more pluralistic in his politics, and, as Andrew Davies asserts, 'he was always very popular, but never a conventional politician and "one of them". I think his lasting achievement was that the Assembly would not have achieved its legitimacy without him.'[76]

Mike Sullivan's interviews with Rhodri Morgan's political allies and foes show a real love and affection for Rhodri Morgan that was shared across political parties. But an understanding of his magnanimity and generous spirit should not mask his will and determination to drive through political change and policy implementation. As David Melding testifies, Rhodri Morgan's lack of vanity was one of his appealing charac-teristics, but he was also an aggressive and doughty 'political scrapper':

It's important not to portray Rhodri as political saint. He was comfortable in the political process, he could rough it, and he was a formidable opponent and he was capable of real anger, and blood was shed in battle. But there was an irascible generosity about the man, and I think the broad success of politics in Wales mattered to him.[77]

Rhodri Morgan's legacy, arguably, was to save devolution after its disastrous beginning, when the future of the NAW was threatened by the deeply flawed nature of the institution as a corporate body, and by the limitations imposed by the lack of a clear majority to govern. WG and its weak leadership was prone to being ambushed by the other political parties, Alun Michael lacked political credibility and was seen as being imposed by Tony Blair's New Labour, and the constant bickering, including for example, an unseemly saga about allocation of seating arrangements in the Assembly, all combined to give a sense of drift and a possible shipwreck. Rhodri Morgan identified and acted upon the weaknesses of the newly created institution, and through his ability to create a greater consensus through coalition, ensured the development of the institution throughout his period as first minister.

His legacy is marked by progressive policies adopted and implemented in the context of a growing economy and increased budgets for the Welsh block grant between 2000 and 2009. Thereafter, the financial collapse of the banking sector brought about a recession, a lengthy period of austerity and a break to ten years of economic growth. At the end of devolution's second decade, the Senedd and WG share with parliaments and governments everywhere the need to respond to the massive challenges of recovery from the COVID-19 pandemic, the consequences of the United Kingdom's departure from the European Union and effective action on climate change. Rhodri Morgan's observation that the Assembly's role in dealing with early crises such as foot-and-mouth helped draw attention to the legitimacy of devolved governance and political leadership, resounds strongly in this context, and WG's confident response to the pandemic underlay Welsh Labour's victory in the 2021 General Election. It is a remarkable achievement for Welsh Labour to have retained its grip on government for over twenty-two years and six elections, and it is testimony to the efficacy of the 'Welsh Labour' brand, built up by Rhodri Morgan, and advanced by Carwyn Jones and Mark Drakeford.

The following essays in this book consider the major areas of public policy, its performance and the extent to which devolution has enabled the melding of Welsh Labour's national identity with commitment to its communitarian values.

Notes

1. *Mike Sullivan Dialogues*, conducted in 2017–18, with nineteen of those politicians and advisers intimately involved with the development of devolution in the period 1997–2011. These transcripts are in the hands of Mike Sullivan's widow and co-editor, Prof. Jane Williams.
2. Rhodri Morgan, *Rhodri: A Political Life in Wales and Westminster* (Cardiff: University of Wales Press, 2017), p. xx.
3. Interview with Prys Morgan, *Mike Sullivan Dialogues* (hereafter *MS Dialogues*), p. 9.
4. Hilary Marquand and Gwynne Meara, *South Wales Needs a Plan* (London: Allen and Unwin, 1936).
5. Interview with Prof. K. O. Morgan, *MS Dialogues*, p. 7.
6. Nick Edwards, Secretary of State for Wales (1979–87), made Lord Crickhowell (1987–2018), and chairman of Associated British Ports; Sir Geoffrey Inkin, chairman of the Cardiff Bay Development Corporation (1987–2000); Saunders Lewis, one of the founders of the Welsh National Party (later Plaid Cymru), prominent Welsh language writer, poet and dramatist. Interview with Lawrence Conway, *MS Dialogues*, p. 3.
7. Lord Jack Brooks of Tremorfa was the hard-nosed Labour leader of South Glamorgan Council during the 1980s and became deputy chairman of the Cardiff Bay Development Corporation (1987–2000). He had been Rhodri's best man at his wedding in 1967; the 'Riverside Mafia' were 'soft left' Labour councillors on South Glamorgan County Council, 1989–93. Jane Davidson, the future education minister, and sustainable development minister, was also a councillor here during the same period; Russell Goodway, leader of South Glamorgan County Council (1992–6), and Cardiff Council (1996–2004). Interview with Andrew Davies, *MS Dialogues*, p. 4.
8. BBC Wales News, 'Goodway Resigns as Leader', 14 June 2004.
9. Interview with Edwina Hart, *MS Dialogues*, p. 7.
10. Interview with Jane Hutt, *MS Dialogues*, p. 2.
11. Interview with Jane Hutt, *MS Dialogues*, p. 4.
12. Interview with Jane Hutt, *MS Dialogues*, p. 3.
13. Interview with Paul Griffiths, *MS Dialogues*, p. 1.
14. Mike Sullivan in interview with Edwina Hart, *MS Dialogues*, p. 1.
15. Morgan, *Rhodri: A Political Life in Wales and Westminster*, p. 114.
16. Morgan, *Rhodri: A Political Life*, p. 120.
17. Quoted in J. Barry Jones, 'Labour Pains', in J. Barry Jones and Denis Balsom, *The Road to the National Assembly for Wales* (Cardiff: University of Wales Press, 2000), p. 210.
18. Interview with Paul Griffiths, *MS Dialogues*, p. 1.
19. Morgan, *Rhodri: A Political Life in Wales and Westminster*, p. 150.

20. Interview with Prys Morgan, *MS Dialogues*, pp. 10–11.
21. Interview with Prys Morgan, *MS Dialogues*, p. 1.
22. Interview with Prys Morgan, *MS Dialogues*, pp. 1–2.
23. Interview with Prys Morgan, *MS Dialogues*, p. 3.
24. Interview with Prys Morgan, *MS Dialogues*, pp. 3–4.
25. Morgan, *Rhodri: A Political Life in Wales and Westminster*, p. 159.
26. Paul Flynn, *Dragons Led by Poodles: Inside Story of a New Labour Stitch Up* (London: Politicos Publishing, 1999). An entertaining, virulently anti-Alun Michael and anti-Tony Blair description of the contest for the Labour leadership in Wales.
27. Interview with Helen Mary Jones, *MS Dialogues*, p. 1.
28. Morgan, *Rhodri: A Political Life in Wales and Westminster*, p. x.
29. Interview with Julie Morgan, *MS Dialogues*, p. 3.
30. Interview with David Melding, *MS Dialogues*, p. 1.
31. Interview with Mark Drakeford, *MS Dialogues*, p. 6.
32. Interview with Mark Drakeford, *MS Dialogues*, p. 5.
33. Morgan, *Rhodri: A Political Life in Wales and Westminster*, p. x.
34. Interview with Edwina Hart, *MS Dialogues*, p. 2.
35. Interview with Lawrence Conway, *MS Dialogues*, pp. 3–4.
36. Interview with Edwina Hart, *MS Dialogues*, p. 2.
37. Interview with Gwenda Thomas, *MS Dialogues*, p. 5.
38. Gwenda Thomas, AM for Neath (1999–2016), deputy minister for social services (2007–11), deputy minister for children and social services (2011–16). Morgan, *Rhodri: A Political Life in Wales and Westminster*, p. 279.
39. Interview with Paul Griffiths, *MS Dialogues*, p. 10.
40. Interview with Gwenda Thomas, *MS Dialogues*, p. 5.
41. Interview with Gwenda Thomas, *MS Dialogues*, p. 4.
42. Kevin Brennan and Mark Drakeford, 'Foreword', in Rhodri Morgan, *Rhodri: A Political Life in Wales and Westminster* (Cardiff: University of Wales Press, 2017), p. x.
43. Interview with David Melding, *MS Dialogues*, p. 23.
44. Nick Bourne, member of the NAW (1999–2011), leader of the Welsh Conservative Party (1999–2011); Mike German, member of the NAW (1999–2010), deputy first minister (2000–1, 2002–3), Liberal Democrat leader (2007–8). Interview with Ieuan Wyn Jones, *MS Dialogues*, p. 3.
45. Interview with Ieuan Wyn Jones, *MS Dialogues*, p. 2.
46. Interview with David Melding, *MS Dialogues*, p. 4.
47. Leanne Wood, member of the NAW for Rhondda, (2003–21); leader of Plaid Cymru (2012–18); Helen Mary Jones, member of the NAW for Llanelli (1999–2011, 2018–21); Alex Carlile (Lord Carlile of Berriew), formerly Liberal Democrat MP for Montgomeryshire (1983–97). Interview with Ieuan Wyn Jones, *MS Dialogues*, p. 4.
48. Peter Hain, MP for Neath (1991–2012); Secretary of State for Wales (2002–8). Interview with Ieuan Wyn Jones, *MS Dialogues*, p. 5.
49. Morgan, *Rhodri: A Political Life in Wales and Westminster*, p. 297.
50. The Labour Party in Wales agreed to the plan in a special conference on 6 July

2007, and Plaid Cymru did so on 7 July. The negotiations on Cabinet posts were scheduled to take place on Monday, 9 July.

51. Neil Kinnock, now Baron Kinnock, former leader of the Labour Party (1983–92); former MP for Bedwellty and then Islwyn (1970–95).
52. Interview with Prys Morgan, *MS Dialogues*, p. 10.
53. Interview with Lawrence Conway, *MS Dialogues*, p. 16.
54. Interview with Adam Price, *MS Dialogues*, p. 3.
55. Interview with Jane Hutt, *MS Dialogues*, pp. 10–11.
56. Rhodri Morgan, 'Clear red water' speech to the National Centre for Public Policy, Swansea University, 11 December 2002.
57. Interview with Lawrence Conway, *MS Dialogues*, pp. 21–3.
58. Mike Sullivan, during his interview with Edwina Hart, *MS Dialogues*, p. 4.
59. Mike Sullivan's comment, in interview with Andrew Davies, *MS Dialogues*, p. 1.
60. Interview with Paul Griffiths, *MS Dialogues*, pp. 6–7.
61. Brennan and Drakeford, 'Foreword', p. xii.
62. Interview with Edwina Hart, *MS Dialogues*, p. 4.
63. Interview with Andrew Davies, *MS Dialogues*, p. 8.
64. Private correspondence from Prys Morgan to Jane Williams, 22 February 2021.
65. Interview with Edwina Hart, *MS Dialogues*, p. 5.
66. Interview with Edwina Hart, *MS Dialogues*, p. 5.
67. Interview with Adam Price, *MS Dialogues*, p. 3.
68. Interview with Adam Price, *MS Dialogues*, pp. 1–2.
69. Interview with Andrew Davies, *MS Dialogues*, p. 6.
70. Interview with Helen Mary Jones, *MS Dialogues*, pp. 7, 10.
71. Interview with Mark Drakeford, *MS Dialogues*, p. 6.
72. Interview with Paul Griffiths, *MS Dialogues*, pp. 12–13.
73. Interview with Paul Griffiths, *MS Dialogues*, p. 12.
74. Interview with David Melding, *MS Dialogues*, pp. 5–6.
75. Interview with Mark Drakeford, *MS Dialogues*, pp. 7–8.
76. Interview with Paul Griffiths, *MS Dialogues*, p. 13; interview with Andrew Davies, *MS Dialogues*, p. 6.
77. Interview with David Melding, *MS Dialogues*, p. 6.

Select bibliography

Flynn, Paul, *Dragons Led by Poodles: Inside Story of a New Labour Stitch Up* (London: Politicos Publishing, 1999).

Jones, J. Barry and Denis Balsom, *The Road to the National Assembly for Wales* (Cardiff: University of Wales Press, 2000).

Marquand, Hilary and Gwynne Meara, *South Wales Needs a Plan* (London: Allen and Unwin, 1936).

Morgan, Rhodri, *Rhodri: A Political Life in Wales and Westminster* (Cardiff: University of Wales Press, 2017), p. xx.

2

IECHYD DA? DEVOLUTION AND HEALTHCARE

Ceri J. Phillips

Introduction

The title of this chapter is often used to wish people well at the end of a conversation. It is used in this context to question whether the people of Wales would have been in better (or worse) health if policies relating to health and healthcare in Wales had been more closely aligned to those pursued by successive UK governments. The health agenda, encompassing the provision of healthcare services and the extent of resources required, has been among the most contentious political issues in the relatively short history of the Welsh Government (WG), and indeed for virtually all governments across the world.

This chapter will not attempt to answer the question as it is impossible to arrive at a definitive conclusion. Comparisons of the state of health between nations and between communities in relation to their health status is highly complex and multifaceted and requires thinking about a number of factors, including the respective determinants of health, which include the quality and quantity of healthcare facilities available, but also include the level of education, the state of the housing stock, nutrition and diet of the population and the economic state of the nation and its citizens. Neither is it a question of funding since the relationship between expenditure on healthcare services and the health status of a population is not directly proportional. It is far too simplistic to argue that to improve the health of the nation and reduce inequalities additional resources need to be channelled into healthcare services. It is known that the stock of the Welsh nation's health increases following a rugby victory over England or a semi-final appearance in the football Euros, but health policies cannot be framed to embrace such events.

This chapter considers the directions pursued by successive ministers and government, both pre- and post-devolution, in relation to health policies, the degree to which the Welsh stripe has been evident and the impact that such deviations might have had on the performance of the healthcare system and the health status of the nation.

The healthcare dilemma

Current expenditure on health and social care, at just under £9 billion, in Wales represented 53 per cent of the total WG budget in 2020/1[1] and, given levels of demand, even before the Coronavirus pandemic, the percentage of WG budget consumed by the NHS alone will inevitably rise, even without any consideration of the need for social care resources and other areas of WG expenditure. Management of the pandemic serves to further emphasise the complexity and challenges confronting politicians and policy makers in seeking to address what has been termed the healthcare dilemma.[2] The health service (or healthcare) dilemma is part of a wider economic problem which characterises every area of society and affects individuals, organisations, communities, societies, economies and the global community, whereby demand far outstrips the resources available to deliver. In Wales and elsewhere, demand for healthcare is ever-increasing despite improvements in population health and well-being and life expectancy, and notwithstanding variations and inequalities. While politicians continue to highlight the increase in the number of healthcare professionals, the availability of resources has declined (in real terms) and certainly failed to keep pace with the increase in demand. It is important to emphasise that there is no single, correct answer or solution to the problem, but successive governments of all shades and colours have aimed to place their own particular stamp on addressing the healthcare dilemma, while issues relating to health (and social) care continue to be a regular feature in the media and made even more apparent during the Coronavirus era.

The Welsh stripe in health policy pre-devolution

The management of the health agenda in Wales was very interesting politically even pre-devolution, with plenty of evidence of the Welsh stripe being apparent. Delving deep into the historical health archives, the origins of the NHS were firmly rooted in Wales and, even to this day, the alignment and commitment to the so-called 'Bevan principles' within health policy in Wales remain firm. Edwina Hart, for example, highlighted the support she had received as health minister from Rhodri Morgan in relation to private finance initiative schemes:

> he wanted to maintain the health service in the spirit of Nye Bevan in Wales, and that was when the division started to emerge with the politics of London, and especially as time went on when you saw the Labour Party starting a privatisation process in England.[3]

Rhodri Morgan's 'clear red water' speech provided further evidence that, in Wales, providing universal services, free at the point of delivery, overrode New Labour's mantra of increased marketisation.[4] The background to the speech and the key role played by Mark Drakeford, as special adviser, in its drafting, as described by Lawrence Conway, reflected Drakeford's 'collectivist, universalist view about public service' and which has been very evident during his period as Health Minister and latterly as First Minister.[5]

Wales had witnessed significant, innovative developments in fields of public health, health promotion and strategic planning during the 1980s, with the Welsh Office, through its NHS Directorate and first director, John Wyn Owen, taking a more active role in determining and managing health policy in Wales. For example, 'Heartbeat Wales' was launched in 1985 to reduce the level of heart disease and generally address the chronic health problems that beset the population in Wales,[6] and which were subsequently identified by Rhodri Morgan as a major cultural constraint in developing policies for the second term of the assembly in 2003.[7] Another development that emerged during the 1980s was the establishment of the Welsh Health Planning Forum, by Secretary of State, Peter Walker. One of its early outputs was the publication of the *Strategic Intent and Direction for the NHS in Wales* in 1989, as a vision for a health service fit for the twenty-first century,[8] pioneering the concept of 'health gain' and being recognised internationally with its status of a World Health Organization Collaborating Centre for Regional Health Strategy and Management Development. During this innovative period in relation to health policy, Wales also took the lead – in many senses on the global stage given interest and visitations from other systems – with strategies for mental illness and learning disabilities, which were identified as marking 'a divergence from the UK policy map'[9] and reinforced the need for system-wide perspective in the management of health and social care.[10]

Peter Walker had succeeded Nicholas Edwards as Secretary of State for Wales, having been 'sent to Wales' by Margaret Thatcher – which, according to Rhodri Morgan, was 'the equivalent in the Thatcher Government to the Siberian power station in the Stalin era, ideal for dissidents you couldn't completely dispose of'.[11] Walker claimed it gave him more influence as it gave access to key economic committees. He certainly made his mark, with the Welsh Health Planning Forum, as an advisory subgroup of the Executive Committee of the Health Policy Board of the NHS, making a clear distinction between the health policy in England and that to be pursued in Wales. Walker stood down from the Cabinet shortly before Thatcher herself was ousted in 1990 and was succeeded by David Hunt, who also pursued a direction of travel for health that was distinct from the policies being followed in England.

In 1988, Margaret Thatcher had announced a review of the NHS and in 1989 two White papers – 'Working for Patients' and 'Caring for People: Community Care in the next decade and beyond'[12] – were produced in response. These papers outlined the introduction of what was termed the 'internal market' and its components: the purchaser-provider split, the advent of GP-fundholding and the creation of NHS trusts. District Health Authorities and the newly established GP fundholders were to act as the purchasers in the system and to negotiate contracts with providers of health services, which were predominantly NHS trusts, and which included hospital, community and mental-health/learning-disability services. There were no Welsh trusts established in the first wave in 1990, with the first Welsh trust coming to fruition in 1991, when Pembrokeshire NHS Trust was established. Despite resistance by the health authorities, gradually all the provider units became NHS trusts over the next few years, eventually totalling thirty-one, fuelled in large part by the re-election of a Conservative Government in 1992 under John Major, which gave added weight to the reforms and their implementation. However, the appetite for GP fundholding was at best variable across Wales, with resistance from the trusts and health

authorities, and differences in structural underpinning and policy direction between Wales and England. This difference began to become even
more apparent, driven, in part, by the philosophy and vision emanating
from the Welsh Health Planning Forum and its project 'Health and
Social Care 2010', which was designed to provide a 'context for local
strategies, giving health planners and professionals a longer-term framework within which they could plan the development of services during
the coming decade'.[13] This led, eventually, to the creation of local health
groups and then local health boards.

Hunt's departure from the Welsh Office in May 1993 resulted in the
appointment of John Redwood as Secretary of State for Wales. Rhodri
Morgan's depiction of John Redwood speaks volumes, including the infa-
mous attempt to mime the Welsh national anthem, but it is worth giving
emphasis to one aspect of the description: 'mostly, Redwood helped the
case for devolution simply by being John Redwood'.[14] However, the
consequences of Redwood's tenure at the Welsh Office had far-reaching
implications for health policy within Wales, as one of his actions was to
stop central planning processes, including the Welsh Health Planning
Forum with its creative and forward thinking. The establishment of
health gain protocols in several specific areas (for example, cancer, mental
health, children, older people, cardiovascular disease, injuries, physical
activity, respiratory conditions), underpinned by three pillars of health
gain, people centredness and resource effectiveness,[15] resonated very
closely with the principles of Prudent Healthcare, established when Mark
Drakeford was Health Minister.[16] It is not inconceivable that we still bear
the scars of John Redwood's actions nearly thirty years on, as organisations grapple with the constraints that hinder the need to change the
shape of services to improve the health of the population across Wales.

David Hunt briefly returned to the Welsh Office before handing over
the reins to William Hague, another keen to utilise his position to make
his mark on the political stage. During his time in office, the structure
of NHS Wales was changed again in 1996 through the merger of district
health authorities and family health services authorities into five health
authorities covering the whole of Wales – the latest in a series of structural
reorganisations, following the NHS reforms, that would continue to be
a regular feature of NHS Wales for the subsequent thirteen years or so.

The landslide Labour victory in the General Election of May 1997,
with its commitment to devolution for Scotland and Wales, did not

result in a ministerial position for Rhodri Morgan. One of the reasons which he personally attributed for his non-selection was the disagreement he had with David Miliband over the wording of the health aspects of the Welsh Labour manifesto. UK Labour was keen not to dismantle all of the previous government's health reforms, whereas Rhodri Morgan and colleagues had placed greater emphasis on the role of the NHS as the delivery vehicle, without any encouragement to private provision, in alignment with the spirit of Bevan and the more recent restatement of Bevan's principles by the Bevan Commission.[17] It was therefore evident that even where the political colour of governments in Westminster and Cardiff Bay were the same, there was to be a clear divide between their respective health agendas. Devolution simply served to reinforce the differences in approaches either side of Offa's Dyke, with Welsh policy firmly embodied in the 'Bevan principles' notion of 'universalism' and its emphasis on the citizen, in contrast to the consumer exercising a degree of choice and the quasi-market approaches advocated and adopted by New Labour. This was clearly evidenced by Rhodri Morgan's indication that the second term of a Labour, or Labour-led, Welsh Assembly Government (WAG) would, in social policy as elsewhere, make obvious the emergence of 'clear red water' between Labour in Cardiff and Labour in Westminster, with descriptors such as 'Welsh way' reflecting new and imaginative approaches;[18] a Welsh version of 'democratic socialism', which distanced the administration in Cardiff from some of the principles and many of the policy actions of the UK New Labour project; and 'socialism with a Welsh stripe', where the intention was to provide distinctive policies that were consistent with Welsh Labour values and with an aspiration to improve the lives of all Welsh citizens. Health and health policy, according to Sullivan, was viewed as part of a contract between government on the one hand and communities on the other – the legitimate response to the social needs of a population rather than to the consumer preferences or demands of individual customers.[19]

The Welsh stripe in health policy post-devolution

Jane Hutt was the first Health Minister post-devolution and she vainly tried to articulate the need to pursue the 'Welsh way', which was an overarching public health approach to tackling the upstream determinants of inequalities in health and deal with the chronic health problems, which were placing ever-increasing demands on healthcare services. The commitment to redressing the inequalities in health that existed within Wales and in comparison to the rest of the UK was documented in the Assembly's NHS plan published in 2001, *Improving Health in Wales: A Plan for the NHS with its partners*.[20] The Minister's foreword to the document indicated the intent:

> I am delighted to introduce proposals, which place the citizen at the centre of the NHS and building on an enviable record in Wales, establish firm lines of accountability to the people and communities of our nation. The NHS will, as part of its renewal, truly become the people's NHS. This involves not only maintaining the patient-centred focus of our services but also making the NHS answerable to all citizens – patients and potential patients alike. It also means involving communities in the collective development of policies for health and well-being and makes the process of health policy-making inclusive.

One of the noticeable features of the plan was its focus on collaboration and cooperation across agencies through formal and informal alliances, which were given further emphasis in the *Well Being in Wales* consultation, published in 2002.[21] This document demonstrated a commitment to increase the effectiveness, efficiency and financial management of health and social services, and highlighted the need for these organisations to be more responsive to the needs of increasingly well-informed patients and clients and ensure better access to those most in need. The early years of devolution therefore saw the reconfiguration of the NHS to reflect the policy agenda, as reflected in the plan *Improving Health in Wales: A Plan for the NHS with its partners*. The Wales Centre for Health was established in 2005 to oversee and advocate on public health issues, while the removal of GP fundholding and the establishment of twenty-two local health groups (LHGs) as committees of the health authorities – their boundaries being coterminous with the local authorities created under the John Redwood period as Secretary of State – laid the foundations for the abolition of the five health authorities in 2003, with the LHGs becoming twenty-two autonomous local health boards (LHBs). This was the ideal opportunity to secure greater alignment and integration between health and social care via partnerships and joint working across public services and the third sector, with clear demarcation from the policy developments that were continuing in England. Wales retained community health councils, which were abolished in England in 2003, and did not adopt either payment by results (2003/4) or the foundation trust model (2004) designed to complement the quasi-market approach being driven in England.[22]

However, as indicated above, the relatively poor health status of the Welsh population represented a major constraint on the implementation and accomplishment of policy intentions and goals in the early years of devolution. The *Welsh Health Survey* for 2003–4 showed that:[23]

- 16 per cent of adults reported that their health was excellent, 34 per cent that it was very good, 28 per cent that it was good, 15 per cent that it was fair, 6 per cent that it was poor
- 54 per cent of adults in Wales were classified as overweight or obese
- 18 per cent of adults were being treated for high blood pressure
- 14 per cent were being treated for arthritis
- 13 per cent were being treated for a respiratory illness
- 12 per cent were being treated for back pain
- 10 per cent were being treated for a heart condition
- 9 per cent were being treated for a mental illness.

In overall terms, 28 per cent of adults and 5 per cent of children were reported to have a limiting long-term illness, which were generally higher than rates reported in England, while the age-old issue of health inequalities continued to haunt policy makers and politicians alike. The Chief Medical Officer's report at the time had demonstrated that death rates in Merthyr Tydfil were almost 50 per cent higher than those in Ceredigion but also highlighted the significant differences between communities within areas, accounted for by levels of deprivation.[24] Life expectancy at birth for males in Merthyr Tydfil was the lowest in Wales at 73.3 years compared with 78.5 years in Ceredigion – a difference of over five years; while the life expectancy for females in Merthyr was 78.1 years compared with 81.9 years in Ceredigion.[25] The differential in relation to healthy life expectancy was even more stark, with people in relatively affluent communities expected to live for eighteen years longer before experiencing significant health problems than those in relatively deprived communities, while the infant mortality rate between 1998 and 2001 in the most deprived fifth of areas in Wales was 60 per cent higher than in the most affluent fifth of areas.[26] The 'opening of the purse strings by Gordon Brown', whilst welcome, did not serve to alleviate the problems caused by the behaviours and attitudes of the people of Wales in relation to smoking, obesity, inactivity and poor diet.[27] Unfortunately, the prevalence of unhealthy behaviours and chronic conditions, along with the challenges associated with health inequalities, remain very much on the agenda for today's politicians and policy makers.

Problems in implementing the Welsh stripe

Despite positive intentions, as well as the relatively poor health of the population, the early years of devolution saw considerable media attention on the difference in 'performance' between Wales and England in relation to waiting lists and waiting times, which was to bedevil attempts to drive the public health agenda forward. In the years following devolution, Wales pursued a far less aggressive approach to managing NHS waiting times than the target and sanction model employed in England.[28] During those years, England sustained a comprehensive focus on reducing excessive waiting times and continued to achieve shorter maximum waiting time targets. In contrast, the Welsh response to excessive waiting times was characterised by specific initiatives with intermittent injections of funds and while there was some improvement, this was attributed to waiting list management as opposed to enhanced access to services.[29]

In January 2005, the Assembly was criticised by the Auditor General of Wales for the absence of a clear strategy to reduce waiting times and for what it described as unacceptably long waiting times for some patients, arguing that the waiting list funding initiative had been neither cost-effective nor achieved sustainable reductions in waiting times.[30] The casualty of this perceived poor performance was the minister Jane Hutt, moved by Rhodri Morgan due to 'exhaustion', but given this occurred a few days prior to the publication of the Auditor General's report, a less favourable view was to avoid her having to resign in the face of its findings.[31] Her successor was Brian Gibbons, a GP who had practised in the same area and similar time to Julian Tudor Hart, the author of the 'inverse care law' whereby the availability of good quality care varies inversely with the need of the population served. It was Brian Gibbons who was to work closely with the First Minister on the 'delivery' of the

26-week waiting time for all referrals pledged in the 2005 general election manifesto. However, this was not to satisfy the ongoing political and media opposition, who pointed to the 18-week target in England, often without recognising that the English target only applied to GP referrals. Performance issues continued to dog attempts to implement the policies that were indicative of the Welsh stripe.

One of the most significant developments took place in October 2002, when the then Finance Minister, Edwina Hart, announced a substantial increase in the future resources to be allocated to health in Wales. She also made clear that the use of these resources needed to be allied to improved performance and modernisation of health and social care services. At the same time, she announced that WAG had asked Derek Wanless, the author of the report for the Chancellor of the Exchequer, *Securing our Future Health: Taking a Long-Term View*, to act as advisor to a team set up to review health and social care in Wales and to examine how resources should be translated into reform and improved performance.[32]

The Wanless Report, *The Review of Health and Social Care in Wales*, clearly emphasised that the situation facing the NHS in Wales was not sustainable, and that action was needed on a number of fronts to remedy system deficiencies, secure developments in the Welsh health service, generate improvements in health outcomes for the population and redress the inequalities in health that existed within Wales and in comparison to the rest of the UK.[33] In May 2005 WAG released *Designed for Life*, which set the policy for addressing these issues and highlighted its ambition to create a world-class health and social care service in a healthy, dynamic country by 2015.[34] The three design aims of *Designed for Life* were: lifelong health; fast, safe and effective services; and world-class care. It supported the goals, made in previous strategic documents and a recurring theme in subsequent policy initiatives, to concentrate on delivering a healthy Wales through partnership. A plan of action was set out to describe the health and social care services that the people of Wales could expect in 2015, delivered through a series of 3-year strategic frameworks. An emphasis on user-centred services was prefaced by the statement that 'optimum improvement will be achieved if people become fully engaged with their own health and wellbeing and also take seriously their responsibilities to adopt healthy lifestyles'.[35] A series of other strategic documents were produced, recognising that the NHS and its partners needed to demonstrate their commitment to the philosophy and aims of *Designed for Life*, by adherence to a series of key milestones with specific targets in place to provide a short-term focus. The document stated that the targets would, among other things, 'prompt a sharp shift towards preventing problems rather than waiting for them to occur' – which recalls *Strategic Intent and Direction*, some fifteen years previously.[36] The intention was that the NHS, local government and their partners would continue to focus attention on strengthening the efforts to promote prevention at all levels and greater efforts would be made to help people look after their own health better – balancing clearer service entitlements and greater individual responsibility for healthy choices relating to lifestyle and behaviour. Health Challenge Wales was established to act as the focal point of efforts to improve health and well-being, recognising that a wide range of factors impact on health and well-being and that co-ordinated action could help to create a healthier nation.[37] The scheme was launched in January 2005 and was a key feature of several initiatives, which were branded with the Health Challenge Wales logo. However, the extent to which the aims of *Designed for Life*, and other policy aspirations that were reflective of a distinctive Welsh stripe to health policy, were achieved was constrained by a range of factors, as documented by a number of commentators.[38] One of the major issues was the ongoing, constant flow of criticism of Welsh health performance, from politicians and media, as compared to that in England. This reached its climax when David Cameron – at a speech to the Welsh Conservatives conference at Llangollen in April 2014 – said that Wales was witnessing a 'national scandal' as Offa's Dyke had 'become the line between life and death'.[39] Further, at the time, WG was also reeling from comments made by Ann Clwyd MP following the death of her husband. She had subsequently led a UK Government-commissioned inquiry on how NHS hospitals in England handled complaints, following the Francis Report into events at Mid Staffordshire NHS Trust.[40] The Francis Report has been something of a landmark in highlighting major quality deficiencies in healthcare provision, with its 290 recommendations having major ramifications for all health organisations and systems. Ms Clwyd alleged that 'the key warning signs that Francis mentioned – accumulation of patient stories detailing adverse incidents, bad practice, unusually high mortality statistics, signals from staff and whistle-blowers, poor governance, dysfunctional hospital wards and also weak regulation' were also evident in Wales.[41] Such negative publicity further contributed to a retreat into policies that were more akin with those from Westminster, with a focus on relatively narrow performance targets and micro financial management. Financial pressures have been a regular feature in the performance of NHS organisations over the twenty years of devolution and the annual budgetary cycle is writ large in media analyses of NHS Wales. The performance against targets, including finance, continued to be benchmarked against what was happening in England, and led to a dilution of the clear red water, as envisaged by the First Ministers of Wales and successive Health Ministers.

The quality of provision has continued to be a significant factor in the dilution of the contrast between the 'Welsh stripe' and other parts of the UK. NHS Wales has experienced a number of major problems relating to quality of provision, as evidenced for example in the *Trusted to Care* inquiry following concerns at Neath Port Talbot and Princess of Wales hospitals,[42] the Royal College of Midwives and Royal College of Obstetricians and Gynaecologists review of maternity services at Cwm Taf Health Board,[43] and with Betsi Cadwaladr Health Board being placed under special measures after a number of issues, including a report which found 'institutional abuse' at the Tawel Fan mental health unit.[44] The *NHS Wales Escalation and Intervention Arrangements* were introduced in April 2014 to identify and respond to serious issues affecting NHS services, quality and safety of care and organisational effectiveness.[45] The four levels of escalation, which reflect increasing levels of concern, are routine arrangements, which reflects normal business; enhanced monitoring; targeted intervention; and special measures. Most health boards have been subject to some form of escalation since the process was initiated and it continues to be in place at present.

The energies and efforts required to address such quality deficits, along with the raft of other issues, were and remain major constraints in seeking to implement the necessary changes to deliver the 'world-class' health system for Wales envisaged in *Designed for Life*. Another major impediment in the attempts to implement policy in a distinctly Welsh manner has been the limited powers afforded to Wales under devolution and the lack of separate Welsh institutions. For example, the National Assembly for Wales (NAW) was the first administration in the UK to back a motion to end smoking in all enclosed public places in January 2003. However, it took more than four years to bring this to fruition, with the ban on smoking in enclosed public places and workplaces coming into force in April 2007. Scotland had introduced a ban in March 2006, while England did so in July 2007. Rhodri Morgan testified that such a scheme was one of the most significant realised by the assembly government:

> this is the single most important public health measure that the Assembly has brought in. Second-hand smoke in public places is estimated to cause 400 premature deaths a year. This is an unacceptable toll. There is now strong support and acceptance from businesses and members of the public alike in Wales for a ban on smoking in enclosed public places. That support is gathering momentum as people become more aware of the damaging and deadly effect of breathing in second-hand smoke. The health benefits of smoke-free public places are already apparent in Ireland and Scotland where public support has grown since their bans.[46]

However, it took several years to be implemented from its inception – and at the cost of the premature deaths that had arisen as a result.

Further constraints to the implementation of the Welsh stripe emerged because of attempts to address structural issues with the NHS in Wales. Any suggestions of service reconfiguration were basically terminal for those with political aspirations, as communities corralled support for their local hospitals in the face of 'attempts' to downgrade or even close such facilities. For instance, Angela Burns was elected as AM in Carmarthenshire West and Pembrokeshire South in the election of 2007. It was reported that 'no-one was more surprised than herself' as the Conservatives moved from third place with 20.5 per cent of the vote in 2003 to take the seat with 30 per cent of the vote.[47] It was strongly argued that a threat to downgrade Withybush Hospital in Haverfordwest was a major factor in securing her victory, with a leaflet circulating during the campaign which suggested that 'whatever our normal political hue we need to make it clear that any threat to our services by any political party will not be tolerated by the voters'.[48] Ironically, it is not political parties, per se, that propose structural changes and service reorganisation, but the blame is laid very much at their door. Interestingly, following a review by the Royal College of Physicians into cardiac services within Hywel Dda in 2014, Mark Drakeford said the review 'bears out many of the things I have said over the year I have been Health Minister – that we try to do too many things in too many parts of Wales'.[49] A few years previously, in November 2011, the fourth Health Minister, Lesley Griffiths, published the policy document *Together for Health: A Five Year Vision for the NHS in Wales*, which again set out a vision for healthcare in Wales that challenged the NHS and its partners to aspire to match the standards of the best in the world, and to aim at achieving excellence everywhere.[50] In response to the document, five of the health boards in south Wales established the South Wales Programme in 2012 to create plans for sustainable services and collectively respond to the fragility of some clinical services, as highlighted by clinicians through their royal colleges and to adhere to professional standards. The South Wales Programme was, in principle, an excellent example of collaboration both across the NHS and with stakeholder groups and organisations. It was recognised that the current configuration, where eight hospitals were involved in the provision of a range of services, was unsustainable and that there was a need to concentrate provision in fewer hospitals. While there was general acceptance that there should be a reconfiguration and rationalisation, the debate was on the number – three, four or five – and the location of such 'chosen hospitals'. The consensual and collaborative approach that had been intended at the outset of the programme was to unravel once the recommendations were evident. One of the proposals emerging from the deliberations was that accident and emergency services would no longer be available at Royal Glamorgan Hospital. This resulted in the obvious and expected criticism from opposition parties, but this was starkly reinforced by the involvement of local Labour MPs and, significantly, from the education minister, Leighton Andrews. This led to a major fall-out between the first minister Carwyn Jones and Leighton Andrews, who had been his campaign manager for his bid to become first minister following Rhodri Morgan, and was yet another example of the obstacles that have stacked up over time to frustrate the aims of the Wanless Review and the implementation of the 'Welsh stripe' in Welsh health policy. The current configuration of NHS Wales was established under the watch of Edwina Hart as Health Minister. She had commissioned the Wanless Review as Finance Minister and became Health Minister, in succession to Brian Gibbons, during the coalition government in July 2007. According to Rhodri Morgan, she 'preferred to be given a job to do and the money to do it, and then go away and get on with it'.[51] There are seven local health boards and three NHS trusts, which emerged from the plethora of organisations that had existed up until 2009. The local health boards in Wales plan, secure and deliver healthcare services in their areas, while the three NHS trusts provide 'specialist' service but have an all-Wales focus – the Welsh Ambulance Services Trust for emergency services, Velindre NHS Trust offering specialist services in cancer care and a range of national support services and Public Health Wales. This structure has remained intact for over a decade, subject to some tweaking in recent years, but any suggestion of hospital closure or downgrading is met with considerable vocal opposition from local communities and their elected representatives, which coupled with the significant challenges in relation to finance, performance and service quality, has meant that the expectations as to what the health and social care system would look like in 2015, envisaged by *Designed for Life*, did not materialise.

Another publication emerged in 2016 that painted more or less the same picture as that portrayed in *Designed for Life*. The Health Foundation report – *The path to sustainability: Funding projections for the NHS in Wales to 2019/20 and 2030/31* – presented the same message.[52] It found that immediate and sustained action was needed to both address the urgent funding pressures facing the service and secure the long-term future of the NHS in Wales. In November 2016, the sixth health minister since devolution, Vaughan Gething, announced, with cross-party support, an independent review into the future of health and social care in Wales by an international panel of experts. The resultant report, *The Parliamentary Review of Health and Social Care in Wales*, published in January 2018, highlighted that spending on health and social care in Wales was outpacing the growth in the country's wealth, and while the emphasis was on achieving greater value in relation to the resources allocated, it was clearly evident that 'sustainability' required a radical, multifaceted series of approaches if the healthcare dilemma was to be addressed.[53] The terminology may be different, but the intent and focus contained within the messaging resonated very closely with those produced by Derek Wanless, fifteen years previously, and with the aims of *Strategic Intent and Direction*, thirty years ago. A scrutiny of policy documents during the intervening years would demonstrate, without the need for any detailed analysis, that while all of the policy documents were consistent with the notion of 'clear red water' and 'Welsh stripe', with the emphasis on systems, improved population health and enhanced service quality, the implementation of such policies have not been enacted and the requisite changes necessary have not emerged to the extent necessary to deliver a distinct and different 'Welsh' health system.

The current WG health policy document, *A Healthier Wales: Our Plan for Health and Social Care*, again aspires to move towards the 'Welsh way', opening with the statement:

> We will build on the philosophy of Prudent Healthcare, and on the close and effective relationships we have in Wales, to make an impact on health and well-being throughout life. We will have a greater emphasis on preventing illness, on support-ing people to manage their own health and well-being, and on enabling people to live independently for as long as they can, supported by new technologies and by integrated health and social care services which are delivered closer to home.[54]

Prudent Healthcare was developed by the Bevan Commission in 2013 as a means to assist in reducing demands, enhancing quality, limiting risk, improving overall care and driving down costs. It was argued that prudent healthcare is conceived, managed and delivered in a cautious and wise way characterised by forethought, vigilance and careful budgeting, which achieves tangible benefits and quality outcomes for patients.[55]

Time will determine whether Wales will reach such a position, envis-aged in *A Healthier Wales*, and the population will be healthier. The current data does not represent any significant deviation from the preva-lence figures and statistics highlighted in the 2003 *Welsh Health Survey*. The final *Welsh Health Survey* was published in 2015 and Table 2.1 high-lights the comparative position.[56]

The *Welsh Health Survey* was superseded in 2016 by the *National Survey for Wales*, of which health status is but one component. The latest figures fail to point to any improvement in the health of the population with 33 per cent of those sampled in 2018/19 indicating that their health was very good; 38 per cent that it was good; 20 per cent that it was fair; 7 per cent that it was bad and 2 per cent that it was very bad. The differ-ent classification approach makes a more direct comparison difficult, but the percentage that were at least good is similar but those who indicated that their health was fair or poor was probably greater.[57] Life expectancy

Table 2.1: Comparison of Welsh health surveys, 2003 and 2015

	Welsh Health Survey 2003	Welsh Health Survey 2015
Percentage of adults reporting that health was excellent	16	15
Percentage of adults reporting that health was very good	34	35
Percentage of adults reporting that health was good	28	30
Percentage of adults reporting that health was fair	15	14
Percentage of adults reporting that health was poor	6	5
Percentage of adults classified as overweight or obese	54	59
Percentage of adults currently smoking	26	19
Percentage of adults treated for high blood pressure	18	20
Percentage of adults treated for arthritis	14	12
Percentage of adults treated for respiratory problems	13	14
Percentage of adults treated for back pain	12	12
Percentage of adults treated for heart condition	10	8
Percentage of adults treated for mental health problems	9	13
Percentage reporting limiting long-term illness	28% adults; 5% children	33% adults

would appear to be plateauing, while there is a slight widening in mortality rates between the least and most deprived communities.

Examples of the Welsh stripe

Despite the relative failure to achieve a distinctive and different health system, there are examples of significant policy initiatives that have reaffirmed the commitment to establish 'clear red water' between Wales and other UK systems. Probably the most noticeable was that of free prescriptions. Rhodri Morgan needed 'something suitably eye-catching to win back those seats in the Labour heartland' lost in the 1999 election in preparing the manifesto for the May 2003 election.[58] On 1 April 2007 Wales became the first UK country to abolish charges for prescriptions, to be followed in subsequent years by Northern Ireland and Scotland. The opposition to such an abolition came from the Welsh Conservatives and UK Government, but the evidence would point to minimal impact in relation to dispensing and purchasing of previously non-prescribed medicines and in relation to expenditure incurred.[59]

Another example of the universalist approach to policy employed by the Rhodri Morgan government and one of the early initiatives introduced by Edwina Hart as Health Minister was the abolition of car parking charges at Welsh NHS hospitals.[60] This was seen very much as an additional tax on patients and their families and should therefore be removed. However, due to contractual obligations with car parking firms, it was to take a decade for this policy to be fully implemented.[61] Wales was again the first of the UK countries to adopt such a scheme, followed by Scotland a year or so later, but in England and Northern Ireland parking charges still apply.

Another legacy from the Edwina Hart era as Health Minister was the establishment – on the sixtieth anniversary of the NHS – of the Bevan Commission, established as an independent, expert group to advise the minister responsible for the NHS in Wales on taking forward health and health services improvement, and to ensure that Wales could draw on best practice from across the world, while remaining true to the principles of the NHS as established by Aneurin Bevan. It was the Bevan Commission that authored the initial paper on Prudent Healthcare.[62] The notion of Prudent Healthcare was first introduced to underpin health policy in Wales in early 2014 and its principles have been generally welcomed and had a positive reception across all professional groups, patient representatives and NHS Wales organisations.[63] They are designed to achieve health and well-being through co-production; to care for those with the greatest health needs first; to do only what is needed; and to reduce inappropriate variation. The notion of prudent healthcare still underpins the health policy agenda in Wales, but the conditions needed for its successful implementation, as advocated in 2014, remain some way off:

> delivery of these benefits will require leadership and clear policy from Welsh Government and health boards including clarity on performance management. It will require politicians, public service leaders and clinicians to have challenging conversations with citizens around shared responsibilities[64]

One of the most significant pieces of legislation emerging during post-devolution was the Human Transplantation (Wales) Act, passed in July 2013 and becoming law in December 2015. It presumes that people aged eighteen and over provide 'deemed consent' for their organs to be donated unless they have specifically objected. The Act has resulted in an increase in donors across Wales and in 2017/18 Wales had the highest consent rate for the whole of the UK at 70 per cent. In England, there is now an opt-out system, whereby all adults agree to become organ donors when they die, unless they have made it known that they do not wish to donate. There are close similarities with the Welsh system, but the English system only became operational in 2020. A new system, similar to that of Wales, came into effect in Scotland in March 2021, while the Organ and Tissue (Deemed Consent) Bill is currently going through its legislative process in Northern Ireland. The data would appear to be positive but this is somewhat of a niche area and one that does not have significant reach in terms of health policy per se.

The Well-being of Future Generations (Wales) Act 2015 was another example of the innovative nature of policy-making. It requires public bodies to consider the long-term impact of their decisions and to engage meaningfully with people, communities and other public bodies to prevent persistent problems such as poverty, health inequalities and climate change. The Act is unique to Wales, attracting interest from countries across the world as it offers a huge opportunity to make a long-lasting, positive change to both current and future generations. The intentions are well meant but only in the longer term will the extent of the benefits realised as a result of the Act become evident.

The Social Services and Well-being Act 2014 provided a legal framework for improving the well-being of people who need care and support and carers who need support, and for transforming social services in Wales to deliver services that are focused on achieving the outcomes necessary to promote a person's well-being. It has four themes, which as can be seen, resonate with other policy aims in the field of health and social care:

- people: putting an individual and their needs at the centre of their care, and giving them a voice in, and greater control over, reaching the personal outcomes that help them achieve well-being

- well-being: supporting people to achieve their own well-being and measuring the success of this support
- earlier intervention: promoting the use of preventative approaches within the community to address people's needs before they become critical
- collaboration: stronger partnership working across all organisations to better support people in achieving positive outcomes.

This Act is in the process of being evaluated to determine the extent to which the intentions have materialised and how the Act has affected the well-being of people who need care and support, and their carers. Preliminary findings from the evaluation demonstrated that the Act clearly has legitimised change and has been a catalysing force in the development of social services, and local authorities' relationships with key partners in health, the voluntary sector and the independent sector. Four years after the Act came into force, there is considerable evidence of the difference made, but also in respect of the difference still to be made.

Conclusion and overall reflection

Obviously, the Coronavirus pandemic has further derailed policy intentions from 2020 onwards, and healthcare systems will not recover for many years. However, the extent to which the healthcare dilemma applies will, in all probability, become even more evident as pressures on public finance intensify during the post-COVID-19 recovery phase. Healthcare systems have been likened to the course of a river, from the relative simplicity of its structure and form at source to the complexity, magnitude and power at its confluence with the sea. As patients enter the system and present with their healthcare problems, their interaction with healthcare professionals is relatively straightforward and simple to comprehend. However, as they journey through the system the degree of complexity intensifies, with many obstacles and problems to negotiate and at the hospital the patient is subjected to an entirely different environment, with its significantly higher costs. The current incentive schemes and performance measures reflect such a pathway, with onward referral of patients to more specialised services, whereas a revised approach would reward efforts to remove patients from the river at the earliest possible opportunity, or even empowering them not to enter the river in the first place. It is much less expensive to 'fish patients out of the NHS river' nearer its source than when it enters the sea, and even more efficient to prevent the patient from falling into the river in the first place.[65] The tendency has been to ensure that patients are equipped with the best buoyancy aids and aqua-craft as they float down the NHS river towards the ocean, having been referred to the specialist professional that resides in the nearest district general hospital. Indeed, it has been suggested that 'a society that spends so much on healthcare that it cannot spend adequately on other health-enhancing activities may actually be reducing the health of its population'.[66] The adoption of a broader agenda in health policy – as in *A Healthier Wales* and aligned with the Welsh stripe – would require an investment of resources at early stages in the healthcare spectrum, dealing with problems in their very early stages and with the aim of removing people from the healthcare system rather than 'moving them on' to a more complex and expensive part of the system or even investing in other public services – education, environment, economic development – that are likely to enhance the health of the population.[67]

In reflecting on the issues that have bedevilled the aspirations and intentions of successive WGs post-devolution, it is ironic that the performance of the NHS in Wales was and has continued to be measured against the metrics of the UK health policy agenda, rather than seeking to measure the indicators that would reflect progress against all of the goals and aspirations that have appeared in all of the health policy documents that have been penned since devolution. It was Mark Drakeford, the primary author of the 'clear red water' speech, writing in 2006, who had recognised that while health policy-making 'has been far-reaching, the implementation of that policy agenda has proved problematic', concluding that:

> both social policy academics and politicians have underestimated the ways in which barriers to reform can be mobilised, including the way in which health policy debates are presented in the media, even when radicalism has been established in policy intent.[68]

The health of the population of Wales is probably on a par with what it was when devolution began. Life expectancy has slightly increased in general, but inequalities remain and will, in all probability, widen – not least as a result of the Coronavirus pandemic. The question as to whether these indicators would be different if successive administrations had persevered with the aspirations contained in their respective policy documents, and the Welsh stripe had been more apparent, is a theoretical one, but it is of note that expert reviews of the respective performance of the health systems within each of the four UK countries have found no difference between them.[69]

Notes

1. WG Final Budget 2020/1. Available at: *https://gov.wales/final-budget-2021-to-2022* (accessed 15 March 2021).
2. Ceri J. Phillips, *Health Economics: an introduction for health care professionals* (Oxford: Blackwell BMJ Books, 2005).
3. *Mike Sullivan Dialogues*, conducted in 2017–18, with nineteen politicians and advisers intimately involved with the development of devolution in the period 1997–2011. These transcripts are in the hands of Mike Sullivan's widow and co-editor, Prof. Jane Williams. Interview with Edwina Hart, *Mike Sullivan Dialogues* (hereafter *MS Dialogues*), p. 4.
4. Rhodri Morgan, 'Clear red water' speech to the National Centre for Public Policy, Swansea University, 11 December 2002.
5. Interview with Lawrence Conway, *MS Dialogues*, p. 21.
6. C. Tudor-Smith et al., 'Effects of the Heartbeat Wales programme over five years on behavioural risks for cardiovascular disease: quasi-experimental comparison of results from Wales and a matched reference area', *British Medical Journal*, v. 316 (7134) (14 March 1998), 818–22; C. J. Phillips and M. J. Prowle, 'The economics of a reduction in smoking: A case study from Heartbeat Wales', *Journal of Epidemiology and Community Health*, 47 (1993), 215–23.
7. Rhodri Morgan, *Rhodri: A Political Life in Wales and Westminster* (Cardiff: University of Wales Press, 2017), p. 258.
8. Welsh Health Planning Forum, *Strategic Intent and Direction for the NHS in Wales* (Cardiff: Welsh Office/NHS Directorate, 1989).
9. Mike Sullivan, 'Wales, Devolution and Health Policy: Policy Experimentation and Differentiation to Improve Health', *Contemporary Wales*, 17/1 (2005), 44–65.
10. M. Longley, C. Riley and M. Warner, 'A health service fit for the 21st century: the Welsh "Health and Social Care 2010" project', *Futures*, 27/9–10 (1995), 967–77.
11. Morgan, *Rhodri: A Political Life in Wales and Westminster*, pp. 58–9.
12. 'Working for Patients', Cm. 555 (London: HMSO, 1989); 'Caring for People: Community Care in the next decade and beyond', Cm. 849 (London: HMSO, 1989).

13. Longley, Riley and Warner, 'A health service fit for the 21st century', 968.
14. Morgan, *Rhodri: A Political Life in Wales and Westminster*, p. 104.
15. J. Gabbay and A. Stevens, 'Towards investing in health gain', *British Medical Journal*, v. 308 (6937) (30 April 1994), 1117–18.
16. Mansel Aylward, Ceri Phillips and Helen Howson, *Simply Prudent Healthcare – achieving better care and value for money in Wales – discussion paper* (Swansea: Bevan Commission, 4 December 2013).
17. Morgan, *Rhodri: A Political Life in Wales and Westminster*, p. 109; Mansel Aylward, *Are Bevan's principles still applicable in the NHS?*, Improving Healthcare White Paper Series, 3 (2011).
18. Sullivan, 'Wales, Devolution and Health Policy', 63; Rhodri Morgan, 'Making Social Policy in Wales', Lecture for the National Centre for Public Policy, 11 December 2002.
19. Sullivan, 'Wales, Devolution and Health Policy', 55.
20. *Improving Health in Wales: A Plan for the NHS with its partners* (Cardiff: WAG, 2001). Available at: *http://www.wales.nhs.uk/publications/NHSStrategydoc.pdf* (accessed 15 March 2021).
21. *Well-being in Wales* (Cardiff: WAG, 2002). Available at: *http://www.wales.nhs.uk/documents/file1-full-doc-e.pdf* (accessed 15 March 2021).
22. John Appleby et al., *Payment by Results: How can payment systems help to deliver better care?* (London: The King's Fund, 2012); R. Lewis, 'NHS foundation trusts', *British Medical Journal*, 331/59 (2005). DOI: *https://doi.org/10.1136/bmj.331.7508.59.*
23. Stats Wales, *Welsh Health Survey, Illnesses by gender and year* (2003–4). Available at: *https://statswales.gov.wales/Catalogue/Health-and-Social-Care/Welsh-Health-Survey/illnesses-by-gender-year* (accessed 15 March 2021).
24. *Digest of Welsh Local Area Statistics 2004: Population and Migration: Expectation of Life at Birth 2000–02* (Cardiff: NAW, 2004). Available at: *https://gov.wales/digest-welsh-local-area-statistics* (accessed 15 March 2021).
25. *Health Status Wales 2004–05: Report 1, Chief Medical Officer's Report Series* (Cardiff: WAG, 2005). Available at: *http://www.wales.nhs.uk/documents/health-status-wales-e.pdf* (accessed 15 March 2021).
26. Peter Kenway et al., *Monitoring poverty and social exclusion in Wales* (York: Joseph Rowntree Foundation, 2005).
27. Morgan, *Rhodri: A Political Life in Wales and Westminster*, p. 258.
28. Scott Greer, *The Politics of Health Policy Divergence. Devolution in Practice. Public Policy Differences within the UK* (London: The Constitution Unit, 2004).
29. IWA, *Time to Deliver: The Third Term and Beyond – Policy Options for Wales* (Cardiff: IWA, 2006), p. 72.
30. IWA, *Time to Deliver*, p. 73.
31. Morgan, *Rhodri: A Political Life in Wales and Westminster*, p. 267.
32. Derek Wanless, *Securing our Future Health: Taking a Long-Term View* (London: HM Treasury, 2002).
33. WAG, *The Review of Health and Social Care in Wales. The Report of the Project Team advised by Derek Wanless* (Cardiff: WAG, 2003).

34. WAG, *Designed for Life: Creating World Class Health and Social Care for Wales in the 21st Century* (Cardiff: WAG, 2005).

35. WAG, *Designed for Life*, p. 13.

36. WAG, *Designed for Life*, p. 26.

37. Health in Wales, 'Welcome to Health Challenge Wales'. Available at: *http://www.wales.nhs.uk/news/2991* (accessed 29 January 2021).

38. C. Riley, 'The challenge of creating a Welsh NHS', *Journal of Health Services Research and Policy*, 21/1 (2016), 40–2; M. Drakeford, 'Health policy in Wales: making a difference in conditions of difficulty', *Critical Social Policy*, 26/3 (2006), 543–61; S. L. Greer, 'Devolution and health in the UK: policy and its lessons since 1998', *British Medical Bulletin*, 118 (2016), 17–25.

39. 'David Cameron claims Offa's Dyke has become the line between life and death', *Daily Post*, 11 April 2014.

40. *Report of the Mid Staffordshire NHS Foundation Trust Public Inquiry chaired by Robert Francis QC*, HC 898 I, II, III (February 2013).

41. BBC News, 'MP Ann Clwyd to continue calls for Welsh NHS changes'. Available at: *https://www.bbc.co.uk/news/uk-wales-26678347* (accessed 29 January 2021).

42. June Andrews and Mark Butler, *Trusted to Care: An Independent Review of the Princess of Wales Hospital and Neath Port Talbot Hospital at Abertawe Bro Morgannwg University Health Board*, Dementia Services Development Centre and The People's Organisation. Available at: *https://gov.wales/sites/default/files/publications/2019-04/trusted-to-care.pdf* (accessed 29 January 2021).

43. Royal College of Midwives and Royal College of Obstetricians and Gynaecologists, *Report of the Review of Maternity Services at Cwm Taf Health Board* (15–17 January 2019). Available at: *http://www.wales.nhs.uk/sitesplus/documents/903/review-of-maternity-services-at-cwm-taf-health-board_0.pdf* (accessed 29 January 2021).

44. Androulla Johnstone, *Independent Investigation into the Care and Treatment Provided on Tawel Fan Ward: a Lessons [sic] for Learning Report commissioned by Betsi Cadwaladr University Health Board* (Hascas Consultancy Limited, May 2018). Available at: *https://bcuhb.nhs.wales/news/updates-and-developments/updates/archived-updates/tawel-fan/tawel-fan/full-hascas-report-may-2018/* (accessed 29 January 2021).

45. WG, *NHS Wales Escalation and Intervention Arrangements* (March 2014). Available at: *https://gov.wales/sites/default/files/publications/2019-04/nhs-wales-escalation-and-intervention-arrangements.pdf* (accessed 29 January 2021).

46. WAG press release, 26 March 2007, available at The National Archive, archived on 14 January 2008. Available at: *https://webarchive.nationalarchives.gov.uk* (accessed 16 March 2021).

47. John Osmond, *Crossing the Rubicon: Coalition Politics Welsh Style* (Cardiff: IWA, 2007), p. 4.

48. Osmond, *Crossing the Rubicon*, p. 4.

49. BBC News, 'Hywel Dda hospital cardiac care review criticised in report', 14 March 2014. Available at: *https://www.bbc.co.uk/news/uk-wales-26550529* (accessed 29 January 2021).

50. WG, *Together for Health: A Five Year Vision for the NHS in Wales* (2011). Available at: *http://www.wales.nhs.uk/sitesplus/documents/829/togetherforhealth. pdf* (accessed 29 January 2021).

51. Morgan, *Rhodri: A Political Life in Wales and Westminster*, p. 261.

52. Toby Watt and Adam Roberts, *The path to sustainability: Funding projections for the NHS in Wales to 2019/20 and 2030/31*, Health Foundation (October 2016). Available at: *https://www.health.org.uk/publications/reports/ the-path-to-sustainability* (accessed 31 January 2021).

53. Ruth Hussey et al., *The Parliamentary Review of Health and Social Care in Wales* (2018). Available at: *https://gov.wales/sites/default/files/publications/2018-01/Revie w-health-social-care-report-final.pdf* (accessed 31 January 2021).

54. WG, *A Healthier Wales: Our Plan for Health and Social Care* (Cardiff: WG, 2019), p. 3. Available at: *https://gov.wales/sites/default/files/publications/2019-10/ a-healthier-wales-action-plan.pdf* (accessed 31 January 2021).

55. Aylward, Phillips and Howson, *Simply Prudent Healthcare*.

56. Stats Wales, *Welsh Health Survey* (2015). Available at: *https://statswales.gov.wales/ Catalogue/Health-and-Social-Care/Welsh-Health-Survey* (accessed 31 January 2021).

57. WG, *National Survey for Wales: Headline results, April 2019–March 2020*. Available at: *https://gov.wales/sites/default/files/statistics-and-research/2020-07/ national-survey-wales-headline-results-april-2019-march-2020-947.pdf* (accessed 31 January 2021).

58. Morgan, *Rhodri: A Political Life in Wales and Westminster*, p. 255.

59. S. Groves et al., 'Abolition of prescription charges in Wales: the impact on medicines use in those who used to pay', *International Journal of Pharmaceutical Practice*, 18/6 (2010), 332–40; F. Alam et al., 'Impact of the phased abolition of co-payments on the utilisation of selected prescription medicines in Wales', *Health Economics*, 27/1 (2018), 236–43; D. Cohen et al., 'Abolition of prescription co-payments in Wales: an observational study on dispensing rates', *Value Health*, 13/5 (2010), 675–80; BBC News, 'Free prescriptions "saving Welsh NHS money for 10 years"', 1 April 2017. Available at: *https://www.bbc.co.uk/ news/uk-wales-politics-39457033* (accessed 31 January 2021).

60. Statement by Edwina Hart, Minister for Health and Social Services, 3 March 2008. Available at: *https://senedd.wales/Ministerial%20Statements%20Documents/ Reform%20of%20Car%20Parking%20Charges%20in%20the%20NHS%20 in%20Wales%20(PDF,%2010.8kb)-03032008-80126/dat20080303-e-English. pdf* (accessed 31 January 2021).

61. BBC News, 'All NHS hospital car parking charges scrapped in Wales', 1 September 2018. Available at: *https://www.bbc.co.uk/news/uk-wales-45347166* (accessed 31 January 2021).

62. Aylward, Phillips and Howson, *Simply Prudent Healthcare*.

63. S. Addis et al., 'Implementing Prudent Healthcare in the NHS in Wales; what are the barriers and enablers for clinicians?', *Journal of Evaluation in Clinical Practice*, 25/1 (2019), 104–10.

64. P. Bradley et al., 'Achieving prudent healthcare in NHS Wales', *Public Health Wales* (2014). Available at: *https://pureadmin.uhi.ac.uk/ws/portalfiles/*

portal/1921669/Achieving_prudent_healthcare_in_NHS_Wales_paper_Revised_ version_FINAL_.pdf (accessed 31 January 2021).

65. Phillips, *Health Economics*, p. 142.
66. R. G. Evans and G. L. Stoddart, 'Why are some people healthy and others are not? The determinants of health of populations', in R. G. Evans, M. L. Barer and T. R. E. Marmor (eds), *Why are some people healthy and others not: the determinants of health of populations?* (New York: Aldine de Gruyter, 1994).
67. Phillips, *Health Economics*, p. 142.
68. Drakeford, 'Health policy in Wales', 543.
69. G. Bevan et al., *The four health systems of the UK: How do they compare?* (London: The Health Foundation/Nuffield Trust, 2014); OECD, *Reviews of Health Care Quality: United Kingdom 2016* (Paris: OECD Publishing, 2016).

Select bibliography

Aylward, Mansel, Ceri Phillips and Helen Howson, *Simply Prudent Healthcare – achieving better care and value for money in Wales – discussion paper* (Swansea: Bevan Commission, 4 December 2013).

Morgan, Rhodri, *Rhodri: A Political Life in Wales and Westminster* (Cardiff: University of Wales Press, 2017).

Phillips, Ceri J., *Health Economics: an introduction for health care professionals* (Oxford: Blackwell BMJ Books, 2005).

Watt, Toby and Adam Roberts, *The path to sustainability: Funding projections for the NHS in Wales to 2019/20 and 2030/31*, Health Foundation (October 2016). Available at: *https://www.health.org.uk/publications/reports/ the-path-to-sustainability* (accessed 31 January 2021).

WG, *A Healthier Wales: Our Plan for Health and Social Care* (Cardiff: WG, 2019). Available at: *https://gov.wales/sites/default/files/publications/2019-10/ a-healthier-wales-action-plan.pdf* (accessed 31 January 2021).

3

EDUCATION IN WALES SINCE DEVOLUTION

David Egan

Overview

Powers over the education system and education policy was one of the major areas devolved to Wales after 1999. The National Assembly for Wales (NAW) and its government was thereby presented for the first time in Wales's history with the chance to develop distinctive educational provision for the nation. This chapter, which focuses on the compulsory phase of education in Wales up to the age of 18, considers the educational legacy inherited by devolved government, the opportunities presented and the responses that have ensued over the last two decades.

It suggests that whilst there have been many achievements over this period, the significant barriers that have been faced and insufficient boldness in addressing these has resulted in a mixed track record. In offering this analysis comparisons are made with other nations that in recent times have had more success in utilising opportunities to transform their education systems.

It concludes by arguing that if over the next decade and beyond the opportunities offered by devolution are to be fully realised, then more radical and transformative change is required. Enacting such changes could result in an education system characterised by excellence of achievement and equity of outcomes, that has so often been aspired to by the education community in Wales since devolution.

The legacy

Whilst the history of education in Wales stretches back to Roman and early medieval times, the education system inherited by devolution had its roots in the Wales of the mid-nineteenth century.[1] Young people in Wales at this time were fortunate if, through provision made by the established and nonconformist churches, they were able to receive the basics of an education. In 1847 a notorious report prepared by commissioners sent by the Westminster Government to enquire into the state of education in Wales scathingly impugned the moral character of the Welsh people and blamed much of the ills it found on the paucity and poor quality of education provision.[2]

What followed in the period up to the First World War was an expansion in education provision in Wales at school, further and higher education level. The first state-provided elementary and grammar schools emerged, technical education expanded to meet the need of Wales's booming industrial economy and university colleges and eventually the federal University of Wales was established. As this period saw the growing ascendancy of the Liberal Party in Welsh politics and its promotion at Westminster of all Welsh causes, often these developments took place ahead of similar ones in other parts of the UK. This created two strong and enduring typologies: one that depicted educational developments in Wales as an ongoing process of expansion and improvement, the other creating a popular perception of a nation and people that held education particularly close to its heart.

Although these developments led to a range of educational bodies being established in Wales to support and regulate the work of this expanding system, the true bastions of educational power were the thirteen county councils of Wales, their local education authorities, directors of education and education committees. The Glamorgan Local Education Authority, for instance, in the most populous part of Wales, traversed an educational terrain now covered by eight of the twenty-two local authorities that currently administer education in Wales.[3]

It was the county councils who oversaw secondary school provision which relied on an IQ-based intelligence test that pupils sat at the age of 11 to select how many would be allocated grammar or secondary modern school places. They also oversaw curriculum provision in these schools. In grammar schools this in essence aped that of the fee-paying public schools with the provision of traditional academic subjects including Latin, very limited if any attention to practical or vocational subjects and the separating of pupils into arts and science streams once public examination courses were commenced. Secondary modern schools offered a basic education in what would now be called literacy and numeracy, with a leavening of practical subjects fully gendered to provide needlework, cooking and secretarial skills for girls and woodwork, metalwork and technical drawing for boys.

Whilst in general local authorities in Wales provided far more grammar school places than in other parts of the UK, this represented an elitist and conservative approach to education that operated within a nation that was always progressive in its dominant politics. The grammar schools were portrayed as allowing opportunities for social mobility for the large working class and much smaller middle-class population that provided routes to university, teacher training college and employment in good public- and private-sector skilled jobs. The reality, however, was often different. A relatively small percentage of working-class children accessed grammar school places and with some exceptions, the small numbers who proceeded to university-level education were largely drawn from the upper strata of the working classes and the middle classes.

Progression from secondary education into employment was unproblematic in the buoyant economy of mid- and late nineteenth-century Wales, and although much harder times were faced in the interwar years and during the long, slow decline of Wales's manufacturing and extractive industries in the 1960s and 1970s, and the much faster death throes of the 1980s and 1990s, the basic education provided by secondary schools enabled most young people to access semi-skilled or unskilled employment.

By the 1970s much of this education, for former grammar and secondary pupils, was taking place in comprehensive schools. Although Wales was able to claim the setting up of the first comprehensive school in the UK in 1949 at Holyhead,[4] the reorganisation of selective education in other parts of Wales was a long, drawn-out and often controversial process. In many areas of Wales that were politically radical, they were nevertheless also deeply committed to their grammar schools, including the former domains of the Glamorgan County Council, where stubborn resistance was put up to the proposed changes.

The eight county councils that had resisted re-organisation of their secondary schools were themselves to become a victim of local government reorganisation, when in 1974 they and their district councils were replaced by twenty-two all-purpose local authorities. Whilst there may have been merit in bringing educational administration closer to local communities, having so many local authorities is generally depicted as having introduced a dead weight around the necks of the policy makers and administrators who, with the coming of devolution in 1999, set about establishing a fit-for-purpose educational system based on partnership between government and local authorities. This is a theme that will be returned to below.

Under both county councils and the new local authorities, the period since the 1970s has seen an ongoing expansion of Welsh-medium education to the point where it now provides for approximately 22 per cent of Wales's children. Whereas in the past bilingual education had experienced a long and slow decline, the period leading up to devolution saw its revival in traditionally strong Welsh-speaking areas of Wales and a new popularity in parts of Wales where the percentages of the population who spoke the language was low and often declining.[5]

Whether in Welsh- or English-medium comprehensive schools or a smattering of faith schools, we know little of the educational standards achieved in Wales's schools from the mid-nineteenth century through to the 1980s, since which time standards have come to almost dominate educational discourse in Wales. What can be of little doubt is that outside those who attended grammar schools these standards were extremely basic, to the extent that by the dawn of devolution 28 per cent of Wales's adults had problems with basic literacy and 32 per cent were unable to master basic numeracy.[6] We can surmise with equal confidence that the lower the socio-economic status of children and their families the greater likelihood it was that they would lack these basic attributes.

Until the 1980s these low and inequitable levels of educational achievement had limited implications as there were sufficient opportunities for semi-skilled and unskilled employment in the Welsh economy to provide access to the labour market for young people leaving school. Following the 1984–5 miners' strike, the implosion of what was left of the traditional Welsh industrial economy and attempts to replace it with more skilled employment opportunities found the education system wanting. By the early years of devolution, academic studies comparing the former coalfield areas of the UK found that the south Wales coalfield was by far the slowest to regenerate its economy and its industrial communities for which low levels of educational achievement and skills were one of the fundamental reasons.[7]

In the 1980s, for the first time academic and public enquiries began to be undertaken on the health of the Welsh education system. They suggested that a 'long-tail' of academic achievement existed in Wales's new comprehensive schools, with many young people, particularly those from the most disadvantaged backgrounds, leaving schools with either no or very low-level qualifications.[8] It was suggested that one of the main reasons for this was the way in which a traditional grammar school curriculum had been transported to the new schools in a way that excluded many young people. Whilst 'Ordinary' level examinations had been supplemented in 1965 by the Certificate in Secondary Education intended for 'less academic' pupils, it was still assumed by those who ran the education system that 40 per cent of children, the 'non-examinable', would not have the ability to sit either of these examinations at age 15.

In responding to similar concerns in England, the UK Conservative Government after 1979 brought forward a raft of education measures, including its 1988 Education Reform Act which included the introduction of the first National (England and Wales) Curriculum. It also ratcheted up system accountability through increased testing, the publication of school league tables, the privatisation of the inspection system, and allowed schools to break away from local authority control and adopt various forms of direct-grant special status, all in the name of the increased neo-liberal marketisation of education.

Wales had no choice but to take up the 'national' curriculum but was able to include provision for the teaching of Welsh for all children until at least the age of 14 and ensured that a Welsh dimension (Y Cwricwlwm Cymreig) was reflected in a number of other subject areas within the curriculum. It also moved to the privatisation of its school inspection system, the adoption of national testing at the ages of 7, 11 and 14 and the publication of league tables based on these and public examination outcomes. Despite the best efforts of the Welsh Office, with very few exceptions, schools eschewed the opportunity to break away from local authority control to be directly funded. Not surprisingly, the Welsh Office was sometimes depicted as a vehicle for transporting Whitehall policy to Wales, only stopping off at the translators to ensure that it emerged in both languages and reflected the legal status of the Welsh language.[9]

For the few years prior to devolution that the Welsh education system was governed by the new Labour administration that came to power at Westminster in 1997, things proceeded much as they had before. The academy school model promoted by 'New Labour' was resisted in the same way as the attempts of the previous Conservative Government to lure Wales away from comprehensive education. One development that did have longer term consequences was the recommendation of the Education and Training Action Group (ETAG) for far greater focus to be given to vocational education, leading to the creation of Education and Learning Wales (ELWa) to oversee all post-16 education in Wales other than school sixth forms and universities.[10]

This brief narrative account suggests, therefore, that the education legacy betrothed by the UK Government and the Welsh Office to the pioneers of devolution can be summarised as follows:

- the growth, despite significant resistance and attempts to dilute it, of a comprehensive education system
- a continuing expansion in the Welsh-medium sector
- a relatively weak profile for vocational education
- an apparently unwieldy structure for the local administration of education
- relatively low levels of overall educational achievement, especially by those from more socio-economically disadvantaged backgrounds
- a dependence on policy-making largely decided in England.

Opportunities, responses and track record

The powers devolved to NAW in 1999 included control over all aspects of education policy and the education system other than the wages and conditions of employment of teachers, which was not devolved until 2018. Following the referendum of 2011, legislative powers in education also became available to the Assembly. Thus, the Assembly, its government and civil service and the wider education community now had the opportunity to shape an education system for Wales in a way that had never been possible before.

Looking back over twenty years it is possible to discern three broad periods of education policy in Wales since devolution, with inevitable overlaps between each period and the current phase still in progress.

Within each period key facets of policy have seen developments in the structure of the education system, the curriculum, teaching pedagogy, leadership, educational standards and system accountability. Underpinning these phases and facets has been a constant underlying philosophy that envisions the education system in Wales as being a public sector service, equitable at the point of access, bilingual, egalitarian in its aspirations and subject to local democracy through local management of schools under the control of local authorities.[11]

Phases
The first phase of education under devolution in Wales began at the turn of the millennium and lasted through to the end of its first decade. For much of this period education policy was strongly influenced by Rhodri Morgan as First Minister of Wales and Jane Davidson who, as Education Minister from 2000 through to 2007, can lay claim to being thus far the longest serving holder of this portfolio not only in Wales but across the UK. In Rhodri Morgan's typically evocative phrase, the policies of his government, including those in education, were seen to be discrete from those espoused by the UK Government led by his own party at Westminster because 'clear red water' separated them from the 'New Labour' approaches being adopted there.[12] In particular, the policies followed in Wales rejected the market- and consumer-driven approaches adopted in England that exerted much greater control and accountability over schools and teachers through increased national testing, centralised strategies, the publication of league tables of school performance and more regular school inspections.[13]

The appointment of Leighton Andrews as Education Minister in 2009 led to a fundamental reconsideration of this policy stance. From his perspective the ethos underpinning education policy in Wales had led to complacency about the health of the system and its achievements. Influenced particularly by Wales's disappointing record in 2007 and 2010 in the Programme for International Student Assessment (PISA), which administered standardised, skills-based tests for 15-year-olds in those countries across the globe that were members of the Organisation for Economic Cooperation and Development (OECD), he decided to significantly change the direction of education policy in Wales and adopt approaches very similar to those being pursued in England and many other countries.[14] These involved much greater system accountability through more regular national testing, a recalibration of the judgements made of schools by Estyn, the school inspectorate, the strengthening of local accountability over schools through the work of four regional education consortia and more centralised control over what happens in classrooms through a stronger emphasis on literacy and numeracy.[15]

Following Andrews's replacement as Education Minister in 2013 by Huw Lewis, a gradual departure from this 'high-stakes' accountability approach to education policy commenced, and this led to a renewed focus on the school curriculum, the professional development of teachers and achieving greater equity in educational achievement.[16] Under his successor, the Liberal Democrat Kirsty Williams (the only non-Labour Party politician to hold the post of education minister since devolution), who took office in 2016, these developments morphed into a fully-fledged 'reform programme' which is still in process and can be seen to be a synthesis between what can be depicted as a 'too loose' phase adopted in the first decade of devolution to the 'too tight' period which ensued thereafter, and one where international examples of how to develop an education system are more influential than what is happening in England.[17]

Facets: structure
There have been minimal changes to the structure of the education system in Wales under devolution. At school level there had been a steady reduction in the number of small primary schools, but this has slowed down under the current administration. A small number (six) of 'all-through' schools for pupils aged 3 to 16 (or 18) have been opened and this might be a presager of future developments. In some local authorities (Merthyr Tydfil and Blaenau Gwent) there has been a controversial and contested re-organisation of education provision for the 16 to 18 age group that has led to school sixth forms being closed and new tertiary provision being provided in further education. This has built upon pre-devolution developments of this kind in Neath Port Talbot and parts of the old county of Gwent. Although the reorganisation proposals were based on rigorous 'pathfinder' research studies undertaken by ELWa and premised on providing higher quality and more cost-effective provision for young people, they were strongly resisted by some pupils and their parents, which in some cases led to proposals being delayed or abandoned.[18]

Education continues to be controlled by twenty-two local authorities at county level, although since 2012, four regional education consortia have been added to the system (building in most cases on less formal collaborative arrangements which existed previously between local authorities) to maximise capacity to both support and challenge schools. The challenge function has been undertaken by challenge advisors who have responsibility for the ongoing monitoring of schools proportionate to their performance within the banding or categorisation of schools, which was introduced by Welsh Government (WG) after 2010 as part of greater system accountability.[19]

The support function provides a range of professional learning opportunities for teachers and schools, much of which increasingly relies upon schools supporting other schools as part of what is termed a 'self-improving system'. Headteachers often reflect, however, that former local authority advisory services provided much richer support, particularly for subject pedagogy. This is one of the areas where the overall success of the consortia is still a matter of debate. Many educationalists in different parts of the system are still unconvinced about the logistics and the worth of having a middle layer in the education system of a small country between WG and local authorities. In one of the four consortia, the regional model has, at the time of writing, recently begun to break up and there are constant rumblings of possible similar developments in the others. How the consortia will adapt to current changes being planned for school improvement and accountability, including a different role for Estyn, remains to be seen.

At national level there have been perhaps more fundamental structural changes than at local or regional level. As part of Rhodri Morgan's commitment to light 'a bonfire' to the many quangos (non-governmental public bodies) that had been established by the former Welsh Office, the not long-established, but troubled, post-16 body ELWa and the Qualifications, Curriculum and Assessment Authority (ACCAC) were brought into government in 2006.[20] As a result of uneasiness about the appropriateness of qualifications being located within the ambit of a government department, in 2015, however, Qualifications Wales was created as an independent, but WG-sponsored organisation. Proposed legislation currently under consultation would establish a new tertiary commission for post-16, non-university education in Wales, suggesting that the appetite for assimilating specialist education bodies into government has been lost. With Wales currently developing for the first time its own national school curriculum, due for commencement in September 2022, there are some who wonder if this might also be a function better moved out of government.[21]

New additions to the architecture of education governance in Wales are the Education Workforce Council, which was set up in 2015 having evolved from the former General Teaching Council for Wales, established in 2000. Whereas the remit of the former is to act as a registration and regulation body for school support staff, further education lectures and teachers, the purview of the former was solely for teachers. In 2018 the National Academy for Educational Leadership was established as a WG-sponsored body, to provide leadership development opportunities initially for school leaders but with a wider locus across the education sectors intended for the future.

Facets: curriculum

During the first phase of devolution much emphasis was placed within policy-making on developing discrete and innovative aspects to cur-riculum provision in Wales. The defining development of the early years of devolution in education was the creation of the foundation phase, a new curriculum for the 3 to 7 age group, which the First Minister was fond of calling 'the Nordic model'.[22] It was indeed strongly influenced by approaches to early years' education systems adopted in many parts of the world, including Europe, although interestingly this provision often sat outside formal schooling in pre-school kindergartens, whereas Wales, which had a long tradition of making free nursery education available, was intent on melding this into existing 3 to 11 primary schools. Based on these international examples and high-quality academic research and following a pilot, an evaluation and supported by considerable enthu-siasm from early years' professionals, the foundation phase was fully introduced from 2008 and is now a settled part of education provision in Wales.[23]

The other prominent development within the Welsh curricu-lum in the first phase of devolution was the introduction of a Welsh Baccalaureate. This was intended to broaden the education of 14- to 19-year-olds in Wales through developing their broader skills and their awareness of the wider world in which they lived, and providing them with an additional qualification. The 'Bac' has evolved over time and is now an accepted feature of the education system: the degree to which it has succeeded in its aims is, however, open to question and to a large extent often depends on how much it is valued and fully used by individual schools.[24]

The other curriculum area that attracted a great deal of attention in the first decade of devolution was what became known as '14–19 Learning Pathways'.[25] The influences behind this policy stretched back to the debate about Welsh education and the grammar school tradition of traditional 'academic' education and an undervaluing of vocational education, and continued into the report produced by the ETAG group. The policy was designed to provide all 14- to 19-year-olds in school further education, work-based learning and partnerships between these sectors, with high-quality vocational as well as academic qualifications, accessed through a range of pathways and supported by learning coaches who would help them to make the right choices to open future career progression.

Learning Pathways did lead to significant short- to medium-term reconfiguration of the curriculum and qualification profile available to young people and some of this has endured. However, despite large amounts of funding, the attention of the Education Minister and a deputy minister specifically appointed to provide leadership in this area, specialists seconded into the civil service and one of the first legislative measures introduced by the Assembly, ultimately the policy had little long-term impact. After 2010, at the behest of a new Minister, attention became focused again on traditional qualifications as the key metric for system performance. The worth of vocational qualifications and the way in which, in some cases, they were being used to inflate the performance profile of pupils was questioned and Learning Pathways was quietly side-lined.

Work on developing more continuity in the transition of pupils from primary to secondary education, in both their curriculum and pedagogical experiences, suffered the same fate. The continuity and progression between these phases were regularly highlighted as being a weakness of the education system, with a concern that Key Stage 3 (for 11- to 14-year-olds) could become almost a 'waiting room' for pupils before they commenced their examination courses, leading to pupil disengagement and later low achievement. Policy work commissioned in this area was, however, brushed aside as being a further distraction from focusing on preparing pupils for national tests in literacy and numeracy prior to the age of 14 and GCSE examinations thereafter.[26]

Although the direction of education policy in the first years of the second decade of devolution meant that there was more focus on assessment than the curriculum, Ministers did commission a series of reviews on aspects of the curriculum, including arts education, the foundation phase, the teaching of Welsh history and bilingual education. After becoming Minister of Education in 2013, Huw Lewis was persuaded that a wider review should be commissioned on the curriculum that would use these studies as part of the evidence base. This was undertaken by Graham Donaldson, a former chief inspector of schools in Scotland, and resulted in a report, *Successful Futures*, published in 2015.[27]

The report was to represent a turning point in that it, first, returned the focus of Welsh education policy to one that placed the school curriculum at the forefront, and secondly called into question the efficacy of an existing curriculum, which, other than in the foundation phase, had become a vehicle for performance-driven assessment rather than a broad and balanced entitlement to pupils. Influenced by developments in Scotland and internationally, it proposed what in effect would be a first national curriculum developed in and for Wales, based on six areas of learning and experience and driven by four underpinning purposes. The report was enthusiastically received by teachers and WG, and since 2016 significant time and energy has been expended by educational professionals, civil servants and others in fashioning a final version of the new school curriculum which, subject to legislative assent, will be introduced from September 2022.

Facets: teacher pedagogy
The success of the new curriculum for Wales will ultimately be decided by the two things that research on education has long identified as being the key determinants of achievement by pupils. First, and most importantly, that they grow up in a home learning environment that fosters and supports their education.[28] Secondly, and by far the most important feature of the experience they have when they attend school, namely the quality of teaching that they receive.[29] This, for example, has been one of the main findings of research, evaluation and inspection undertaken on the foundation phase in Wales, and has been a constant theme of Estyn's reporting throughout the devolution period.[30]

How has education policy under devolution responded to this and allowed teachers to develop high-quality pedagogy? After a challenging phase during the period of high-stakes accountability after 2010 when the quality of provision offered by university/school partnerships was generally found to be wanting, from September 2019, there has been a major reform of initial teacher education (ITE) and newly accredited programmes, which allow much greater involvement for schools.[31]

Teacher development after ITE and a statutory induction period, where they receive support from a mentor within their school and the regional consortia, is not a compulsory part of their terms and conditions of employment and inevitably is, therefore, variable in quality and extent.[32] Performance management systems in school and the Professional Standards for Teaching and Leadership produced by WG, the most recent version of which were introduced in 2018, provide the stimulus for professional learning.[33] This may be undertaken within the school, through working in networks of teachers and through provision offered by the regional education consortia or other providers.

Following its creation in 2000, WG provided the General Teaching Council for Wales with considerable funding to promote the individual entitlement of teachers to professional learning. The very popular and oversubscribed schemes that it offered through to 2010 were generally successful, but also became a victim thereafter of the policy shift to more prescriptive approaches to pedagogy designed to improve system performance.[34]

WG during this period promoted a pedagogy initiative designed to identify and share effective practice: despite considerable investment, little discernible outcomes resulted.[35] For a period after 2009, professional learning communities – which brought together practitioners to share and develop effective practice – were promoted, but ultimately, they too were not sustained.[36]

Borrowing from the experience of Finland, during Leighton Andrews's period as Minister, a 'Masters' in Educational Practice was developed and offered at no cost to newly qualified teachers. Although it was almost certainly offered to the wrong target group, leading to a significant drop-out of teachers beset by all the challenges they faced in establishing themselves in their first teaching posts, it did have success and has left a cadre of teachers who are often identified as exceptional practitioners. It too, however, was eventually discontinued.[37] The ultimate demise of this and many other initiatives of the type suggest that developing the quality of teachers in Wales has been one of the least successful areas of activity by WGs since devolution, resulting in Estyn regularly identifying this as one the weaknesses of the education system.[38]

As part of the recent wider reform programme, there has been a renewed interest in promoting teacher pedagogy. This has included the reforms to ITE mentioned above, new professional standards, an imminent change to induction arrangements designed to retain more teachers in the profession, an emphasis on teachers developing research-informed enquiry skills, a framework for schools developing as learning organisations[39] and, commencing in 2022, a new national MA education programme developed jointly by universities in Wales and targeted at early career teachers. These strands are encompassed in the first coherent strategy for professional learning by teachers developed since devolution – *The National Approach to Professional Learning*.[40] Time will tell if this represents a sustained breakthrough in sustaining the high-quality teaching profession that will be so critical to future success.

Facets: leadership

Whilst high-quality teaching is the most important determinant of pupils succeeding in their schools, research and inspection evidence points also to the importance of school leadership.[41] Effective leadership is identified as being distributed, so that it involves a wide number of staff, and focused above all else on improving the quality of teaching and the learning experience of pupils.

As has been the case with developments in teaching, the record of devolved government in this area has been mixed. Whilst in England a National [*sic*] College for School Leadership was established in 2000 (only to be effectively closed by the coalition government after 2010), WG in the first period of devolution rejected proposals from the headteacher unions to establish something similar in Wales. Despite being misnamed, many Welsh headteachers did in fact access provision offered by the college. A leadership programme for intending headteachers has operated throughout the devolution period with some success, although not sufficient to avoid shortages of candidates for rural primary, Welsh-medium and the most disadvantaged secondary schools.[42]

A well-regarded, but expensive to provide, professional development programme for serving headteachers was discontinued in the mid-2000s and has never been replaced, and a less successful programme to assist new or acting headteachers also experienced a fleeting existence.[43] Headteachers seeking to develop their own staff for middle and senior roles within their schools were left to their own devices or accessed programmes offered by professional associations or the private sector, until this became part of the work of the regional education consortia after 2012.[44]

Given this lack of focus on developing leadership within the education system it is unsurprising that Estyn often pointed to variability and frequent weaknesses in the leadership of schools. As part of the current education reform movement, WG announced in 2016 its intention to create a National Academy for Educational Leadership (NAEL) in Wales and asked the former chief inspector at Estyn to lead this development. The academy came into existence in 2018, and one of its main areas of responsibility is to validate a range of leadership development courses that are generally provided by the regional consortia working in partnership with higher education institutions to allow for the possibility of academic accreditation.

Currently the focus of the NAEL is school leadership, although its remit is to expand into other education sectors. The reasoning behind this is sound. It could be suggested that at the outset of devolution something like a staff college should have been established to develop a new leadership class across the education system– within schools, local authorities, Estyn and WG. The concept of 'system leadership' has often been espoused in the devolved education system but far too little has been done to turn this aspiration into a reality.

Facets: system accountability
The devolution period in Wales has coincided with far greater emphasis on holding public sector institutions to account for their performance. The author was a classroom teacher, head of department and senior teacher for thirteen years between 1976 and 1989. As with other teachers he exercised complete autonomy over the methods he and his colleagues used in the classroom and the results that were achieved with pupils were never critically reviewed. Other than a visit from a local authority adviser during his induction period or the one school inspection by HMI that he experienced (the average school was inspected once every twenty-three years at this time) his teaching was not observed by anyone else internally or externally.

This 'hidden world' of the classroom and professional practice has disappeared over the last thirty years. This gained momentum in the 1990s through firstly increasing emphasis by politicians (particularly the Westminster Labour Government after 1997) on accountability and the evidence from research on school effectiveness and improvement that whilst such autonomy might be prized by the teaching profession it was often not conducive to system improvement.[45] The new accountability era has passed through three phases during devolution: what might be termed a period of relatively benign accountability, followed by one that was 'high stakes' and more recently a move to more 'intelligent' approaches.

For the first decade of accountability, whilst the privatisation of the inspection system in Wales led to more frequent inspection of schools (once every five or six years with repeat visits for schools that needed further monitoring), the outcomes generally suggested that a 'good' education system was getting better. Local authority inspections, reviews of schools and visits from advisers came to similar conclusions. At national level, WG moved away from national testing of pupils (SATs) at the ages of 7, 11 and 14, relying on teacher assessments of pupils at these ages, and ceased to publish statistical information of these outcomes and GCSE AS/A Level results in a way that could be turned into school performance league tables.[46]

During a period of breaking away from an 'England and Wales' education system, comparisons were inevitably regularly made between data on the pupil achievement in the two countries. Given that England had retained standardised testing for earlier age groups, comparison for these pupils were not possible (although teacher assessment outcomes were generally favourable for Wales), but examination outcomes – particularly at GCSE – represented a more valid basis for comparison. Although improving in both countries, the Wales figures for key indicators at GCSE began to fall behind those for England. This was particularly stark in relation to pupils from disadvantaged backgrounds. At national level pupils in England fared far better than their counterparts in Wales, although given that socio-economic disadvantage in Wales was much greater than in England this might not have been surprising. Comparisons with regions of England including those with similar post-industrial socio-economic profiles to Wales, were also unfavourable, however, and suggested that Wales might be the lowest performing part of England and Wales.

By 2006–7 the picture painted by these comparisons and the variabilities in school and pupil achievement highlighted by Estyn persuaded WG that not all was as well in the Welsh education system as it might have seemed. Additional funding received as part of the Barnett formula was used for the first time to target low-achieving pupils from disadvantaged backgrounds,[47] and work began to develop a major school and system improvement strategy, namely the *School Effectiveness Framework* (SEF). Drawing upon research on highly effective international education systems and the practice of some of Wales's most successful schools, this offered a cohesive framework for system improvement at school, regional and national level.[48]

Turning the SEF from high-level vision into a programme of practical improvement practice became a protracted process. Just as this was finally gaining momentum, a major change in policy direction to the next period of system accountability beckoned. In time the SEF was to become redundant – another victim of the move to 'high-stakes' performance-driven accountability after 2010, and probably one of the great missed opportunities in education in Wales since devolution.

As has been indicated above two factors can be seen to explain the change in policy direction in relation to accountability. The first was the appointment in 2009 of Leighton Andrews to become Education Minister, someone who was critical of the direction that education policy in Wales had taken since devolution, who was far more attached to 'New Labour' thinking in England and who perceived complacency to be endemic within the Welsh system. The publication of disappointing PISA results in 2010 played directly into his mindset and resulted in a policy earthquake that moved the system to the high-stakes accountability system already described above.[49]

The jury remains out as to whether this change in policy direction led to improvements in standards, but there seems to be a lack of compelling evidence to suggest that it did so. Much more apparent is a series of deleterious consequences that did flow from this change in policy direction: which may have been unintentional, although why these should not have been foreseen stretches credibility. Increasingly most school leaders responded to this new environment through adopting behaviours that were driven by feeding the performativity machine rather than drawing upon sound educational thinking.

These included 'gaming' examination courses and qualifications, focusing on certain categories of pupils (the moving a 'D' to a 'C' syndrome) in order to achieve marginal gains in overall performance, commencing examination courses as soon as possible and entering pupils as early as possible in the hope that they would gain the 'C' pass grade even if this depressed what they might have been capable of if they were entered at the intended age.[50] For earlier age groups the pressure on teachers to improve teacher assessment outcomes meant that year-on-year they improved to an extent that led the chief inspector at Estyn to doubt the reliability and validity of these indicators.[51]

Inevitably the increased pressure placed on headteachers and teachers by this intense accountability atmosphere affected teacher workload, morale, recruitment and retention. For the last decade recruitment to secondary ITE programmes in Wales has been challenging, particularly in attracting Welsh-medium applicants: this had long been the case for subjects such as mathematics and physics, but it now became the case for subjects like English where previously recruitment had been healthy. Schools found it increasingly difficult to recruit teachers with strong subject backgrounds in English, mathematics and science and Welsh-medium teaching and this was particularly true for schools in the most disadvantaged communities. Retention of teachers and the recruitment of headteachers, as has been pointed out above, also became increasingly difficult.[52]

After 2015, growing awareness of the difficulties caused by this accountability regime has led to a gradual and phased move away to a different policy trajectory. Data on school performance is no longer so readily available, the role of challenge advisers at local authority level and of Estyn is evolving, school categorisation was suspended due to the COVID-19 pandemic and is unlikely to return. A new accountability and school-improvement approach based on school self-evaluation has been developed and is due to be piloted.[53] This represents a move towards a more intelligent and commensurate form of accountability that can be interpreted as a synthesis between the more benign and invasive approaches that have preceded it. If this is to be an approach that can be sustained into the future, it is inevitable that as the SEF attempted to do, perhaps before its time, that this new approach to accountability is brought into synergy with improvements in the quality of teaching and leadership and the new school curriculum.

Facets: standards

Throughout the narrative and analysis offered above there has been a sub-text related to standards. Whether devolved education policy has led to an improvement in educational standards is a reasonable question to ask. It is not, however, a straightforward one to answer! There can be little doubt that compared to the situation that existed before devolution, as set out in the first section of this chapter, there has been a significant improvement in education achievement, particularly at examination level. More children are entered for examinations and pass rates have increased as teachers have become more focused on how important these indicators are for the pupils and their future progression, their own reputation and the performance of their school. What has happened in Wales in this respect is replicated across the UK and internationally.

Beyond this there is a lack of empirical evidence to enable reliable judgements to be made. The pressures of performativity inevitably have called into question the reliability and validity of teacher assessment at the ages of 7, 11 and 14, all of which have increased exponentially over the period of devolution. Comparisons with England are no longer valid as standardised assessments are still used there for earlier age groups, and GCSE-level assessment and grading systems have significantly diverged between the two countries. For similar reasons, comparisons with the other UK nations are also problematic.[54]

International comparisons draw upon the outcomes of PISA. Initially WG decided not to participate in these three-yearly exercises after their introduction by the OECD. The Education Minister was of the view that Wales should participate for the first time in 2006 as this would provide a true indication of Wales's standing and move the focus away from unfair England/Wales comparisons. The First Minister, having forensically 'sat' the tests himself and concluding that they were not in sync with the curriculum and pedagogy as it currently existed in Wales, was far less sanguine. The disappointing outcomes for Wales in three successive PISA rounds might suggest that, as so often was the case, that Rhodri Morgan was a sage judge of this situation.

Since commencing its participation in PISA, the three-yearly outcomes have not reflected well upon Wales and have, therefore, provided powerful ammunition for academics, politicians and members of the media who questioned the onward trajectory and virility of the Welsh education system since devolution.[55] They perceive PISA to be a statistically valid exercise capable of producing a robust single metric that can be reliably used to make comparisons between different national education systems. Such certainty is inevitably open to challenge. There are statisticians and epidemiologists (including interestingly those who have come to the fore in the COVID-19 crisis) who question the reliability of the PISA method.[56]

More tellingly there are issues about whether single comparisons between very different education systems are fair and valid. Wales experiences significant socio-economic disadvantage and it is not clear that PISA takes full account of this, seeing equity as being more associated with access to schooling than low family-income backgrounds. Secondly, and perhaps of the greatest importance, PISA does not allow for the fact that part of the sample of 15-year-olds it assesses in Wales are pupils who are being taught through the medium of Welsh, which they have learnt as a second language and this leads to outcomes that inadvertently depresses overall performance in Wales.[57]

Given that, therefore, it might be one of the inevitable consequences of devolution that comparisons with other countries become increasingly difficult, if not redundant, it might be better to recalibrate the national conversation about standards in Wales to one that is framed by the aspirations that we have for our children and their progression, rather than one that compares them erroneously with other countries at the behest of neo-liberal-inspired dogma.[58]

Summary

The above account of the overlapping phases that the education system in Wales has passed through since devolution and the main facets of policy that have operated across this timespan can be summarised as follows:

- the devolved education system has developed within three broad phases which could be characterised as initially embracing innovation/loose accountability, followed by control/high accountability and currently reform/proportionate accountability
- minimal changes have been made to the structure of the education system that existed prior to devolution

- innovative curriculum developments have taken place, some of which have been more successful than others and the latest and most profound of which is, as yet, unrealised
- insufficient attention has been paid for most of the devolution period to the key determinants of school effectiveness – teacher quality and school leadership – although most recently these are beginning to be addressed
- overall progress has taken place in raising educational standards, but the extent of this improvement is contested

Barriers and limitations

The analysis offered above suggests, therefore, that the achievements of the Welsh education system since devolution have generally been worthwhile; in some cases impressive, but in others less so. This section of the chapter will consider the barriers that have impeded progress and how these have limited the overall progress that has been secured.

The major weakness of the Welsh education system since devolution is the same fault-line that existed prior to 1999. Whilst, in relation to school choice, the system is largely but not completely equitable at the point of entry, it remains highly inequitable in terms of pupil achievement.[59] Given that the private school sector is extremely small in Wales, nearly all children attend a local state-provided primary school and proceed at the age of 11 to a local secondary school. Whilst most of these schools use English as the main language, an increasing percentage are Welsh medium and there are also Church in Wales and Roman Catholic schools. Within this overall ecology, and influenced by the socio-economic demography of Wales, parents are able to exercise choice in finding a school place for their children and particularly in secondary education this often leads to structural inequalities.

Given the demography of Wales and the size of primary schools, a significant number of the nation's schools have a high concentration of pupils from more disadvantaged socio-economic backgrounds. At secondary level, the size and catchment of schools generally leads to a more balanced spread of pupil socio-economic backgrounds. Parental choice of schools often leads, however, to the composition of secondary schools being skewed, with significant numbers of more aspirational parents choosing to send their children to schools outside the catchment area of local secondary, largely English-medium, comprehensive schools.[60]

These trends result in a significant number of secondary schools in the most disadvantaged areas of Wales being faced by serious challenges that generally lead to them having lower attainment and accountability outcomes. Through a combination of historical legacy, parental choice and a lack of appetite for structural reform, the Welsh education system has created what are often pejoratively referred to as 'sink schools', which are almost doomed to fail given the accountability yardsticks and processes in play.

Beset by these structural inequalities and through a lack of attention to other determinants of school effectiveness considered below, the system continues to be highly inequitable in the outcomes which pupils achieve. There are four key points to be made here. First, the socio-economic background of our pupils is a major determinant of what they will achieve by the end of their time in school, and their progression into further/higher education and the labour market after school. By the age of 16 only approximately 30 per cent of young people from disadvantaged backgrounds achieve good outcomes compared to about 62 per cent from higher-income homes.

Secondly, through greater focus on this area since devolution, progress has undoubtedly been made, but the extent of this is overstated at primary/early secondary level due to 'grade inflation' in school-based assessments. The more limited progress made by disadvantaged pupils in external examinations taken at the age of 15 and above supports this interpretation. Thirdly, whilst the improvement that has been made will have been greatly assisted by additional funding provided by WG for schools proportionate to their need, attempts to develop a coherent strategy to tackle the cause of this underachievement by the large majority of the one-third of our pupils who live in poverty have generally not succeeded. Fourthly, the lack of major progress in this area has a massive effect in holding back the overall achievement of the Welsh education system, particularly when compared to some of the most successful and equitable education systems in other parts of the world.

What might a coherent strategy in this area look like and what barriers would it need to overcome? There are four areas to consider: parental engagement, teaching and leadership, curriculum and qualifications, and community schools. An important consideration here is that whilst overcoming barriers in these areas would benefit all pupils in Wales, it would particularly impact upon those who are most disadvantaged.

Educational research and inspection evidence finds that the influences which have the greatest impact on the educational achievement of children is their family background and the home learning environment which exists there.[61] Children who live outside poverty have much greater social capital to draw upon in supporting their aspirations and their learning experiences in and out of school. Many children who grow up in poverty also do so in a nurturing family environment but most, through no fault of their parents and families, do not enjoy the same enriched and aspirational environment experienced by their more privileged peers. Awareness of the importance of family backgrounds and the need to better engage parents in the education of their children has grown throughout the devolution period, but the gaps that exist here between the life experience of pupils from different backgrounds in Wales continues to be substantial.

As has been highlighted above, when children enter the education system the most important influences that schools have on them are the quality of teaching they receive, the extent to which school leaders focus on maximising the amount of high-quality teaching and, of course, support for their general well-being. Because of the deficits that many disadvantaged pupils experience outside school, these factors are proportionately far more important for them within their schools.[62]

Too little attention has been given to addressing these issues in our most disadvantaged schools. Many of these schools face significant challenges in recruiting and retaining staff, and spend so much of their time dealing with issues relating to pupil well-being that developing the expertise of their teachers and the quality of leadership in their school is relatively marginalised. The Welsh education system has failed to come up with an approach that addresses these problems, enabling the leaders of these schools, who are nearly always highly dedicated and motivated individuals, to have the intellectual and capital resources that they require to bring about sustained change.

Whilst the school curriculum might not have the same impact upon outcomes as the factors considered above, it is the means through which pupils are introduced to rich experiences that will shape their lives and eventually to the qualifications system that will determine their futures. The promise offered by the new school curriculum in Wales is that a curriculum narrowed to suit the dictates of high-stakes accountability will be replaced by one that again offers a rich and balanced experience to pupils from all backgrounds.

It should, however, be accompanied by a major reform of qualifications, particularly if the more innovative approaches to assessment which will be introduced up to the age of 14 are to be in sync with what follows thereafter. There are two issues here. First, what educational justification can there be for standardised assessments of pupils at the ages of 15/16, 17 and 18? What we have currently is an 'exam industry' that has developed to meet the needs of high-stakes assessment. The detrimental cost in resources, time and pupil well-being hardly justifies what is in place. What the COVID-19 pandemic has also highlighted – as we probably have always known but become inured to – is the way in which this system is slanted against our most disadvantaged pupils. More affluent parents will ensure that their children receive private tutoring and other support to reach the goal of entry into the mass higher-education market that has increased in the UK far more than any other nation, the yardstick for success.[63] The subliminal and overt messages that this situation conveys to many young people is both the cause and the representation of their disengagement.

The second issue is closely related. The attempt made up to 2010 to broaden educational experiences and qualifications in Wales to provide parity of esteem between traditional programmes of study and qualifications (GCSE and GCE) and those of a more vocational nature (GNVQs, BTEC, pre-apprenticeship) ultimately was sacrificed on the altar of high-stakes accountability. Thereby our young people have been denied a range of experiences and qualifications that might attract young people who have a variety of interests, preferred styles of learning and career objectives. Whilst this is true for all young people, the potential for greater engagement of pupils from disadvantaged backgrounds through a more diverse curriculum and qualifications offer has been largely lost in pre-16 education. The message, again as much overt as subliminal, is 'take traditional qualifications and aspire to go to university'. It can hardly be surprising that many young people, including significant numbers of those from less privileged backgrounds, decide that this does not interest them and may be beyond them.

Finally, it is time for Wales to recognise that the structure of the education system that it inherited at the point of devolution should now be reviewed. There is no great appetite for further changes to local authorities. The regional education consortia are still an unproven layer and further thought may need to be given to their role. Overall, it is to be wondered if a small nation like Wales requires separate regional school improvement organisations, an inspectorate, a leadership academy and a workforce registration body.

It is at the level of schools, however, that the most profound and urgent attention is required. The issue can be expressed straightforwardly: in situations where schools already engage well with their parents, high-quality teaching and leadership are in place and expected outcomes are achieved, there is probably no justification for any change to existing structures. In other contexts where these key determinants of success are not present – many of our primary schools and a significant number of our secondary schools – there is a case for structural change that will enable these schools to break out of the current cycle of low achievement to realise the aspirations they have for their pupils and the potential which those young people possess. How this might be achieved is considered further below.

Fulfilling the devolution dividend: a vision for the next decade

Policy learning

In crafting a transformative vision for education in Wales over the next decade that would allow the promise of devolution to be realised, what guidance might be garnered from the experience of other countries that have used independence to develop successful education systems. Three examples are briefly considered here: Singapore, Estonia and Finland.

Singapore, a country of 5.5 million people, achieved independence from British rule in 1965. Since then, it has developed from 'a nation where education was the province of a tiny, affluent minority to a thriving state with among the highest levels of student achievement in the world'.[64] Approximately 75 per cent of post-school students complete a degree, including technical degrees, and the remainder complete a programme through the Institute of Technical Education that prepares them for work. It is, thereby, a highly equitable system where all pupils regardless of background achieve success.

Other features of the system include high-quality pre-school education between the ages of 4 and 6, bilingual education for all with English and the 'mother tongue' being studied, a variety of schools and pathways (based on streaming), an inter-disciplinary curriculum that seeks the holistic development of pupils and is not fixated on academic performance, and recognises that talents as well as abilities are important.

Teachers are highly regarded, well qualified and are provided with time during their working week to undertake professional learning and undertake research and networking with other teachers. They are expected to be facilitators of learning developing the creativity, innovation and independence of their pupils. School leaders work together in clusters to share effective practice and take responsibility for high-quality teaching across the cluster.[65]

Estonia, a nation of 1.3 million regained its independence following the break-up of the Soviet Union in 1991. Since that time, it has transformed its education system to become one of the most high-achieving and equitable in the world. Although overseen by a Ministry of Education and Research and local authorities, there is a high degree of school autonomy with pupils attending pre-school childcare between the ages of 3 and 7, 'basic' schools until the age of 14, followed by three years either in upper secondary general or vocational schools, both of which provide a national curriculum that ensures a broad education and can be adapted to meet local and cultural needs.

The status and quality of the teaching profession has been a major area of development and teachers undertake ongoing, mandatory programmes of professional learning. The system is strongly committed to all children, regardless of their situation, achieving to high levels and to that end seeks to ameliorate the impact of negative background and experiential influences upon children. To achieve this, specialist support centres work alongside schools to provide, for example, mentors, psychologists, special needs professionals and anti-bullying resources. Digital exclusion has been overcome by providing free access to all school pupils in their homes and the impact of this on equity of learning outcomes has had a significant positive impact both before and through the COVID-19 pandemic.[66]

Finland is well known to have one of the most successful and highly equitable international education systems. A country of 5.4 million people, it has long been an independent nation, but following invasion and civil war between 1939 and 1945, in the 1990s it determined to transform its previously average education system that had long been based on German gymnasia-type influences. Whilst in a federal state the national government establishes the basic requirements of the system, such as a framework national curriculum, the 300 municipalities and schools have considerable licence to interpret this and to promote innovation. Pupils are encouraged to develop the skills of inquiry, thinking and independent learning and other than matriculation tests at the end of compulsory schooling, assessment is school-based and focused on these skills.

At school level, teaching is held in high esteem in Finnish society, and developing the quality of the teaching profession has been one of the major factors leading to success. Teachers are provided with earmarked time within their working week to collaborate with other professionals and to undertake research and enquiry. Trust is placed in teachers and they are encouraged to be innovative and creative. No child is allowed to underachieve in the Finnish education system and schools are supported by multidisciplinary teams of welfare officers, special needs professionals, healthcare providers, social workers and other services with approximately 20 per cent of pupils and their families accessing these services.[67]

What Wales might learn from these other relatively small nations should be set in the context that research evidence convincingly demonstrates that 'policy borrowing' almost always never works. There are, however, important policy lessons that can be learnt from these and other successful nations which could be adapted and used by Wales in developing a more successful and equitable education system in future. These include:

- the development of a high-quality teaching profession, involving a trade-off between expectations that teachers will throughout their careers update their knowledge and proficiency with allowing teachers considerable autonomy and space to innovate, undertake research and inquiry, and be creative
- a flexible curriculum and qualifications framework that emphasises the skills that learners require to achieve success and provides general and vocational pathways
- in addition to the above, specialist professional support for pupils, families and schools that enables all children to succeed and the education system to be highly equitable
- system structures that support these factors

A vision for Wales

The reform programme began by WG prior to 2016 and accelerated under the regime that will be in power to May 2021 has made good progress in moving Wales's education system towards the learning that can be derived from these successful systems. Teacher education has been reformed, the career-long professional learning of teachers is being shaped in a way that has been neglected in the past and a new, innovative curriculum is being developed.

Promising as these developments are, by themselves they are unlikely to lead to the high-quality and equitable education system that devolution has aspired for since 1999. Additional transformative change is needed in three areas: further improving the quality of teaching in our schools, a major initiative to improve the levels of engagement and achievement of our most disadvantaged pupils, and changes to the structure of the education system to support these developments.

Developing the quality of teaching should include an ongoing focus on improving recruitment and retention to the teaching profession, and, in particular, changes to teachers' working conditions that allow them far greater time within their working hours to develop their pedagogy, collaborate with other teachers and undertake research and enquiry. This is the direction that many other professions are taking in making themselves more attractive, improving recruitment and retention, and developing professional competence.[68] If the new school curriculum is to realise its full potential, putting in place opportunities for greater teacher autonomy, more proportionate accountability, less high-stakes testing and greater teacher assessment will be of critical importance.

A strategy to break the link between poverty and low achievement should deny the naysayers who think this is too ambitious and affirm that this is possible for Wales as it has been for other countries. It requires a high level of resolve that might best be enabled by the next WG either introducing a legislative measure to require the education system (not just schools) to focus unswervingly on eliminating the achievement gap, or by extending to schools the current socio-economic duty to reduce inequalities in public service delivery that has been introduced by the Senedd.[69] The key elements of a strategy to support such statutory intent have been set out above, with a key aspect of this, drawing upon international examples, being the much closer alignment of the work of schools and other professional services for children and families.

The current structure of the school system in Wales should be transformed to support these developments. In the more affluent parts of Wales the current structural arrangements work well enough and should remain unchanged. In the significant numbers of primary and secondary school contexts that are impacted by the effects of disadvantage, new structures should be established on a 'community-school' model that brings together groups of primary schools and single secondary schools with other agencies, community organisations, further and higher education, to offer a quality of support and enrichment for pupils and families that the current system is unable to provide.

The community schools would be local authority-provided organisations rather than the independent academy entities that have been created in England. Work has already begun by the current WG in re-imagining schools for the future: this type of structural reform would provide it with the organisational form to achieve transformation from a nineteenth-century model of schooling that increasingly is not fit for purpose to serve the needs of the majority of our pupils, parents and communities.

Structural change might not stop at this point. Comparisons with other countries suggest that what is called the middle tier in Welsh education (twenty-two local authorities, four regional education consortia, a school inspectorate, a qualifications body, a workforce regulation body and a leadership academy) might be disproportionate to the needs of a country of fewer than 3 million people. Within any configuration at this level, much greater emphasis could be placed on ensuring that the system was supported by high-quality education research, something which is deficient within our current arrangements, particularly when international comparisons are made.

At the outset of the devolution journey, Wales's education minister suggested that the nation was now 'at a turning point for education and lifelong learning'.[70] This article suggests that whilst over the last twenty years, despite one major misstep on the way, good progress has been made in preparing for such a manoeuvre, a full turn has not yet been successfully executed. If the rich promise of devolution of power over education is to be fully realised, further bold steps will be required over the next five to ten years.

Notes

1. The first section of this chapter draws upon Gareth Elwyn Jones, *Controls and Conflicts in Welsh Secondary Education, 1889–1944* (Cardiff: University of Wales Press, 1982); Wynford Davies, *The Curriculum and Organization of the County Intermediate Schools, 1880–1926* (Cardiff: University of Wales Press, 1982); Gareth Elwyn Jones, *The Education of a Nation* (Cardiff: University of Wales Press, 1997); Robert Smith, *Schools, Politics and Society: Elementary Education in Wales 1870–1902* (Cardiff: University of Wales Press, 1999); Richard Daugherty, Robert Phillips and Gareth Rees (eds), *Education Policy-making in Wales: Explorations in Devolved Governance* (Cardiff: University of Wales Press, 2000); Gareth Elwyn Jones and Gordon Wynne Roderick, *A History of Education in Wales* (Cardiff: University of Wales Press, 2003); Gareth Elwyn Jones, 'Education and Nationhood in Wales: an Historiographical Analysis', *Journal of Educational Administration and History*, 38/3 (2006), 263–77. For a treatment which places education within broader developments in the history of Wales since 1939, see Martin Johnes, *Wales since 1939* (Manchester: Manchester University Press, 2012), and for one that sets developments in education in Wales within the wider United Kingdom context, see Ken Jones, *Education in Britain: 1944 to the Present* (Cambridge: Polity Press, 2016).
2. *Reports of the Commissioners of Inquiry into the State of Education in Wales* (London: William Clowes and Sons, 1847).
3. Gareth Elwyn Jones, 'Education in Glamorgan since 1780', in Prys Morgan (ed.), *The Glamorgan County History: Volume VI, Glamorgan Society, 1780–1980* (Cardiff: University of Wales Press, 1988).
4. A. O. Rost, 'The significance of the Welsh dimension: the pioneering of comprehensive education in Anglesey, c.1930–1953', *Welsh History Review*, 29/3 (2019), 436–60.
5. Huw S. Thomas and Colin Williams, *Parents, Personalities and Power: Welsh Medium Schools in South-East Wales* (Cardiff: University of Wales Press, 2013).
6. Robat Powell, Robert Smith and Angharad Reakes, *Basic Skills and Key Skills: A Review of International Literature* (Slough: National Foundation for Educational Research, 2003).
7. Stephen Fothergill, 'The Most Intractable Development Region in the UK', in J. Osmond (ed.), *Futures for the Heads of the Valleys* (Cardiff: IWA, 2012).
8. Frank Loosmore, *Curriculum and Assessment in Wales: An Exploratory Study* (Cardiff: Curriculum Council for Wales, 1981).
9. Russell Deacon, *The Governance of Wales: The Welsh Office and the Policy Process 1964–1999* (Cardiff: Welsh Academic Press, 2002).
10. The Education and Training Action Group for Wales, *An Education and Training Action Plan for Wales* (Cardiff: Welsh Office, 1999).
11. G. Rees, 'Democratic Devolution and Education Policy in Wales: The Emergence of a National System', *Contemporary Wales*, 17 (2002), 28–43; D. Reynolds,

'New Labour, Education and Wales: the devolution decade', *Oxford Review of Education*, 34/6 (2008), 753–65; S. Power, 'The politics of education and the misrepresentation of Wales', *Oxford Review of Education*, 42/3 (2016), 285–98.

12. Rhodri Morgan, 'Clear red water' speech to the National Centre for Public Policy, Swansea University, 11 December 2002.

13. NAW, *The Learning Country* (Cardiff: NAW, 2001); NAW, *Vision into Action, The Learning Country 2: Delivering the Promise* (Cardiff: NAW, 2006).

14. Jenny Bradshaw, Robert Ager, Bethan Burge and Rebecca Wheater, *PISA 2009: Achievement of 15 Year Olds in Wales* (Slough: National Foundation for Educational Research, 2010).

15. Leighton Andrews, *Teaching Makes a Difference* (Cardiff: IWA, 2011).

16. WG, *Qualified for Life: An Education Improvement Plan for 3 to 19 Year Olds in Wales* (Cardiff: WG, 2014).

17. WG, *Education in Wales: Our National Mission* (Cardiff: WG, 2017).

18. See, for example, ELWa, *Report of the Geographic Pathfinder on 16–19 Education Provision in Merthyr Tydfil*, Report to Merthyr Tydfil County Borough Council (ELWa, 2005).

19. WG, *National Model for Regional Working* (Cardiff: WG, 2014).

20. A. Thomas, *The Reform of Assembly Sponsored Public Bodies* (Cardiff: NAW, 2004).

21. Ellen Hazelkorn, *Towards 2030: A framework for building a world-class post-compulsory education system for Wales* (Cardiff: WG, 2016).

22. Amanda Thomas and Alison Lewis, *An Introduction to the Foundation Phase Early Years Curriculum in Wales* (London: Bloomsbury, 2016).

23. I. Siraj-Blatchford et al., 'Developing the Foundation Phase for three to seven-year-olds in Wales', *Wales Journal of Education*, 14/1 (2007), 43–68.

24. David Greatbatch, John Wilmut and Wyn Bellin, *External Evaluation of the Welsh Baccalaureate Qualification Pilot* (Cardiff: WAG, 2006).

25. David Egan, *14–19 Developments in Wales: Learning Pathways* (London: Nuffield Foundation, 2004).

26. David Egan, *Report of the Task and Finish Group on 8–14 Education Provision in Wales* (Cardiff: WG, 2009).

27. Graham Donaldson, *Successful Futures: Independent Review of Curriculum and Assessment Arrangements in Wales* (Cardiff: WG, 2015).

28. I. Siraj-Blatchford, 'Learning in the home and at school: how working-class children "succeed against the odds"', *British Educational Research Journal*, 36/3 (2010), 463–88.

29. Michael Barber and Mona Mourshed, *How the world's best-performing school systems come out on top* (London: McKinsey and Company, 2007); Robert Coe et al., *What makes great teaching? Review of the underpinning research* (London: The Sutton Trust, 2014).

30. WG, *Evaluating the Foundation Phase: Final Report* (Cardiff: WG, 2015); Estyn, *Improving Teaching* (Cardiff: Estyn, 2018).

31. John Furlong, *Teaching Tomorrow's Teachers: Options for the future of initial teacher education in Wales. A Report to Huw Lewis, AM, Minister for Education and Skills* (Oxford: Oxford University, March 2015).

32. Mick Waters, *Learning to be a teacher for Wales: The induction of teachers into the profession* (Cardiff: WG, 2020).
33. WG, *Professional Standards for Teaching and Leadership* (Cardiff: WG, 2017).
34. David Egan and Roy James, *Evaluation for the General Teaching Council Wales of the Phase 3 Professional Development Pilot Project: Final Report* (Cardiff: General Teaching Council for Wales, 2004).
35. WG, *The National Approach to Professional Learning (NAPL)* (Cardiff: WG, 2018). Available at: *https://hwb.gov.wales/professional-development/nationa l-approach-to-professional-learning* (accessed 6 May 2021).
36. A. Harris and M. S. Jones, 'Professional Learning Communities: A Strategy for School and System Improvement', *Wales Journal of Education*, 19/1 (2017), 16–38.
37. M. Hadfield et al., 'Developing the Capacity to Support Beginning Teachers in Wales: Lessons Learnt from the Masters in Educational Practice', *Wales Journal of Education*, 19/1 (2017), 90–106.
38. Estyn, *Annual Reports of Her Majesty's Chief Inspector of Education and Training in Wales 1999–2019* (Cardiff: Estyn, 1999–2019).
39. Marcus Kools and Louise Stoll, *What Makes a School a Learning Organisation?* (Paris: OECD, 2016).
40. WG, *NAPL*.
41. David Egan and Ann Keane (eds), 'Special Number on School Leadership in Wales', *Wales Journal of Education*, 20/2 (2018).
42. A. J. Davies et al., 'Headteacher Recruitment, Retention and Professional Development in Wales: Challenges and Opportunities', *Wales Journal of Education*, 20/2 (2018), 204–24.
43. David Egan and Roy James, *Evaluation of the Leadership Programme for Serving Headteachers in Wales* (Cardiff: WAG, 2003); David Egan and Roy James, *Evaluation of the Professional Headship Induction Programme in Wales* (Cardiff: WAG, 2003).
44. David Egan and Ann Keane, 'The Leadership Challenge in Wales: Voices from the Front Line', *Wales Journal of Education*, 20/2 (2018), 116–37.
45. D. Egan, 'School effectiveness in *The Learning Country*: Wales and School Improvement', in Christopher Chapman et al. (eds), *School Effectiveness and Improvement Research, Policy and Practice* (Abingdon: Routledge, 2012), pp. 109–24.
46. WAG, *The Daugherty Report: Learning Pathways Through Statutory Assessment at Key Stages 2 and 3* (Cardiff: WAG, 2004).
47. D. Holtom, 'Narrowing the Gap: Lessons from RAISE Ten Years On', *Wales Journal of Education*, 19/2 (2017), 118–42.
48. WAG, *The School Effectiveness Framework* (Cardiff: WAG, 2008).
49. Gareth Evans, *A class apart: Learning the lessons of education in post-devolution Wales* (Cardiff: Welsh Academic Press, 2015).
50. WG, *Teaching: A valued profession working towards a Career, Conditions and Pay Framework for School Teachers in Wales: The report of the independent review* (Cardiff: WG, 2018).

51. Estyn, *The Annual Report of Her Majesty's Chief Inspector of Education and Training in Wales 2016–2017* (Cardiff: Estyn, 2018).

52. Davies et al., 'Headteacher Recruitment, Retention and Professional Development in Wales Challenges and Opportunities'; Anusha Ghosh and Jack Worth, *Teacher Labour Market in Wales* (Slough: National Foundation for Educational Research, 2020).

53. WG, *School improvement guidance: framework for evaluation, improvement and accountability* (Cardiff: WG, 2021).

54. G. Rees and C. Taylor, 'Is There a Crisis in Welsh Education?', *Transactions of the Honourable Society of Cymmrodorion* (2015), 97–113.

55. Leighton Andrews, *Ministering to Education* (Cardigan: Parthian, 2014).

56. B. Lingard, W. Martino and G. Rezai-Rashti, 'Testing regimes, accountabilities and education policy', *Journal of Education Policy*, 28/5 (2013), 539–56.

57. G. Johnes, 'Medium Efficiency: Comparing Inputs and Outputs by Language of Instruction in Secondary Schools in Wales', *Wales Journal of Education*, 22/2 (2020), 53–68; L. Swaffield, 'Never Waste a Crisis: Understanding the Welsh Policy Response to PISA in the Context of the Globally Structured Reform Agenda', *Wales Journal of Education*, 19/1 (2017), 178–87.

58. Power, 'The politics of education and the misrepresentation of Wales', 285–98.

59. D. Egan, 'Educational Equity in Wales', *Wales Journal of Education*, 18/1 (2016), 21–44; D. Egan, 'Shifting Paradigms: Can Education Compensate for Society?', in S. Gannon, R. Hattam and W. Sawyer (eds), *Resisting Educational Inequality: Reframing policy and practice in schools serving vulnerable communities* (Abingdon: Routledge, 2018), pp. 236–44.

60. Jens Van den Brande, Jude Hillary and Carl Cullinane, *Selective Comprehensives: Great Britain* (London: The Sutton Trust, 2019), pp. 38–54.

61. Janet Goodall, *Narrowing the Achievement Gap: Parental Engagement with Children's Learning* (Abingdon: Routledge, 2017).

62. Steve Higgins et al., *The Sutton Trust-Education Endowment Foundation Teaching and Learning Toolkit* (London: Education Endowment Foundation, 2014). Available at: *educationendowmentfoundation.org.uk/evidence-summaries/teaching-learning-toolkit* (accessed 6 May 2021).

63. E. Keep, in A. Mann and P. Huddlestone (eds), *How should schools respond to the demands of the twenty first century labour market? Eight perspectives* (Education and Employers Research, Occasional Taskforce Research Paper 4, 2015), pp. 18–20.

64. Linda Darling-Hammond et al., *Empowered Educators* (San Francisco: Jossey-Bass, 2017), p. 43.

65. C. Tan, K. Koh and W. Choy, 'The education in Singapore', in S. Juszcyzk (ed.), *Asian Education Systems* (Torun: Adam Marszalek Publishing House, 2016), pp. 129–48.

66. Amanda Ripley, *The Smartest Kids in the World* (New York: Simon & Schuster, 2013); Fenton Whelan, *Lessons Learned* (2009); Eurydice, *Key Features of the Education System*. Available at: *https://eacea.ec.europa.eu/national-policies/eurydice* (accessed 30 April 2021); Kevin Dickinson, 'Equity Made Estonia an Educational Front Runner', Big Think (2020). Available at: *https://bigthink.*

com/politics-current-affairs/estonia-education?rebelltitem=1#rebelltitem1 (accessed 30 April 2021); OECD, 'Education Policy Outlook in Estonia', *OECD Education Policy Perspectives*, 13 (Paris: OECD Publishing, 2020). Available at: *https://doi. org/10.1787/9d472195-en* (accessed 30 April 2021).

67. Linda Darling-Hammond et al., *Empowered Educators*; Ripley, *The Smartest Kids*; Whelan, *Lessons Learnt*; Pasi Sahlberg, *Finnish Lessons: What can the world learn from educational change in Finland?* (New York: Teachers College Press, 2011).
68. David Egan, Julia Longville and Emmajane Milton, *Graduate Recruitment: Teaching and Other Professions* (Cardiff: Education Workforce Council, 2019).
69. The Equality Act 2010 (Authorities subject to a duty regarding Socio-economic Inequalities) (Wales) Regulations 2021 SI 2021/295 (W. 72).
70. NAW, *The Learning Country*.

Select bibliography

Daugherty, Richard, Robert Phillips and Gareth Rees, *Education Policy-making in Wales: Explorations in Devolved Governance* (Cardiff: University of Wales Press, 2000).

Egan, David, 'School effectiveness in *The Learning Country*: Wales and school improvement', in Christopher Chapman et al. (eds), *School Effectiveness and Improvement, Research Policy and Practice* (Abingdon: Routledge, 2012).

Egan, David, 'Poverty and Education in Wales: enabling a national mission', in Ian Thompson and Gabrielle Ivinson (eds), *Poverty in Education across the UK: A Comparative Analysis of Policy and Place* (Bristol: Policy Press, 2020).

Jones, Gareth Elwyn and Gordon Wynne Roderick, *A History of Education in Wales* (Cardiff: University of Wales Press, 2003).

Wales Journal of Education, 18/1 (2016).

Wales Journal of Education, 19/1 (2017).

Wales Journal of Education, 20/2 (2018).

WG, *Education in Wales: Our National Mission* (Cardiff: WG, 2017).

4

ECONOMIC DEVELOPMENT IN WALES: EVOLUTION AND REVOLUTION

Gareth Davies

Introduction

The introduction of democratic devolution for Wales in 1999 has been presented as a process enabling Wales 'to make our own decisions and set our own priorities', and as a driver 'to improve economic performance and productivity (and) to create more and better jobs'.[1] Debate has since followed over whether Welsh devolution's purpose has been to improve economic performance as well as to address a democratic deficit.[2] It has, however, been argued that the nation's future economic performance is potentially the most critical measure of devolution's success.[3] Studies suggest that an expectation of a 'devolution dividend' would be unfounded, and indeed that devolution may actually bring negative economic effects.[4] The fact remains though that with the coming into force of the Government of Wales Act 1998, Wales was now responsible for its own economic development.

In this context, the prospect of devolution providing less uneven economic benefit across the UK was unlikely, despite being 'elevated into one of the principal goals' for Welsh devolution.[5] It should be noted though, that those wider goals include the reduction of economic inequality and achieving sustainable development. In this chapter, the relationship between economic performance and devolution is examined in the context of the emergence of City and Growth Deal regions across Wales, which introduce a new level of spatial governance and activity. Combined with Brexit and the establishment of a new UK internal market, this is redefining the relationship of regions with the Welsh and UK governments.

Pre-devolution

Prior to the creation of the National Assembly, Wales already languished as one of the poorer parts of the UK, and its economic performance was in stark contrast to the prosperity it fuelled through the Industrial Revolution. The challenges faced by the Welsh economy can be traced back to the economic restructuring that saw the UK established as the world's first industrial nation.[6] Having powered an empire, as part of the 'Outer Britain' of regions which were home to heavy industry, Wales had served its purpose as the Industrial Revolution turned full circle.

At the turn of the millennium Wales was performing poorly across a broad range of economic measures, despite its comparatively vibrant and productive manufacturing sector.[7] This weak overall performance included limited indigenous new enterprise, and low levels of business investment in research and development (R&D), compared with other UK regions. Since records began at the beginning of 1970s, the Gross Domestic Product (GDP) of Wales broadly tracked that of the wider UK, but at a lower level. This continuing gap relative to the UK (and Europe) resulted in most of Wales qualifying for the highest level of EU Regional Aid (Objective One) in 2000. This phenomenon was reflected across much of the UK with the deindustrialisation of many regions which saw their fortunes fall behind the growth of London and south-east England.

To arrest this decline, economic development policy in Wales, led by the UK Government's Welsh Office and delivered through the Welsh Development Agency (WDA) from 1976 onwards, focused on pursuing inward investment. The approach involved what Cooke and Clifton termed the 'field of dreams' approach of 'build it and they will come'.[8] This strategy produced a significant impact, particularly during 1983–93, with Wales attracting 15 to 20 per cent of inward-UK Foreign Direct Investment (FDI).[9] Despite this impressive FDI performance, the overall Welsh economy continued to decline.[10]

Partly as a result of successfully attracting FDIs, the contraction of primary industries since the 1970s was largely offset by a partial restructuring of the Welsh economy with 200,000 jobs absorbed into a modernised employment base of services and advanced manufacturing.[11] Alongside this was also a redistribution of UK public sector employment, with the Driver and Vehicle Licensing Agency, Companies House and the Office of National Statistics moving location to Wales. The new employment and shift in industry mix was also accompanied by a gender restructuring of the workforce that saw the proportion of women employed in Wales rise from 38 per cent in 1975 to 50 per cent in 1994.[12] However, the opportunities for tempting FDIs to Wales declined during the 1990s, due to a slowing UK economy and emergence of competitor regions for low-skilled manufacturing such as China and India.[13]

The focus on heavy industries, branch plant manufacturing and major regeneration schemes risks overlooking the contemporaneous growth clusters in technology fields, including optoelectronics and biotechnology.[14] The optoelectronics cluster originally identified by the UK Department of Trade and Industry stretched across Wales from optronics and space technology in north-east Wales through to the semiconductor industry in south-east Wales. These technology clusters subsequently became a focus of Welsh Government (WG) economic policy as it aimed to increase activity within higher Gross Value Added (GVA) sectors.

Wales's persistently lagging economic performance had been caused by its heavy reliance on low value-add employment. This resulted in lower productivity per employee and was accompanied by higher rates of economic inactivity (particularly in the west Wales and valleys region). These factors were compounded by almost 60 per cent of Welsh GDP relating to the public sector,[15] and in order to arrest the continued decline, major economic restructuring was required, with a focus on redeveloping and growing private sector activity.

Devolution's early years: 1999–2006

'A Winning Wales'
As Wales took responsibility for its own economic development ambitions, the collapse of the mammoth LG FDI project involving a support package of £250 million became a cause célèbre.[16] The withdrawal of the South Korean conglomerate from this megaproject coincided with an ongoing downturn in Wales's FDI performance, set within increasing competition for such projects, and signalled a turning-point in economic development approach.[17] Observers had also noted weaknesses in the 'embeddedness' of such branch-plant manufacturing activity, together with an imbalance against support for indigenous enterprise and development of more localised clusters.[18] Aiming to address this, the Welsh Assembly Government's (WAG) 10-year economic development plan

'A Winning Wales', published in 2001 and updated in 2003, presented a vision of 'a prosperous Welsh economy that is dynamic, inclusive and sustainable, based on successful, innovative businesses with highly skilled, well-motivated people'.[19]

The strategy sought to rebalance the Welsh economy towards more knowledge-based activity, by promoting R&D and innovation, and targeting growth of the services sector. In 2003, WAG reported on its progress towards achieving the 'winning Wales' vision, prior to delivering an updated version of the strategy in 2004.[20] This restated WAG's aim to increase the prosperity of Wales to 90 per cent of the UK level within a decade and be level with the UK within a generation. There was also a shift to greater regional spatial planning, that foreshadowed the geographical boundaries of the four City/Growth Deals.[21] WAG strategy and policies had included a central role for the WDA, with greater focus on local business support and entrepreneurship schemes.

The WDA had been established by the UK Labour Government in 1976 to further economic development across Wales, promote competitiveness and support employment.[22] Even in its early years it had faced criticism of its activities, and whilst not always justified,[23] this contributed to the government's dissatisfaction with its performance, which was to lead to its disbandment. The agency's initial focus was to attract FDI and evolved to involve further effort in supporting indigenous enterprise, particularly that which was new and/or knowledge-based, along with further integration of the skills agenda. This came as a result of the changing global economic conditions and WAG's economic strategy rather than the Westminster-directed Welsh Office.[24]

The agency's remit included implementation of the *Entrepreneurship Action Plan*, reaching beyond the FDI and commercial/industrial property agenda. The difference is clearly seen in the WDA corporate plan from the period which was developed prior to its absorption into WAG.[25]

The strategy also outlined how European Union (EU) Structural Funds, including Objective 1 funding would be used in economic development for west Wales and the valleys. These economic development ambitions were boosted by the significant EU funding, though Wales's qualification for the highest level of regional aid was itself a dire indictment of the woeful state of much of its economy. Nevertheless, there was also ongoing debate regarding the additionality of this support, as the required match-funding would pressurise existing budgets.[26] This issue ultimately led Rhodri Morgan to the role of first minister, after Alun Michael's government had failed to secure additional match-funding from UK central government.

A notable example of the shift towards entrepreneurship and innovation support with structural funds investment was the controversial Technium initiative. Debate has centred on the aggregate 'network' of these centres, mostly focused upon headline figures. This debate has, however, had limited focus on actual project data except for that from Murphy et al. and Davies et al., or lacks the depth of analysis of underpinning theory such as that provided by Cooke and Morgan.[27] Nevertheless, there is consensus that the initiative struggled initially to increase its impact with the rollout of a pan-Wales network. The original aims of the initiative were to nurture indigenous innovation and to attract 'stickier' higher-GVA inward-investment R&D activities, with an emphasis on drawing upon local universities to support the agenda. This stepped away from the branch-plant focus of the WDA and towards greater knowledge-based activities involving ventures at an earlier riskier stage of their development. Despite its initial success, the initiative became embattled and ultimately ended with the network being disbanded in 2011.[28] The project's key challenges identified during its decade of operation included a lack of coherent management control,[29] together with too great a focus on property development rather than operating as a knowledge/innovation initiative.[30] The emphasis on property development resonated with the original WDA approach of holding industrial/commercial property, albeit within a market that differed significantly from previously targeted inward-investing manufacturing operations.

It is widely acknowledged that there were missed opportunities to learn from the experience of the first Technium site prior to rollout of the network, but some lessons were absorbed.[31] While some commentators were labelling sites such as Technium Pembrokeshire as 'emptiums' as late as 2018, this centre had in 2019 achieved full occupancy, beyond the 85 per cent occupancy rate that DTZ noted in 2009 as 'best practice'.[32] At the time of network disbandment, three sites had only been in operation for three years, with a further three sites having only been open for a further two years. The initiatives themselves and relevant evaluation guidance suggested more meaningful time horizons for incubator and science park initiatives, while the DTZ review of individual centres showed that earlier established centres had started to make progress.[33] The tension between the focus upon property development and innovation-led activities was a continuing theme during the 2000s, in which WG challenged and gradually dismantled the WDA approach. This culminated in a broader shift as WG took firmer control of policy implementation by disbanding a range of its arms-length bodies.

Bonfire of the quangos

The second Assembly term (2003–7) saw the controversial long-threatened 'bonfire of the quangos', as functions undertaken by quasi-autonomous non-governmental organisations (quangos) were absorbed into WAG. This involved the absorption into government of the WDA, Wales Tourist Board (WTB) and Education and Learning Wales (ELWa), each of which had operated independently. This change was articulated in WAG's vision for the future of public services, *Making Connections: Delivering Better Services for Wales*.[34] Its intention was to deliver greater efficiency and impact by creating improved cooperation and coordination between agencies and across the public sector.

While other quangos were lesser known, the WDA had become renowned worldwide in promoting Wales as a location for business activity. Despite notable success through FDI, the WDA had already been targeted for the 'bonfire' as early as 1997. The then Welsh Secretary Ron Davies pledged to merge the agency with other bodies and to make its opaque appointments process more transparent. The 'Making Connections' vision made very clear that the changed lines of political accountability lay with WAG: 'It is this Assembly, with the authority of its democratic mandate, which must assume responsibility and accountability for public policy in Wales. It is for Ministers to determine policy, and for this Assembly to hold us to account.'[35]

These quangos were merged with government in April 2006. Observers critical of this move thought of this as an example of 'moving the institutional deckchairs', and it was noted that the impact of the policy would take some years to become clear.[36] Despite its Labour roots, much of the WDA's success had been during the influence of experienced and respected Conservative Secretaries of State for Wales such as Nicholas Edwards and Peter Walker.[37] This changed however, under Welsh secretary John Redwood, MP for Wokingham, as he sold off public assets with the stated aim of allowing more Thatcherite laissez-faire market forces. This in itself was a rolling back of the Conservative

Government's support for the WDA in addressing market failure that the agency and its investments had been established in order to tackle. The direction was reversed as the new Assembly Government pursued a much more interventionist approach.

One Wales 2007–10

The new coalition Labour-Plaid Cymru government was formed in 2007 on the basis of the 'One Wales agreement'. Its twin priorities were a 'healthy future' centred on investment in the NHS with a focus on equality and overall employment, and a 'prosperous society' based on increasing economic growth and closing the gap with other UK and EU regions.[38] The economic development agenda was led by Plaid Cymru leader Ieuan Wyn Jones who also became deputy first minister as part of the 2007–11 One Wales delivery plan. The plan emphasised an 'all-Wales approach to economic development', bringing further emphasis to activity in northwest Wales, Plaid Cymru's traditional heartland. The plan also reflected a greater emphasis upon social inclusion and sustainability, and showed greater ambition for rail connectivity between north and south Wales.

Alongside longer-term rail and road upgrades, this ambition resulted in creation of an air-link, established as a Public Service Obligation (PSO) route, connecting RAF Valley in Ynys Môn with Cardiff Airport. This subsidised service was rapidly dubbed 'Ieuan Air' after the deputy first minister and frequent flyer on the service which served his constituency.[39] Whilst this may have raised eyebrows, this symbolic development, though limited in scope, did point towards a more interventionist WG approach to transport infrastructure, not least to support its economic development role. This would subsequently include the nationalisation of Cardiff Airport, and the rail network in Wales in 2021.

In the wider economy, a continued comparatively low regional level of business expenditure on R&D brought focus to the capacity and capability of the region's universities to support development of knowledge-based enterprise.[40] This was not only through infrastructure such as the Technium initiative, but also through targeted development of science and technology with the intent to 'anchor companies undertaking industrial R&D in Wales'.[41] This approach targeted sectors that offer potential for higher levels of GVA, including life sciences and health, low-carbon technologies, and advanced engineering and materials.

The One Wales plan initially benefitted from a period of economic growth as Wales enjoyed an increase in employment ahead of the UK as a whole, although productivity continued to lag behind the other UK nations (Figure 4.1). This reflected Wales's growth in public-sector employment, and its continued structural imbalance with lesser higher-GVA service sectors compared with the rest of the UK.

Figure 4.1: Gross Value added by UK nation, 1997–2017[42]

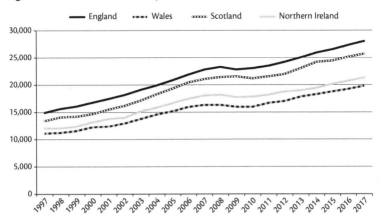

Alongside sectors targeted through the development of science and technology, other high-growth potential sectors focused on by WG economic development policy included the creative industries. While available data were imprecise, employment in this sector in 2004 across Wales totalled somewhere between 22,000 and 30,000 people, representing over 1 per cent of total Welsh economic output.[43] This employment was concentrated in the Cardiff region where at the time it exceeded the number of jobs in financial services. There were notable wider examples of growth in the sector, such as Tinopolis headquartered in Llanelli and which has since grown into a significant multinational group. North Wales, through companies such as Barcud and Cwmni Da, offered further potential for links eastwards with UK-wide initiatives in Liverpool and Manchester regions. Developments during the period included support for the founding of the 'Valleywood' Dragon Studios in Bridgend, within 5 miles of the threatened Ford engine plant, which finally closed in 2020. Despite being driven by well-known industry figures it was initially beset by funding and development issues, and did not deliver on its early promise, which had included a new hospital and theme park on an adjacent site.[44]

This was followed by further restructuring of WG-sponsored support for the sector with the establishment of new development bodies and the creation of new public funds for commercial projects. Such commercial property-related developments would have been the focus of the WDA before 2006, and heralded the more direct challenges and accountability WG would face in subsequent projects.

The expansion of the public sector in Wales was halted by the financial crisis of 2008. Previously, much employment growth and replacement of lost manufacturing jobs had come from new public sector employment, and this dependence provided poor preparation for the austerity in public budgets which followed, including the reduction in the income from the Barnett formula which provided the base for the WG budget. The 2008 financial crisis had less initial impact in Wales than that felt by other parts of the UK due to its lesser reliance on those services, particularly financial services, which were at the epicentre of the crisis. Sensier and Artis demonstrate that Wales had initially weathered the economic crisis well in comparison with many other UK regions, as the experience of previous recessions had already contributed to the major erosion of the heavy industry and manufacturing sectors.[45] The greater diversification of economic sectors together with WG's ProAct employment support programme succeeded in moderating the level of job losses, supporting over 10,000 jobs across a range of sectors.[46]

Despite this challenging context, WG continued to invest in capacity for knowledge-based enterprise within Wales, with a new focus upon the 'smart specialisation' approach, which would become a centrepiece of subsequent development efforts.[47] This place-based approach would focus on localised strengths across industry and academia to support sustainable economic development.

From 2010 up to the present day

WG refreshed its economic strategy in 2010 with *An Economic Renewal*, focusing on the development of skills to improve productivity, and infrastructure.[48] However, in comparison with previous policies, it lacked firm targets and timescales, offering vague goals rather than the previous predominantly economic and employment growth ambitions.[49] The strategy continued to focus upon the strengths and opportunities afforded in the sectors of life sciences, health, low-carbon technologies, energy and the environment.[50] Fostering partnerships across clusters of activity, and targeting new energy technologies, brought an emphasis on innovation in economic development in order to achieve an amalgam of economic, social and environmental goals.[51] This included championing initiatives such as SPECIFIC, which brings together academic research in photovoltaic technology, with industry partners ranging from metals production, manufacturing and housebuilding.

A more interventionist WG approach saw greater investment in activity beyond the provision of built infrastructure. One notable development was the arrival in Wales of the world-famous Pinewood Studios franchise, through a partnership between the studios and WG to develop a complex for creative industries on the outskirts of Cardiff. A £30m fund was established to co-invest and attract productions to the facility, alongside the leasing of a vacant building for studios. The initial number of projects did not realise the anticipated returns, and the arrangement was subsequently terminated following concerns which emerged in 2016, with WG recognising that the collaboration had not resulted in good value for money.[52]

A similar approach had been developed for life sciences with the establishment of the £50m Arthurian investment fund, based at the Life Sciences Hub Wales. Led by celebrated biotechnology entrepreneur Sir Chris Evans, the fund encountered some early criticism, though at the time it was noted it was too early to determine value for money. The fund has subsequently supported the creation of over 200 jobs and provided a 3:1 return on WG investment, which, considering the risk associated with ventures in such a challenging sector, provided both economic development and financial return for the public investment.[53]

The focus on high-growth high-GVA sectors was accompanied by a return to considering entrepreneurship and company growth more broadly. A review of small- and medium-size enterprises' (SME) access to finance identified deficiencies in the support from the UK banking sector for the SME community.[54] This section of the Welsh economy is particularly important with SMEs representing 75 per cent of private sector employment,[55] and the review recommended greater focus on economic development benefit from public investment, rather than pure financial return. The review also set out the rationale for a new entity to ensure that 'every viable business in Wales should get access to funding at an affordable price', with 'the primary role of government-backed funding for SMEs is to drive forward economic development'.[56]

The recommendations were taken forward by WG resulting in the establishment of the Development Bank of Wales in 2016, later branded 'Banc'. It brought together Finance Wales funding together with a range of support for projects in Wales, ranging from technology start-ups seed-funding to property development loans.

However, the most notable WG business investment was the nationalisation of Cardiff Airport. In 2013, WG purchased the airport for £52m from its owners TBI who had put it up for sale. The purchase could be considered as a return of the airport to public ownership, only having been privatised in 1995 following forty years of public own-ership and operation, initially by Glamorgan Council.[57] Since being taken on by WG, there has been new investment into facilities and while there has been volatility in the range of airlines operating from the airport, there have been new links formed, notably to the Middle East with Qatar Airlines. Part of the rationale for WG intervention was to secure the airport's future, with its claimed economic impact measuring over 2,400 aviation-related jobs and over £246m of direct annual economic benefit to Wales.[58] However, as the responsibility for air transport regulation and tax policy, such as Air Passenger Duty, is retained by the UK Government the scope for further WG interven-tion has been limited.[59]

Between 1999 and 2010, devolution operated under the alignment of a Labour UK Government and a Labour-led Government in the National Assembly. The following UK Conservative/Liberal Democrat coalition and its regressive austerity programme pressured the finance available to Wales for economic development. Against this backdrop of imposed austerity and the more challenged UK-Wales political relation-ship, there did exist the prospect of major collaborative initiatives to stimulate economic development. Major energy infrastructure projects fall under the retained powers of the UK Government, though they represent significant regional economic drivers in both their construc-tion and operation. A notable example of the impact of this separation of powers was in Ynys Môn, with the relationship between Anglesey Aluminium and the neighbouring Wylfa nuclear power plant, both established in the 1970s. The aluminium plant was one of the largest employers on the island, with over 500 staff. As one of the UK's largest electricity consumers using the neighbouring Wylfa nuclear plant's baseload, the two entities were inherently interlinked. The planned decommissioning of Wylfa and complexities in extending arrangements, without a timely replacement, led in turn to the loss of both important regional employers.

Despite being too late to potentially support Anglesey Aluminium, the continuation of nuclear power generation in north Wales was given a boost with the endorsement of a new reactor at Wylfa.[60] Significant investment was made in the initial phases of development, despite the opposition of anti-nuclear activists and Plaid Cymru, with the exception of the local Assembly Member and former party leader, Ieuan Wyn Jones. However, the initiative has since been dealt a major blow with Hitachi's withdrawal after the Horizon consortium's negotiations with UK Government failed to progress. A similar ebb and flow featured with another proposed major energy initiative in south Wales. Swansea Bay offers the second largest tidal range in the world, and therefore the prospect of massive reliable renewable energy generation. The concept of a man-made tidal lagoon presented greater potential feasibility than the proposed Severn barrage.[61] Despite initial support from the UK Government and achieving the all-important planning consent, this enthusiasm waned. This was ostensibly due to concern over costs as the scheme competed against government subsidy (mainly UK) for other projects such as those using nuclear and offshore wind technology, though not in itself an insurmountable issue, as highlighted by leading business figures.[62] UK Government support was lost despite a significant independent review giving strong support to the proposal, with the concept of a Swansea lagoon advocated as a 'pathfinder' for future potential developments.[63] The review applauded not only the initial economic impact of the construction and operation, but also the longer-term opportunity for supporting local steel and manufacturing industries.

The fate of these initiatives reflected the limitations of WG and the supremacy of the UK Government in brokering economic development within the energy sector, and highlighted failures to resolve the long-standing challenge of financing long-term major infrastructure projects in Wales.[64]

City Deals

The period from 2010 also ushered in wider UK devolution, with the Localism Act paving the way for greater devolution to English regions, including the creation of elected mayors and a greater role for Local Enterprise Partnerships (LEPs) in regional economic policy.[65] The opportunity for the local retention of business rates by English regions accompanied by additional UK central government funding led to a clamour from counterparts in Scottish and Welsh regions to receive similar potential benefits. However, it is argued that the arrangements do not aid inter-regional competition and favour the existing prosperous regions whilst exacerbating regional inequalities.[66]

This regional economic development approach was set in the context of UK industrial policy's focus on key sectors and technologies.[67] This aligned to an extent with those sectors targeted by WG,[68] albeit with those areas such as nuclear and energy more influenced by the UK Government's powers, as witnessed by the fate of proposed developments at Wylfa and the Swansea Bay tidal lagoon.

Despite those areas of alignment in industrial policy, the City Deals create a layer of complexity in the Welsh context, accentuated by the lack of (as in England) elected mayors as figureheads. In Wales, Senedd Members provide a superficial layer of democratic accountability, although Waite and Morgan note it as an opportunity for WG to support coherence within and between regions.[69] Ultimately Wales has seen a set of deals established, from Cardiff Capital (2016) and Swansea Bay (2017) City Regions and then the subsequent North and Mid Wales Growth Deals (2020).[70] These regions and the partnerships around them broadly reflect Wales's spatial plan,[71] and align the City/Growth Regions with their local 'smart specialisations'. Each deal also gives focus to developing the skills required to support the growth of targeted sectors, with the involvement of universities and further education colleges. While the deals are at different stages of development and delivery, a recent review provided a positive report on their progress.[72]

Much like the previous debate relating to the potential for English Regional Development Agencies (RDAs),[73] the prospect of these regions realising significant economic development with their level of available resources requires a dose of realism. For example, while the launch of the Swansea Bay City Deal was surrounded by a mixture of fanfare, scrutiny and criticism, the combined value of the deal only equates to 0.16 per cent of the region's economy, delivered across a timescale equal to two EU programme cycles. These deals will be only truly transformative if their regional project portfolios are able to leverage significant additional investment.

However, the focus of these deals has not been solely to pursue economic development, but also to address health and wider social inequalities, such as improving access to public services, reduce fuel poverty and improve housing stock.[74] The deals themselves and the individual projects they realise are also being considered within the context of the Well-being of Future Generations (Wales) Act 2015 (WFGA),[75] a novel piece of legislation that has subsequently come to frame all developments, including economic policy and City/Growth Deals, and with the independent Future Generations Commissioner given the power to scrutinise proposals.

Whilst the City/Growth Deals have attracted much interest, the most significant economic development for Wales has been the departure of the UK from the EU. The WDA-era FDI boom had in large part been supported by attracting investors with access to the growing EU single market. Amid assurances that such benefits would be preserved, the majority of voters in Wales, as well as England, voted for Brexit. Considering the significant levels of EU investment into Wales, this may have been a surprising result, although the disgruntlement caused by the UK Government's austerity agenda was fundamental to this outcome.[76] Austerity had hit the poorest communities hardest, resulting in understandable disillusionment amongst voters towards a UK Government that was ostensibly campaigning to remain in the EU.[77] The resulting economic uncertainty and the prospect of friction in trade has impacted upon key sectors in Wales. These effect activities ranging from aerospace, with Airbus's pan-European assembly plants, farming subsidies and the regulation of medical technologies. Wales's manufacturing sector is also precariously placed with Europe as its major export market, particularly as European customers may look to alternative suppliers within the EU single market.

Trade for Wales with its EU neighbours is now embroiled in greater friction and cost, but a positive regional development has been the removal of tolls from the Severn Bridge at the end of 2018. This has reduced trade friction for south Wales and it was projected by the Welsh

Office that this would provide an annual £100m boost to the Welsh economy, removing barriers that the UK Government accepted had 'hindered Wales's economic prosperity for more than half a century'.[78] Projections for WG back in 2012 even then suggested a potential uplift in excess of this figure from productivity uplift and wider benefits.[79]

Emerging context

Two decades on from democratic devolution, the economic context has never been more unsure. Beyond the tragic human consequences of the COVID-19 pandemic, its prevalence has led to huge economic challenges globally. Before its future impact ripples through the economy, following the end of furlough and other support schemes, unemployment in Wales was already starting to rise sharply as firms struggled with lockdowns despite £1.7bn of WG support by the end of 2020, in addition to UK schemes. This support may appear significant but it is small in a context where tourism alone suffered a £6.6bn loss to the Welsh economy in just the first four months of the pandemic.[80] Furthermore, in the longer-term, COVID-19 has compounded the regressive effects of Westminster-driven austerity, falling disproportionately hard upon the most vulnerable, including younger workers and those from Black and minority ethnic backgrounds.[81]

The impact of COVID-19 has coincided with the transition phase of Brexit, and although the separation of the UK from the EU has been enacted, its effects are not obvious or complete. The potential 'No Deal' outcome had been set to hit Wales hardest, along with those other UK regions most reliant on manufacturing and agriculture.[82] While this outcome did not materialise, the deal struck is already creating difficulty for these sectors.[83] Minto and Morgan suggest the challenges and opportunities for Wales to remain engaged with Europe, building upon networks and bilateral regional relationships.[84] They note the need to work more closely with the private sector and civic society to achieve this, although challenged by a poorer political environment. This may, or may not, be helped by the promised Shared Prosperity Fund (SPF) that is due to emerge as a replacement for the regional aid previously delivered through EU structural funds. This is unlikely to be aligned with EU programmes, as indicated by the decision to cease participation in the celebrated Erasmus educational exchange programme. Along with the uncertainty around the quantum and timing of the SPF, it also creates a new policy dynamic, with the tightening of the Westminster purse-strings as the economic lever for economic and social development beyond those policy areas tied directly to the financial mechanism of the Barnett formula and the City/Growth Deals.

It is anticipated that the SPF will focus on regional differentiators, and technology clusters have already become a core part of City Deal strategies in Wales. The first of these, focused on the semiconductors cluster along the M4 corridor has attracted significant investment into the Cardiff city region and beyond. In parallel, the City Deals and other investments are supporting additional clusters including life sciences and health along the M4 corridor, and marine energy on the west and north Wales coast. These deals are presented as part of a solution to improve productivity across the wider UK, distributing investment and opportunity more equitably.

The COVID-19 pandemic has also further exposed spatial and other entrenched inequalities across the UK which has accentuated the UK Government's stated aim of creating a 'levelling up' agenda. This is now reflected in its development of 'place based analysis' to allow for greater spatial distribution of public investment under the Treasury's Green Book guidance.[85] Within Wales, the recent Organisation for Economic Cooperation and Development governance review echoes this notion, reflecting upon territorial economic inequalities across Wales, which bear similarities to the inequalities across the UK as a whole.[86] The importance of physical and digital connectivity to support well-being and economic growth across Wales is also emphasised, along with the need for stronger mechanisms to achieve this.

Conclusion

Wales emerges into its third decade of democratic devolution, faced with notable uncertainty and challenges. Its economic prospects are interwoven with significantly deteriorating relationships both within and beyond the UK. Over this period, WG has not been able to reverse the nation's economic fortunes and there has seemingly not been a devolution economic dividend. Since the creation of the National Assembly for Wales (NAW), the nation's economic performance has continued to fail to catch up with most of the rest of the UK, while other lagging regions such as Cornwall have succeeded in closing the gap. It should be noted though that these two decades, punctuated by a global recession and the retrenchment of Wales's prided FDI-driven manufacturing base, has been a challenging time to drive prosperity forward in the teeth of significant economic headwinds. This makes it difficult to assess economic development against any counterfactual argument, though undoubtedly WG's ambition to narrow the gap with the performance of the wider UK economy has failed.

Certainly, the lack of powers granted in the devolution settlement has limited Wales's ability to act,[87] though bold steps such as disbanding the WDA and pursuing a more interventionist sectoral approach have displayed the ambition 'to make our own decisions and set our own priorities'. An assertive UK Conservative Government may bemoan how Wales has performed, but may be held politically accountable for the period of economic decline before devolution. It is, however, ironic that the extinct WDA's emphasis on inward investment is still relevant and opposition political parties wish to revive it, as Wales recently missed out on two major inward-investment opportunities in the targeted automotive sector, with the British Volt battery Gigafactory preferring Blyth in Northumberland, and the Ineos Grenadier investment, led by a leading Brexiteer businessman, departing for the EU.

The shift towards developing Wales's strength of indigenous companies and clusters shows promise. Successes in the emergence of the semiconductor, life sciences and creative industries have been engendered partly by taking the longer timescales required to achieve more meaningful structural economic development than FDI investment and that Wales requires. The shift from pursuing 'quick-wins' for job creation through the WDA's attraction of inward-investment via arms-length premises and grants to a more interventionist longer-term development of key sectors has received mixed success.[88]

As observed by Pike, any economic benefit from devolution may not be plainly apparent, and with the continued dominance of the central UK Government's influence upon regional development policy, this may continue to be the case.[89] The Internal Market Act 2020, passed despite the objection of WG, gives the UK Government powers for infrastructure and economic development.[90] In the wake of cancelling major initiatives such as Wylfa B and the Swansea Bay tidal lagoon, it remains to be seen what the UK Government will invest in Wales beyond its current contributions to City/Growth Deals. Drawn into the post-Brexit context, EU state aid rules have been cited as to why extended power deals could not be extended to Anglesey Aluminium in the past or to BSC's Port Talbot steelworks. However, we do not yet know how any new arrangements under Brexit will benefit such sectors. The possible nationalisation of critical infrastructure by WG in key sectors beyond transport may well be areas in which it may wish to intervene.

In terms of Wales's future economic prospects, it remains to be seen whether democratic devolution will be a continued evolution, as Rhodri Morgan viewed it, or revolution, returning control of economic policy to Westminster, and strengthening the powers of the UK Government. As such, it will likely be the next Senedd term that indicates whether there is an emergence of the 'dark side' of territorial politics described by Morgan in 2001 which would create rivalry and parochialism, or instead the internal and external cooperation needed to confront the global challenges faced by Wales, the UK and the wider world.[91] As such it highlights how levels of governance should work together for all citizens, a concept partly broken by Brexit. In exemplars such as the steel industry, that BSC Port Talbot provides steel for manufacturing in the Midlands and north of England, Wales has traditionally understood and benefitted from focusing on regional interdependence and collaboration rather than competition. The present political outlook for the UK makes realising that opportunity somewhat more challenging.

Notes

1. Ron Davies, *Devolution: A Process Not an Event*, address to the IWA Gregynog Seminar, 9–10 January 1999, Gregynog Papers, 2/2 (4 February 1999), 1–16; A. Pike et al., 'In Search of the "Economic Dividend" of Devolution: Spatial Disparities, Spatial Economic Policy, and Decentralisation in the UK', *Environment and Planning C: Government and Policy*, 30/1 (2012), 10–28, 10.
2. Adrian Kay, 'Evaluating Devolution in Wales', *Political Studies*, 51/1 (2003), 51–66.
3. John Osmond, *The National Assembly Agenda: A Handbook for the First Four Years* (Cardiff: IWA, 1998).
4. Pike et al., 'In Search of the "Economic Dividend" of Devolution'; D. Bailey, 'Economic Renewal through Devolution? Tax Reform and the Uneven Geographies of the Economic Dividend', *Competition & Change*, 21/1 (2017), 10–26.
5. K. Morgan, 'Devolution and Development: Territorial Justice and the North-South Divide', *Publius: The Journal of Federalism*, 36/1 (2006), 189–206, 197.
6. Peter Mathias, *The First Industrial Nation: The Economic History of Britain 1700–1914* (Abingdon: Routledge, 2013).

7. Osmond, *The National Assembly Agenda*.
8. Philip Cooke and Nick Clifton, 'Visionary, Precautionary and Constrained "Varieties of Devolution" in the Economic Governance of the Devolved UK Territories', *Regional Studies*, 39/4 (2005), 437–51, 439.
9. Hans-Joachim Braczyk, Philip N. Cooke and Martin Heidenreich (eds), *Regional Innovation Systems: The Role of Governance in a Globalized World* (Hove: Psychology Press, 1998).
10. Morgan, 'Devolution and Development'.
11. WAG, 'A Winning Wales: The National Economic Strategy of the Welsh Assembly Government', Economic Policy Division, Cardiff (2001).
12. G. Cameron, J. Muellbauer and J. Snicker, 'A Study in Structural Change: Relative Earnings in Wales since the 1970s', *Regional Studies*, 36/1 (2002), 1–11.
13. S. Young, N. Hood and E. Peters, 'Multinational Enterprises and Regional Economic Development', *Regional Studies*, 28/7 (1994), 657–77; C-H. Chen, 'Regional determinants of foreign direct investment in mainland China', *Journal of Economic Studies*, 23/2 (1996), 18–30.
14. Department of Trade and Industry, 'Business Clusters in the UK: A First Assessment', Department for Trade and Industry (2001), 18–32.
15. K. Morgan, 'The New Territorial Politics: rivalry and justice in Post-devolution Britain', *Regional Studies*, 35/4 (2001), 343–8.
16. N. A. Phelps and M. Tewdwr-Jones, 'Globalisation, regions and the State: Exploring the limitations of economic modernisation through inward investment', *Urban Studies*, 38/8 (2001), 1253–72; Leon Gooberman, 'Business failure in an age of globalisation: Interpreting the rise and fall of the LG project in Wales, 1995–2006', *Business History*, 62/2 (2018), 240–60.
17. Leon Gooberman, 'Welsh Office Exceptionalism, Economic Development and Devolution, 1979 to 1997', *Contemporary British History*, 30/4 (2016), 563–83.
18. N. A. Phelps et al., 'Embedding the Multinationals? Institutions and the Development of Overseas Manufacturing Affiliates in Wales and North East England', *Regional Studies*, 37/1 (2003); Cooke and Clifton, 'Visionary, Precautionary and Constrained "Varieties of Devolution" in the Economic Governance of the Devolved UK Territories'.
19. WAG, 'A Winning Wales', p. 2.
20. WAG, 'A Winning Wales'.
21. *People, Places, Futures: The Wales Spatial Plan* (Cardiff: WAG, 2004).
22. Welsh Development Agency Act 1975. Available at: *https://www.legislation.gov.uk/ukpga/1975/70/contents* (accessed 15 January 2022).
23. Philip Cooke, 'Discretionary Intervention and the Welsh Development Agency', *Area*, 12/4 (1980).
24. WAG, 'A Winning Wales'.
25. WDA, *The Welsh Development Agency Corporate Plan 2003/4–2006/7 'Creating Success Together'* (Cardiff: WDA, 2002).
26. Gillian Bristow and Nigel Blewitt, 'The Structural Funds and Additionality in Wales: Devolution and Multilevel Governance', *Environment and Planning A*, 33/6 (2001).

27. Lyndon Murphy, Robert Huggins and Piers Thompson, 'Social Capital and Innovation: A Comparative Analysis of Regional Policies', *Environment and Planning C: Government and Policy*, 34/6 (2015); Gareth Huw Davies et al., 'Reflections on Technium Swansea: Ambition, Learning and Patience', in David Higgins, Paul Jones and Pauric McGowan (eds), *Creating Entrepreneurial Space: Talking through Multi-Voices, Reflections on Emerging Debates* (Bingley: Emerald Publishing Limited, 2019), pp. 137–51; Philip Cooke, *Re-Framing Regional Development: Evolution, Innovation and Transition* (London: Routledge, 2013); Kevin Morgan, 'The Regional State in the Era of Smart Specialisation', *Ekonomiaz*, 83/2 (2013), 103–26.

28. WG, 'Technium Update Cabinet statement', deputy minister for science, innovation and skills (25 March 2011).

29. DTZ, *Evaluation of the Technium Programme, Final Report to the Welsh Assembly Government, Stage 1: Scoping and Review* (2009). Available at: *https://gov.wales/sites/default/files/statistics-and-research/2018-12/101119techniumstage1en.pdf* (accessed 15 January 2022).

30. Philip Cooke, 'The Regional Innovation System in Wales', in Philip Cooke, Martin Heidenreich and Hans-Joachim Braczyk (eds), *Regional Innovation Systems: The Role of Governance in a Globalized World* (London: Routledge, 2004); Simon Gibson, 'Commercialisation in Wales – A Report by the Independent Task and Finish Group' (2007). Available at: *https://senedd.wales/media/fw2pbd2k/commercialisation_in_wales_-_gibson_review-english.pdf* (accessed 15 January 2022); Rhiannon Pugh, Niall G. MacKenzie and Dylan Jones-Evans, 'From "Techniums" to "Emptiums": The Failure of a Flagship Innovation Policy in Wales', *Regional Studies*, 52/7 (2018).

31. Cooke, *Re-Framing Regional Development*.

32. Pugh, MacKenzie and Jones-Evans, 'From "Techniums" to "Emptiums"'; *Business News Wales*, 'Pembrokeshire's Bridge Innovation Centre Praised as Exceptional Launch Pad ', news release (15 May 2019). Available at: *businessnewswales.com/pembrokeshires-bridge-innovation-centre-praised-as-exceptional-launch-pad* (accessed 7 March 2021).

33. European Commission, 'Guide to Cost-Benefit Analysis of Investment Projects, Economic Appraisal Tool for Cohesion Policy 2014–2020', Directorate-General for Regional and Urban Policy (2014). Available at: *https://ec.europa.eu/regional_policy/sources/docgener/studies/pdf/cba_guide.pdf* (accessed 15 January 2022); DTZ, *Evaluation of the Technium Programme*.

34. WAG, *Making the Connections: Delivering Better Services for Wales: The Welsh Assembly Government Vision for Public Services* (Cardiff: WAG, 2004).

35. WAG, *Making the Connections*, p. 29.

36. Cooke and Clifton, 'Visionary, Precautionary and Constrained "Varieties of Devolution" in the Economic Governance of the Devolved UK Territories', 444; Morgan, 'Devolution and Development'.

37. Aled Eirug, 'The Welsh Development Agency', *Geoforum*, 14/4 (1983), 375–88.

38. Labour and Plaid Cymru, 'One Wales: A Progressive Agenda for the Government'

(2007). Available at: *http://news.bbc.co.uk/1/shared/bsp/hi/pdfs/27_06_07_onewales.pdf* (accessed 11 May 2012).

39. 'Tories Criticise "Ieuan Air" Link', BBC Wales News (13 May 2008). Available at: *news.bbc.co.uk/1/hi/wales/7398506.stm* (accessed 15 January 2022).

40. Mark Rogers, 'R&D and Productivity in the UK: Evidence from Firm-Level Data in the 1990s', University of Oxford, Department of Economics, Working Paper 255 (2006). Available at: *https://citeseerx.ist.psu.edu/viewdoc/download?doi=10.1.1.622.5828&rep=rep1&type=pdf* (accessed 15 January 2022).

41. WAG, *Science for Wales: A Strategic Agenda for Science and Innovation in Wales* (Cardiff: WAG, 2009).

42. Office for National Statistics (ONS), *Regional Gross Value Added (Income Approach) Reference Tables* (Newport: ONS, 2018). Available at: *https://www.ons.gov.uk/economy/grossvalueaddedgva/datasets/regionalgrossvalueaddedincomeapproach* (accessed 15 January 2022).

43. Ian Hargreaves, 'The Heart of Digital Wales: A Review of Creative Industries for the Welsh Assembly Government' (Cardiff: Cardiff University, 2009). Available at: *https://www.cardiff.ac.uk/__data/assets/pdf_file/0006/113586/HeartofDigitalWales.pdf* (accessed 15 January 2022).

44. WG, 'Dragon International Film Studios', WG news release (6 October 2006).

45. Marianne Sensier and Michael Artis, 'The Resilience of Employment in Wales: Through Recession and into Recovery', *Regional Studies*, 50/4 (2014), 437–51.

46. WAG, *Impact Evaluation of ProAct* (Cardiff: WAG, 2011).

47. Dominique Foray, Paul A. David and Bronwyn Hall, 'Smart Specialisation – the Concept', *Knowledge Economists' Policy Brief*, 9/85 (2009); WG, *Innovation Wales* (Cardiff: WG, 2014).

48. WAG, *Economic Renewal: A New Direction* (Cardiff: WAG, 2010).

49. WAG, *Wales: A Vibrant Economy: The Welsh Assembly Government's Strategic Framework for Economic Development Consultation Document* (Cardiff: WAG, 2005).

50. WG, *Innovation Wales*.

51. Morgan, 'The Regional State in the Era of Smart Specialisation'.

52. Wales Audit Office, 'The Welsh Government's Relationship with Pinewood', Welsh Audit Office (June 2018). Available at: *https://senedd.wales/laid%20documents/cr-ld12165/cr-ld12165-e.pdf* (accessed 15 January 2022).

53. Sion Barry, 'The Welsh Life Sciences Firm That's Just Struck a Huge £80m Deal in China', *Western Mail*, 10 April 2019. Available at: *https://www.walesonline.co.uk/business/business-news/welsh-life-sciences-firm-thats-16108291* (accessed 15 January 2022).

54. Dylan Jones-Evans, *Access to Finance Review Stage 2 Review* (Cardiff: WG, 2013). Available at: *https://uwe-repository.worktribe.com/output/926259* (accessed 15 January 2022).

55. Nikos Kapitsinis, Max Munday and Annette Roberts, *Medium-Sized Businesses and Welsh Business Structure* (Cardiff: Cardiff University, Economic Intelligence Wales, 2019).

56. Jones-Evans, *Access to Finance Review Stage 2 Review*.

57. 'Council Take over an Airport', *The Times*, 2 April 1965.
58. Cardiff Airport press release, 'Covid-19 and the aviation industry', Cardiff Airport (19 August 2019). Available at: *https://www.cardiff-airport.com/news/2020/08/19/ceo-statement-cv19-and-the-aviation-industry/* (accessed 15 January 2022).
59. Northpoint Aviation, 'A Review of Cardiff Airport's Performance and Prospects in the Context of Current UK Regional Airport Economics', Submission to the Public Accounts Committee, NAW (February 2020). Available at: *https://business.senedd.wales/documents/s99239/PAC5-08-20-P2%20-%20Cardiff%20Airport%20performance%20and%20prospects.pdf* (accessed 15 January 2022).
60. UK Government, *Nuclear industrial strategy: the UK's Nuclear Future*, UK Department for Business, Innovation and Skills and Department of Energy and Climate Change (March 2013), BIS/13/627.
61. Clive Baker, 'Tidal Power', *Energy Policy*, 19/8 (1991); D. G. Wardle, J. P. Gibson and R. F. McGlynn, 'The Present Status of the Severn Barrage Project Studies', paper presented at the International Conference on Renewable Energy – Clean Power 2001 (1993). Available at: *https://ieeexplore.ieee.org/document/264118/similar#similar* (accessed 15 January 2022).
62. Chris Kelsey, 'Big Drop in Swansea Bay Tidal Lagoon Subsidy Cost Makes Project a "No-Brainer" says Sir Terry Matthews', *Western Mail*, 26 January 2016. Available at: *https://www.walesonline.co.uk/business/business-news/swansea-bay-tidal-lagoon-strike-10817156* (accessed 15 January 2022).
63. Charles Hendry, 'The Role of Tidal Lagoons', final report, UK Government, BEIS (December 2016). Available at: *https://hendryreview.files.wordpress.com/2016/08/hendry-review-final-report-english-version.pdf* (accessed 15 January 2022).
64. WG, *Wales Infrastructure Investment Plan for Growth and Jobs* (Cardiff: WG Strategic Investment Division, 2012).
65. Localism Act 2011, UK Government (2011). Available at: *https://www.legislation.gov.uk/ukpga/2011/20/contents/enacted* (accessed 15 January 2022).
66. Bailey, 'Economic Renewal through Devolution?'.
67. Chris Rhodes, 'Industrial Policy, 2010 to 2015', Economic Policy and Statistics Briefing Paper, House of Commons Library (2 April 2014). Available at: *https://commonslibrary.parliament.uk/research-briefings/sn06857/* (accessed 15 January 2022).
68. WG, *Sectors Delivery Plan* (Cardiff: WG Economy and Transport Departments, 2013); WG, *Innovation Wales*.
69. David Waite and Kevin Morgan, 'City Deals in the Polycentric State: The Spaces and Politics of Metrophilia in the UK', *European Urban and Regional Studies*, 26/4 (2019).
70. House of Commons Report, 'City Deals and Growth Deals in Wales', Second Report of Session 2019, House of Commons Welsh Affairs Committee, HC48 (2019). Available at: *https://publications.parliament.uk/pa/cm201919/cmselect/cmwelaf/48/48.pdf* (accessed 15 January 2022).
71. WAG, *People, Places, Futures*.
72. House of Commons Report, 'City Deals and Growth Deals in Wales'.
73. Morgan, 'Devolution and Development'.

74. Swansea University, 'Internet Coast: Phase 1: City Deal Proposal Impact Appraisal', *V1.26*, School of Management, Swansea University (2017); Cardiff Capital Region (CCR), 'Key Cardiff Capital Region Projects Given City Deal Backing', CCR press release (11 March 2020). Available at: *https://www.cardiffcapitalregion.wales/news-post/key-cardiff-capital-region-projects-given-city-deal-backing/* (accessed 15 January 2022).

75. Well-being of Future Generations (Wales) Act 2015, NAW (2015). Available at: *https://www.legislation.gov.uk/anaw/2015/2/contents/enacted* (accessed 15 January 2022).

76. Thiemo Fetzer, 'Did Austerity Cause Brexit?', *American Economic Review*, 109/11 (2019).

77. Alfie Stirling, 'Austerity is Subduing UK Economy by more than £3,600 per household this year', New Economic Foundation, 21 February 2019. Available at: *https://neweconomics.org/2019/02/austerity-is-subduing-uk-economy-by-more-than-3-600-per-household-this-year* (accessed 15 January 2022).

78. UK Government, 'Severn Crossings to Go to Toll-Free on 17 December 2018', Welsh Office press release (2 October 2018). Available at: *https://www.gov.uk/government/news/severn-crossings-to-go-toll-free-on-17-december-2018* (accessed 15 January 2022).

79. ARUP, 'The Impact of the Severn Tolls on the Welsh Economy: Final Report' (2012). Available at: *https://gov.wales/sites/default/files/statistics-and-research/2018-12/121105severntollsfinalen.pdf* (accessed 15 January 2022).

80. *Business Live*, 'Shocking Wales Tourism Figures Highlight Covid's Devastating Impact on the Sector', Cardiff (11 December 2020). Available at: *business-live.co.uk*.

81. Jesus Rodriguez and Guto Ifan, 'Covid-19 and the Welsh Economy: Shutdown Sectors and Key Workers', Cardiff University, Wales Fiscal Analysis (2020). Available at: *https://www.cardiff.ac.uk/__data/assets/pdf_file/0017/2410343/Covid-19-and-the-Welsh-economy-shutdown-sectors-and-key-workers-briefing-paper.pdf* (accessed 15 January 2022).

82. Institute of Government, *No Deal Brexit and the Union* (London: Institute for Government, 2019). Available at: *https://www.instituteforgovernment.org.uk/publications/no-deal-brexit-union* (accessed 15 January 2022).

83. Ione Wells, 'Post-Brexit Taxes for Steel "Very Damaging" Says Kinnock', BBC Wales News, 31 January 2021. Available at: *https://www.bbc.co.uk/news/uk-wales-55845067* (accessed 15 January 2022).

84. Rachel Minto and Kevin Morgan, 'The Future of Wales in Europe', *Edinburgh Law Review*, 23/3 (2019).

85. H. M. Treasury, *The Green Book: Central Government Guidance on Appraisal and Evaluation* (London: H. M. Treasury, 2020). Available at: *https://assets.publishing.service.gov.uk/government/uploads/system/uploads/attachment_data/file/938046/The_Green_Book_2020.pdf* (accessed 15 January 2022).

86. Organisation for Economic Cooperation and Development (OECD), *The Future of Regional Development and Public Investment in Wales, United Kingdom* (Paris: OECD Multi-level Governance Studies, 2020).

87. OECD, *The Future of Regional Development and Public Investment in Wales, United Kingdom*.

88. Eirug, 'The Welsh Development Agency'.

89. Pike et al., 'In Search of the "Economic Dividend" of Devolution'.

90. United Kingdom Internal Market Act 2020, UK Government (2020). Available at: *https://www.legislation.gov.uk/ukpga/2020/27/contents/enacted* (accessed 15 January 2022); WG Cabinet statement, 'Possible Legal Challenge to the UK Internal Market Bill', WG (16 December 2020). Available at: *https://gov.wales/written-statement-possible-legal-challenge-uk-internal-market-bill* (accessed 15 January 2022).

91. Morgan, 'The New Territorial Politics: Rivalry and Justice in Post-Devolution Britain', 203.

Select bibliography

Cooke, Philip and Nick Clifton, 'Visionary, Precautionary and Constrained "Varieties of Devolution" in the Economic Governance of the Devolved UK Territories', *Regional Studies*, 39/4 (2005), 437–51.

Gooberman, Leon, 'Welsh Office Exceptionalism, Economic Development and Devolution, 1979 to 1997', *Contemporary British History*, 30/4 (2016), 563–83.

Minto, Rachel and Kevin Morgan, 'The Future of Wales in Europe', *Edinburgh Law Review*, 23/3 (2019), 423–8.

Morgan, Kevin, 'The Regional State in the Era of Smart Specialisation', *Ekonomiaz*, 83/2 (2013), 103–26.

OECD, *The Future of Regional Development and Public Investment in Wales, United Kingdom* (Paris: OECD Multi-level Governance Studies, 2020).

Pike, Andy et al., 'In Search of the "Economic Dividend" of Devolution: Spatial Disparities, Spatial Economic Policy, and Decentralisation in the UK', *Environment and Planning C: Government and Policy*, 30/1 (2012), 10–28.

Salvador, Elisa and Rebecca Harding, 'Innovation Policy at the Regional Level: The Case of Wales', *International Journal of Foresight and Innovation Policy*, 2/3 (2006), 304–26.

WAG, 'A Winning Wales: The National Economic Strategy of the Welsh Assembly Government', Economic Policy Division, Cardiff (2001).

5

WELSH DEVOLUTION AND THE QUEST FOR SUSTAINABLE DEVELOPMENT: INTO A NEW ERA

Terry Marsden

Introduction: devolution and environmentalisation

Welsh devolution has always been precariously built, fluid and contested. A quest for identity and difference, and indeed in creating for a small country some freedoms from its neo-colonialist past, Welsh devolution from 1998 has been a major experiment in developing a multi-level governance framework amidst the historically dominant, some might say, hegemonic UK unitary and centralised state.

In parallel, environmental politics and indeed, more generally, the environmentalisation of the state, has also increased in significance and political appeal over recent decades; with the unfolding and multiple crises of climate change, biodiversity loss, resource depletion and growing related social and economic inequalities. It is thus timely to consider the effects and shaping of these agendas in terms of what has been a period of growing Welsh devolution (not least since the devolution settlement itself, and several institutional progressions, such as the enactment of the Silk Commission's recommendations for stronger law-making powers in 2011).[1] Indeed, it has been an incremental 'process and not just an event', as Ron Davies, one of its architects, notably coined it.[2]

In this chapter I wish to critically interpret the process of both environmentalisation and devolution in Wales. This occurs at a rather critical period in governance terms (March 2021), with the UK as a whole, as it enters the post-EU world. The chapter attempts to address three critical questions from the perspective of our current juncture: (i) what has been the lineage of sustainable development (SD) policy in Wales as part and parcel of the wider devolution politics that have ensued? (ii) How effective or otherwise has been policy delivery, especially in those areas (environment, agri-food and rural development) where Wales has held full devolved powers? And (iii), what do we understand about the changing dialectics between English and Welsh politics with respect to these policy fields? I conclude by arguing that the Wales polity now needs to re-discover the innovation it began when creating the Well-being and Future Generations Act (2015), and develop transformative agri-food, environment and rural policies which match its vision with integrated policy delivery.

I want also to more critically argue that, despite the energies and hopefulness that the early devolutionists displayed (from the late 1990s onwards), not least in espousing a sort of a Welsh version of European federalism as part of national identity and empowerment, and the related assumptions that this could unleash powerful forces of endogenous (not to say, possibly 'crypto-nationalist') development, curiously so far it has yet to make the most of its devolved powers. This has then been combined, rather ironically, with a fractured Welsh politics that has been regressively Blairite and watered down in comparison with Rhodri Morgan's early ideas of asserting real 'red water'. During what we may now see as the first phase of Welsh devolution (1998–2011), Welsh Labour has continued to be the dominant party, albeit in varied and occasional coalitions. This has tended to 'water-down' the redness, although it has created an innovative policy framework which can usher in red-green policy approaches.

However, on the statute book, and by exercising its new-found powers (2011), the passing of the Well-being and Future Generations (Wales) Act (WBFGA) in 2015, together with the Environment Act (2016) and the establishment of the unifying body of Natural Resources Wales (NRW), (incorporating the former Countryside Council of Wales, the Forestry Commission in Wales and the Welsh elements of the Environmental Agency) and its attendant duties under both Acts, has been, as Jane Davidson rehearses, both innovative and internationally unique.[3] This can be seen as something of a unique case of framing statute-led policy.

As a result, in the SD field there is no doubt that Wales has proudly employed all its significant devolved abilities and competences in establishing a robust institutional and statutory framework and apparatus unique in the UK (and indeed the world). This is more important than ever, we can suggest, given, as we see below, the disruptive governance and politics that has been unfolding for the past decade in England, and especially in Westminster and Whitehall. It is also important to recognise that the WBFGA was not and should not be pigeonholed as just being about 'the environment'. It is innovative because it encompasses all government decision-making, embraces all the wider UN SD goals, and brings in statutory duties about collaborative and precautionary 'ways of working' in the public sector. In this sense it is revolutionary in governance terms, and it embodies and demonstrates an SD vision for Wales that encompasses social justice and, in particular, inter-generational justice and equity issues into the heart of the Welsh Government (WG).

In Westminster, by significant contrast, we have seen, prior to Brexit, a deinstitutionalisation and related concentration of powers regarding SD. From 2010 onwards successive UK neo-right governments have steadily dismantled former long-standing and, indeed, independent democratic institutional structures put in place to call successive governments to environmental account. The Rural Development Commission (formed in 1909), the Countryside Commission (then Agency, 1950s), the Royal Commission for Environmental Pollution (formed in the 1970s) and the Sustainable Development Commission (formed in the 1990s) were all disbanded.[4] This has left a weakened and financially strapped English Nature as the chief but not-so-independent body for land-based environmental affairs in England.

There is no doubt, then, rather paradoxically, that as the environmental and rural development infrastructure has been dismantled in England, in Wales we have seen a contemporaneous reconstruction of independent environmental governance in the successive Acts and public policy processes that have taken place. Rather ironically a more devolved Wales has created, I will argue, significant 'green water' in comparison with its larger English neighbour over the past decade. However, now – as we shall see in a period of profound disruptive governance – this divergence presents something of a challenge for SD policy development in Wales.[5]

These dynamic shifts and dialectics have not been the only ones to affect SD policy in Wales. From the start, led by the RSPB-supporting Welsh Minister, Ron Davies, and a group of what were to become leading and proactive first assembly Cabinet ministers during the first decade or so of the Welsh Assembly (namely Sue Essex, Jane Hutt and Jane Davidson), Wales was to have from the start a SD duty which would place it at the heart of all succeeding policy development and actions. There was a strong cross-party political commitment to this[6] across the Welsh political spectrum.[7] So as the Assembly found its feet, not least with a proportional representation system, the idea and commitment to SD was almost taken for granted. In fact, SD was a significant party-political binding agency in the early days of the Assembly, and given this was seen as an area of devolved 'competence' and innovation, one that could be exploited to the full, along with of course Welsh language, culture, planning, and to a less extent farming and the rural economy. We should not underestimate, therefore, the power of SD as part and parcel of the new and emerging 'Welsh stripe', as in fact it served as an important binding agent to assuage the tensions between nationalist and 'crypto-nationalist' forces on the altar of a bespoken national and more self-sufficient SD policy, for Wales and of Wales. In this sense it entered and played an important and continuing part in the wider national identity politics that devolution unleashed.

As a result a successive raft of policy statements (SD schemes), such as 'Learning to live differently' (2003–7), 'Starting to live differently' (2004–7) and 'One Wales: One Planet' (2009–11), emerged as an outcome of strong alliances between key Assembly players and environmental NGOs, both eager to assert and position deeper environmentalisation and social justice at the heart of devolved Welsh policy-making.[8] As Nikhil Seth, head of sustainable development (United Nations Development Programme), was to say, 'We hope that what Wales does today, the world will do tomorrow. Action, more than words, is the hope for our current and future generations.'[9]

From the start of devolved government, but especially over the past decade, this policy field, probably more than any others, has indeed defined an authentic Wales and Welsh stripe approach. It was seen as 'not an option' by successive Welsh First Ministers, and delivered with the leadership of innovative cabinet members. Rather ironically, then, as Wales has indeed trailblazed with regard to institutionalising SD over the past decade, England, on the other hand, has effectively been deregulating and dismantling in this policy field. As we shall see below, this contested and dual-evolutionary path has been brought into even more stark relief as a result of the four years of destabilising Brexit preparations that have dominated both Whitehall and Welsh governance arrangements.

The current governance conditions (as of 2021) are now remarkably far removed from the halcyon days depicted in Rhodri Morgan's autobiography where he portrays regular political 'jostling' between the various factions of Welsh Labour, and Westminster did not impede the steady development of wider Welsh powers, nor the development of Wales as an active and more autonomous territory in the emerging 'Europe of the regions'. Continuous and programmed pipelines of funding through the European Regional Development Fund, the European Development Bank, Horizon and Erasmus EU research and training programmes, and the now more diversified Common Agricultural Policy (CAP) frameworks with their growing emphasis upon rural development and LEADER community initiatives, provided First Ministers with a degree of financial largesse and latitude, enabling them to spread financial sweeteners to the more impoverished parts of rural west Wales and the valleys. Moreover, as Rhodri Morgan admits in his account at the time, funding sent down the M4 via the Barnett formula was increasing at the healthy rate of an additional 10 per cent a year during the Blair and Brown years. This fiscal cushion was to be radically removed under the Osborne Treasury as the age of public sector austerity dawned, and just at the point when Rhodri was to hand over the First Ministerial reins to his more managerialist successor Carwyn Jones.

It is interesting to read Rhodri Morgan's autobiography as in many ways the first and last chapter of what we may call the first phase of Welsh devolution (i.e. 1998–2011), with hindsight, a period of stability, state largesse and relative consistency in the political mediations between Whitehall and Cardiff, and indeed Brussels. As a result, Morgan, notably without much reference to real policy development at all during his period of rhetorical politics, could afford to leave real policy development to his trusted Cabinet members and spend far more time on 'shadow-boxing' between Welsh Labour and Blairite Labour, playing identity politics with an increasing differentiation and building up the relatively small capacity of the Welsh Assembly to do things differently, as on plastic bag charges, waste recycling or default organ donations.[10]

This was, as we now see, a prelude to the outcome of the tussles between Welsh Labour and crypto-nationalist politics and the last vestiges of Blairite Whitehall governance. Once the Conservatives regained partial control (the Con-LibDem coalition of 2010–15) and then full successive parliamentary majorities (Cameron, May and then Johnson from 2015 onwards), the Blairite social and political contract between bickering Welsh Labourism and Blairism broke apart, and the politics of austerity and growing populist (English) nationalism took hold so as to seal this political fracture.

As a result we have entered, as I attempt to outline below, a new, long-running, more disruptive governance phase within which there is little social contract or compatibility between the politics of Cardiff and Westminster; where, not least as a result of the Welsh popular referendum vote, the EU becomes a detached player; and where the jostling between Westminster (and its Welsh Office and Ministers) and the Welsh Parliament becomes more acute and indeed politicised. Conservative Westminster Welsh Office ministers tend to strongly demonstrate the funding and supportive role of UK Government policies over and above those of the Welsh Parliament, at the same time as Boris Johnson argues publicly that devolution was one of Tony Blair's biggest mistakes and should never have happened.

Whilst Wales's SD policy and especially its institutional development was a product of the earlier phase of devolution, it now has to contend with a different set of relations between Cardiff and Whitehall, between Wales and the other unevenly devolved territories, and with an increasingly disconnected Europe. The rest of this narrative relates to this new political and governance landscape, raising questions about the continuance or otherwise of a 'Welsh stripe'.

Below we assess the ways in which Wales confronts a new period of disruptive governance with particular reference to the agri-food environmental sector – a sector, unlike energy or transport, where Wales has been granted almost complete devolved competence, but one, as we shall see, where the nation struggles to deliver goals aligned to the Future Generations statutory framework. To be fair, by 2020 the Well-being Future Generations framework (WBFGA) could be seen as still largely embedded, as Jane Davidson admits in conclusion to her recent monograph.[11] Nevertheless, with a decade of fiscal austerity and growing economic and spatial inequalities, the challenges for policy delivery were mounting, and increasing questions being raised about the extent to which the WBFGA provisions were becoming little more than a technocratic and 'box-ticking exercise'.[12]

Moreover, many of the Welsh as well as English national environmental and sustainability indicators were by 2020 pointing decidedly in the wrong direction, not least in many of the areas where WG (agri-food, environmental protection, public health) had strong powers. Food insecurity and the rise in the use of food banks was rising well before COVID-19, with 160,000 children in Wales living in households where living a healthy diet is seen as unaffordable. Meanwhile, rising rates of obesity were costing the health service £73 million per year by 2020, with 28 per cent of children obese and 94 per cent not eating the recommended five portions of vegetables per day. The State of Natural Resources reporting in Wales, set up as part of the WBFGA, also concluded that none of the Wales ecosystems have all of the ecological attributes required for resilience. Wildlife continues to decline with one in six species at the risk of extinction, with unsustainable agricultural management and practices, especially on the vast majority of farmed land in Wales, being the single largest driver of biodiversity decline, with agriculture accounting for 12 per cent of Welsh greenhouse gas emissions. By the time WG signed up to the climate change emergency in 2019, it was clear that overall radical and structural environmental restoration was necessary in Wales if it was to enact its lofty and ambitious SD agenda and framework.[13]

From multi-level governance to disruptive governance

Wales's position in the European and UK multi-level governance system that had been slowly developing over the last half century is being disrupted. A new UK-wide and divisive process of governance re-settlement is underway. This multi-level settlement emerged as a process by which economically weaker regions sought more powers from a strong centralised UK Government, and obtained support from being part of a federated EU and a more devolved UK. The EU counter-balanced its centralisation and harmonisation with its own regional policy, but the arrival of Brexit has disrupted that regime. The EU 'syphon' of support, which came to poorer UK regions, was strongly supported in the referendum in Scotland and Northern Ireland but not in Wales, which voted to leave the EU, although by autumn 2018 signs of regret were evident.

These challenges for Wales, not least in the SD environmental and agri-food sectors, are currently far from being resolved or even adequately debated. Rational policy options and developments (whether dealing with future trading, environmental and food and regional/ rural development policy) are often neglected and replaced by ideological arguments which feed what we can term 'disruptive governance'.[14]

Disruptive governance is often advocated as if it were an end in itself. Most frequently, disruptive governance is intentionally pursued with the aim of shifting the governance system to a radically different type of future, and in the context of Brexit, the hoped-for future is a radically neo-liberal one, with entrepreneurs unencumbered for example, by EU regulatory restrictions, and politicians free to develop policies outside EU strictures, so that they can enjoy a regime allowing for the 'freer movement' of resources, goods, capital and services, but not necessarily labour. Another, not entirely distinct variant of disruptive governance, is a decidedly English-nationalistic, rather than globalist, perspective that consists of rules and regulations, just as long as they serve particular nationalist agendas. These aspirations are, of course, not confined to the UK or Brexit. It can be seen in varied forms in North America, the re-writing of NAFTA trade arrangements, the abolition of US environmental protections, and in Latin America with fiscal austerity and the corporatisation of government, not least agri-business, for example in Argentina and Brazil. Those disruptions are leading to higher levels of environmental and food insecurity for consumers, and greater vulnerability for farming families.[15]

Given the historical centrality of the EU to the agri-food sector, for example, which accounts for around 40 per cent of all EU-wide expenditure and legislation, Brexit is hugely important to farmers and urban consumers and the entire UK food sector. In Wales, this is particularly so. This new disruptive governance exposes the extent to which the UK agri-food system has been ordered by the EC/EU-wide regime during the last half-century. Europe provided a combination of agreed measures to stabilise agricultural markets, and developed programmed systems of support that are all now being disrupted. This has effects, of course, on markets, as well as institutions and their regulatory practices. We now see some of these multi-dimensional effects with the end of frictionless trade with the exit from the single European market and customs union.

Disruptive governance is thus a deliberate political strategy, the eventual goal of which is not always acknowledged by its advocates. The UK governance arrangements that have been in place in recent years are increasingly portrayed by enthusiasts for disrupting those arrangements as if they were outdated and illegitimate.[16] Old-fashioned political narratives focusing on the primacy of nation states, the benefits of liberalised markets and the burdens of regulatory 'red tape' are emerging in the rhetoric of 'taking back control', but without being explicit about what is to be controlled, how or by whom? In this context agri-food and the environment sector is being collaterally embroiled in a new politics – a politics that sits between rationalist and clearly worked through evidence-based perspectives on the one hand and populist ideological promotions on the other.[17] The former proposes more integrated and systems thinking about food security, whilst the latter promotes more fragmentation and disruption, which would seriously compromise food security in the UK.[18]

For Wales, a small country with limited devolved powers, the Brexit crisis has disrupted the established ways in which it can operate within the multi-level governance frameworks that apply in the UK and the EU.[19] In disruptive governance, the political and territorial tectonic plates perturb their locations and what can be done at different governance levels, from the local to the global. A decade on from the financial, food and fuel crises of 2007–8, and while enduring financial austerity, disruptive governance is further destabilising former policy processes.

The UK's legislative approach to leaving the EU legislation ostensibly just rolls over EU rules into UK laws, but there is no clarity on how they will be interpreted or implemented, especially in the environmental, agri-food and rural fields. In July 2017, Lang and others explained that there are dozens of links with food-related institutions and regulatory frameworks that will be disrupted.[20] UK Ministers might profess commitments to high standards, but the UK's compliance can no longer be monitored by the European Environment Agency, and devolved administrations will receive no European Regional Funds to help finance them. The UK will no longer have access to EU-wide research networks to provide relevant data, nor support from the European Food Safety Authority, and also little or no bargaining power in trade negotiations or at international forums.

The new disruptive governance Welsh paradox: de-regulation or re-regulation?

Amidst these multiple disruptions and discontinuities, we can also detect a new disruptive governance paradox: perhaps some hope amidst the turmoil. On the one hand, the UK Government is creating uncertainty as a new norm, and this looks as if it will continue. Uncertainties are unavoidable when ministers protest that they are committed to retaining 'high' food and environmental standards, while also trying to pre-negotiate trade deals with countries, such as the USA, that have lower food standards. On the other hand, severance from the EU could offer new opportunities to all, or parts, of the UK to forge a radically better direction for our agri-food systems. Simultaneously, farmer and environmental interests argue for new subsidy and support-payment systems, and food consumer groups and some trade unions are pressing for higher welfare and food quality standards. In the agri-food system, therefore, disruptive governance may indeed unleash significant public counter-forces that eventually undermines its plausibility. This is a paradox of disruptive governance: it could lead in Wales to the very opposite effects to those originally intended – more public and institutional innovation and regulation rather than less, as food producers and consumers recognise the harm that such disruption will cause.

For years, rational and scientific evidence has emerged from civil society, academia and progressive agri-food sectors that radical transformation is needed in how the British are fed and how food is produced and provided.[21] If the recent Intergovernmental Panel on Climate Change (IPCC) warning was taken seriously, the government and the food industry would recognise that there are just twelve years to contain average temperature rises to within 1.5°C.[22] Given that Wales is a major animal and dairy producer, and that livestock farming is a major contributor to greenhouse gas emissions, Wales ought to be helped to change. Across all of the UK, from the scandal of food banks to the food system's adverse impacts on the environment and public health, the scale of changes now needed is considerable.

In Wales, as in the UK, post-Brexit a great food transformation is needed, on a par with what was accomplished in the post-Second World War period of reconstruction. Now, the redesign should focus on, for example, lowering carbon dioxide and other greenhouse gas emissions, while diminishing dietary inequalities and health outcomes; substantially increasing consumption of fruit and vegetables, while producing more at home; shortening food supply chains where possible; shifting more of the £204 billion UK consumers spend annually on food and drink to primary producers under a 'fair returns' policy, rather than subsidising farmers; encouraging young people into decently remunerated employment on the land. But no such vision has yet emerged from any of the three main Westminster political parties.

If Brexit was really about UK citizens 'taking back control', policy would be directed towards enhanced food security, in the sense of a system that more reliably provides a food supply that is sufficient, sustainable, safe, nutritious and equitable, but that is not the preferred direction of the most enthusiastic pro-Brexit disrupters. The signals from the Department for the Environment, Food and Rural Affairs (DEFRA) Agriculture Act are weak and disturbing. It barely mentions health or devolution or indeed food, and a limited Environment Act, in which targets are set but which emphasises voluntary action rather than compulsion.[23] Creating somewhat hollow statutory bills and Acts, and limited ad hoc committees seems to be a political tactic of UK disruptive governance, and it needs to be challenged in the wider public and consumer interest, for it will encourage wider political and ministerial latitude in a post-Brexit and transitional landscape.[24]

In relation to agri-food, the rhetoric of Brexit is laid bare. Food, like ecosystems services, cross borders; so 'taking back national control' is a recipe for detachment. If the UK chooses to set its own rules, it can do so, but that as we are now seeing will disrupt the international trading on which our system relies.

The Wales case in disruptive governance

The onset of disruptive governance in the UK as a whole presents Wales policy in general, and its SD agenda in particular, with major challenges. Plans and new structures across Wales and the other countries in post-Brexit UK are urgently needed. The current machinery for coordinating policy and practice across the UK and especially between the devolved governments (such as the joint ministerial committees) is 'not fit for purpose'.[25] This has been, as we have seen, exacerbated by the COVID-19 crisis where communications between Whitehall and Cardiff have been spasmodic. So far, Wales governance becomes rendered reactive to these wider profound regulatory and indeed governance changes. For instance, how will the internal market within the UK work? What role will Wales have in new ongoing trade agreements, and how wider economic governance of powers will be applied and shared are current questions to be addressed. For the Welsh polity, these issues are exacerbated by a UK media that tends to downplay or ignore devolved decision-making. The Wales polity has lost the somewhat secure umbrella of the EU in the agri-food, environment and trade field. As such it will have to be far more proactive in forging new intermediations with the Whitehall government, and of course vice versa.

One might have hoped that Whitehall would by now have developed new bespoke coordinating structures and frameworks, which are transparent and accountable to both legislatures and citizens. That has not happened. Rather there is an unfortunate lack of trust between the devolved authorities and Westminster, and so far reduced levels of communication between different executives. It is difficult to avoid the conclusion that Brexit is and will continue to fuel constitutional fragmentation and distrust just when the UK ought to be displaying the pragmatic, clear and integrated thinking for which it used to be celebrated.[26]

UK public sector funding has been far the largest provider of resources enabling the devolved administration in Wales over the twenty years since it was established. Levels of funding have been governed by the so-called Barnett formula.[27] Rural, agricultural and regional policies have also relied heavily on ring-fenced EU funding associated with Regional Development ('Convergence funding') and CAP programmes.

Those programmes (representing something like 6 per cent of all annual public funding in Wales) were based upon a 'needs-based' set of priorities built by reference to the EU's goal of reducing regional economic disparities. It has been used to build regional capacities and support farming families to deliver a combination of public and market goods. They have provided important ring-fenced EU funding for Wales in its first, relatively stable, twenty years of devolution.

Wales's first decade of devolved powers occurred under Labour governments and the second decade has mostly been under Conservative-dominated coalitions in Westminster. Yet across those apparent politically different government periods, there was general consensus between EU, Westminster and Cardiff governments that the distinctive features of Wales's post-industrial and post-productivist landscape and economy were in need of considerable state investment. That consensus is now being undermined by Brexit. Future commitment to the goal of attempting to reduce regional economic disparities in the UK is increasingly uncertain.

Let us pause to consider in more detail the nature of the rupture. Many on the intellectual left in Wales were taken aback by the overall UK referendum result in June 2016. The Welsh electorate, unlike its Northern Irish and Scottish counterparts, mirrored England and voted for majority leave: 52.5 per cent of Wales voted to leave, compared with 53.8 per cent in England, 44.2 per cent in Northern Ireland and only 38 per cent in Scotland. Ironically it was the post-industrial valleys and the large and dispersed rural areas that had been the major recipients of EU investments over the past twenty years; like Cornwall, the largest UK recipient of EU funds, Wales apparently voted to bite the hand which had been helping to feed it. In fact, EU funds were more like compensation payments than core funding for Wales. The resources often came from EU regional funds, set up to act as counterweight to the centralisation and concentration trends unleashed by the completion of the single market, first championed and later denounced by Mrs Thatcher. Uncomfortably for the dominant Welsh Labour administration, which was strongly pro-Remain, it is difficult to deny that this was a major act of collective devolved 'self-harm' by the poorest and most vulnerable Welsh communities. But, as other analysts have argued, the referendum coalesced many sentiments – deserved and undeserved – into one stark yes/no vote. Much of the societal marginalisation from de-industrialisation and fiscal austerity was the responsibility of policymakers in London rather than in Brussels, a result of economic concentration and cost reductions for competitiveness in larger markets rather than just those of Europe.

Whatever the benefits to Wales from the EU's continued support for Wales's agri-food and environmental economy, those benefits were overshadowed by the wider political rhetoric stressing immigration and Brussels 'red tape'. While the European Commission is often derided in the UK as a 'bloated bureaucracy', few acknowledge that there are in fact more civil servants in Edinburgh running Scotland than there are in the entire European Commission. Agri-food and environment concerns were thus ignored or discounted by (what Adorno called) a political 'context of delusion', exhibiting 'false consciousness' (which in German he termed *Verblendungszusammenhang*).[28]

Another macro-governance consequence of the way in which the pursuit of Brexit has disrupted relations of governance amongst the devolved administrations, and between those administrations and the

Whitehall government, stems from the uneven and compromised nature of devolved governance in the UK more generally. As Douglas-Scott aptly puts it, the prevailing arrangements were never actively or rationally designed. The problematic status quo has been reliant upon Westminster; and the current state of devolved regional politics has recently been described as a case of a policy 'without map or compass'.[29] England continues to be far too highly centralised, and arguably has become more so since 2010. The Regional Development Authorities and Regional Government Offices created since 1997 by Labour have been replaced by smaller, less funded and weaker Local Enterprise Partnerships. A competition over which authorities can or cannot have a mayor gives a semblance of concern for the regions. A short-lived burst of enthusiasm for a 'northern powerhouse' championed by George Osborne when Chancellor of the Exchequer (2010) was an attempt at big thinking but was ineffective and ignored in other parts of England. Whilst city mayors are increasingly lobbying for more 'levelling up' consideration in the Johnson government, they suffer from lack of direct representation in Whitehall.

In Wales, England and Scotland, the significance of environmental, agri-food and regional development agendas has been marginalised by the dominant issue of Brexit. This is despite or probably because these are indeed the very areas that had been Europeanised over the past forty years. Brexit particularly will mean the need for new innovative UK and devolved policy development in these key fields.

If one positive long-term development now emerges, it could well be a revitalised regionalisation and decentralisation of the UK state. The rigidity of Whitehall and its reluctance to re-distribute to the devolved administrations any powers that might be repatriated from Brussels to London is not a fault that can be attributed to the EU or Brussels bureaucrats. Other EU member states are far more devolved internally – Germany was deliberately constructed to have relative strong regions and relatively weak central government by the victorious Allies after 1945. Unlike Scotland (and Northern Ireland for obvious reasons), Wales has nominally agreed new devolved arrangements with Westminster about the scope of 'devolved competences', though this is still contested as the post-Brexit process unfolds in ways that are exceptionally difficult to predict. For many parts of the devolved administrations Westminster seems ironically a far more (politically) remote and less trustworthy negotiating partner than Brussels ever did.[30] Several observers and com-mittees have called for greater cooperation amongst civil servants and departments across the UK's governments, while also wanting to see greater autonomy for the devolved administrations. Inevitably Brexit has provoked calls for longer-term and more root and branch reforms across at least the 153 areas where EU law formerly intersected with devolved competences, forty-one of those are closely related to the environment, agriculture and fisheries.[31]

It should be noted that this unfolding and contested process of disruptive governance does not have its roots in the political arenas of environmental, agri-food nor regional economic development. Because these policy fields have been, and are by far, the most Europeanised, they are the policy domains (together with trade) over which the UK Government seeks to regain control. Consequently, they are becoming a key policy fulcrum around which the new and more disrupted domestic UK devolved relations are most likely to be recast.

Brexit has thus set in train a new medium- to long-term need for a domestic and UK-wide contested debate about revising the governance settlements for the devolved administrations. A new governance regime, or set of regimes, is likely to emerge, by default or design; whether an accident or a tragedy remains to be seen. The outcome of those contested debates will alter policy goals, instruments and practices for many years. Another feature of the present disruption concerns the seemingly narrow politics of the London-based DEFRA. Under Secretary of State Michael Gove, DEFRA successfully courted the established environmental inter-est groups seeing a chance of wrenching agri-food policy away from the priorities of productionism, symbolised by the CAP and the entrenched interests of the National Farmers Union.

The CAP is easily demonised by those who question the ecologi-cal impacts of intensive industrial farming. There are good reasons for urgently re-engineering land-use policies to provide improved environ-mental sustainability and enhanced biodiversity. This was the dominant narrative in the DEFRA's *Health and Harmony* consultation paper.[32] It, and the Agriculture Act which emerged, stressed the future financing of environmental public goods, including soil, water, amenity and land-scape. Meanwhile, traditional, farmer productivist and wider ecological concerns and interests are being sidelined. Any consideration of food, as the product of agriculture, is absent from the White Paper and the legislation.[33] Brexit is therefore being used as an opportunity to re-orient and re-frame the power relations between public, private and civic sectors, and indeed to separate 'agriculture' (public) from 'food' (private).[34] The shift in DEFRA policy constitutes a re-orientation of neo-liberal assumptions about environmental protection and agri-food production. It partly means de-regulating, but also re-regulating, empowering some and disempowering others. These developments provide both opportunities and threats to the long-term ecological and social sustainability of the UK agri-food and rural development system.

How should Wales, armed, as we have shown, with the distinctive Well-being of Future Generations statutory machinery take forward its own reforms in these key policy areas?

Taking the policy initiative: what Wales should be doing in the context of disruptive governance?

Wales needs to develop a new and collective vision of its own sustainable environmental, agri-food and rural and regional development. This is the moment when it could set out to restructure policies to deliver on the principles and values embodied in its own ambitious, inspiring Well-being of Future Generations and Environment Acts, and its statutory obligations.[35] Wales could recognise where it has highly integrated economic ties with the rest of the UK – in processing or services, and in many regulatory areas such as food standards, trade and environmental protection – and could use these ambitious Acts as the basis to negotiate those wider UK links. Unlike England, where the Agriculture Act barely mentions food and where an Environment Bill is still being finalised, Wales can build on its commitment to develop an agri-food economy that takes future generations' needs and interests as its core focus. Wales has an opportunity both to participate in evolving UK-wide frameworks, and to develop its own distinctive vision and strategy for agri-food, rural and regional economy based upon a strong ecological-economic approach.[36]

This envisages a strategy and vision designed to facilitate the unfolding transition to a post-carbonised and more inclusive growth-oriented model of sustainable economic development, and in so doing to augment the distinctiveness and potential Wales holds in developing a world-leading innovative green economy. That is an economy and vision which can locate the needs of rural areas and their managed ecosystems (including varied combinations of stakeholders including landholders and foresters) at the heart of the Future Generations agenda over the rest of this century.[37] But solving those problems of the rural areas will necessitate reconciling their requirements, and closely coupling them with those of urban areas.

Clearly the two major areas of potential support for Wales are associated with the UK regional development objectives in its 'Shared Prosperity Fund' (so far still largely unspecified by the UK Government); and 'transitional' and eventual post-Brexit UK agricultural support. Proactive discussions with Whitehall are urgently needed on these issues from WG, to articulate and promote a distinctive vision and strategy, and to justify critical funding for Wales in both these areas. The argument will need to be won that whatever the volume of funding made available for Wales under these schemes, it needs to be based upon (i) reducing GDP disparities across Wales, (ii) based on an assessment of needs, and (iii) allowing support to continue, at least on a tapering model for farm production support based upon a wider multifunctional approach, as outlined above.

There is a distinct danger here that whatever funding is made available and eventually allocated under these schemes it will be (i) highly competitive, especially with regions in England, (ii) linked to a conventional concept of productivity and growth which discriminates against rural and sparsely populated areas, favouring urban agglomerated economies, and (iii) focuses too much on non-marketised public goods instead of a combination of production and services.

This is why it is critical to not get bogged down in 'transition' processes following Brexit, but to create a Welsh vision. Serious considerations should be given to proposing that whatever Westminster funding replaces CAP and Regional Development ('Convergence') this funding should be driven by a transparent formula on a supplemented 'Barnett plus' model. This could be over 5- to 7-year planning periods so as to give some certainty and review of investments over time.[38]

The analysis and arguments above suggest a need for the establishment of a strategic Food, Regional and Rural Development Commission for Wales, which could have within its remit regional development, agrifood and rural economic development for the whole of Wales (urban and rural), and reports to Cabinet and the Senedd. It should deliver the promises set out in *Future Generations*, addressing the restoration of biodiversity, family farming and local rural economies in Wales, food provisioning, and negotiating with Whitehall on funding allocations. The body should also influence devolved allocation across all parts of Wales, including support to delivery agents (rural stakeholders). This approach could avoid the potential increases in transaction costs associated with narrow politically driven 'hand-me-downs' from Whitehall. It would also give a stronger collective voice for Wales amongst the devolved nations, and should forge positive and networked links with the EU (not least regarding future Research and Development EU funding access), and actively participate in debates about food and rural policies.

The targeting and delivery of financial support within Wales should emphasise providing support for and 'scaling out' place-based partnerships on a variety of different spatial scales. These could be aligned to the NRW's sub-regions and to catchment planning and partnerships. Farmers could remain major recipients of these funds as long as they were working in partnership and collaboration with the wider range of place-based stakeholders, and were demonstrating how they were achieving and reconciling sustainable production of high-quality foods with other environmental and social goods and services (including woodlands, water management, renewables and sustainable amenity and tourism). This is at the heart of the 'Farming plus' approach. The designated landscapes of Wales (over 25 per cent of its land surface), for instance, can become innovative beacons for fostering these partnership approaches. Wales holds many excellent and innovative experiments of place-based partnership working. And these now need to be made more mainstream if our visions are to be realised. Two significant examples here concern the work of the Food, Farming and Countryside Commission in Wales regarding its work in progressing agro-ecology and restorative agro-ecological practices; and 'Project Skyline'-funded pilot projects whereby place-based experiments are taking place around opening up public access to land for wider public use.

In July 2018, after a considerable amount of internal stakeholder discussion and scenario planning, as well as discussions between Welsh and Westminster policy officials, the Welsh Minister published the first of a series of new consultation papers on post-Brexit agricultural arrangements.[39] This was far more narrowly framed than what is proposed above. In many ways it still falls into the trap of treating agricultural production very much as a separate and 'exceptional' sector, not least in failing to integrate it into a wider enriched food and environmental strategy.[40] The latter, currently under revision has at least placed some emphasis upon improving food for urban consumers and for public health priorities. These concerns were re-enforced with the publication of the Agriculture (Wales) White Paper (December 2020) consultation. So far these policy proposals in the agri-food and rural sector fail to build upon, and indeed, apply the principles laid down in Wales's innovative future generations and environmental legislation. In order to align these, the following policy considerations are necessary.

First, it builds and integrates its principles and policies directly on the existing and landmark statutory legislation which (fortunately) pre-dated Brexit: the Future Generations and Environment Acts. The Sustainable Development Principle and the seven statutory well-being goals provide an integrated framework for future decision-making which, it is proposed, will establish a new approach to land management in Wales. The central objective of the Environment Act is the Sustainable Management of Natural Resources (SMNR), to maintain and enhance the resilience of ecosystems and the benefits they provide to deliver lasting, sustainable economic, social, cultural and environmental benefits. The Act sets the legal framework for decarbonisation and adapting to the impacts of climate change and other environmental and social shocks and stresses.

The overall aim should be to enhance resilience in ecosystems, businesses and communities. Delivering on the SMNR is the responsibility of a number of statutory bodies, not least the all Wales NRW, which is responsible for delivering regular State of Natural Resources Reports (SoNaRR) to WG. Section 6 of the Environment (Wales) Act also puts in place a biodiversity and resilience of eco-systems duty for public authorities (including Welsh Ministers and local authorities) who must seek to maintain and enhance biodiversity, and in so doing promote the resilience of ecosystems. This recognises the underlying importance of biodiversity in its widest sense for healthy, functioning ecosystems, and the multiple benefits that are derived from them. As part of this framework, 'area statements' and 'well-being plans' are being prepared by local authorities and the NRW.

Secondly, the definition (in *Brexit and our Land*) of 'land manager' is significantly broader than that of 'farmer', and therefore provides opportunities for greater flexibility about the incentives given to land managers operating in partnership and cooperation with each other to deliver SMNR objectives and to receive public funding, rather than targeting 'farmers' only with support. 'Land manager' means farmers, foresters, and 'any other activity drawing on non-urban land to produce goods and services'.[41] There is no ostensible reason therefore, why any future, post-transition funding for rural areas could not be directed to collections and partnerships of land managers, some of which might be farmers, as well as other land-based stakeholders. *Brexit and our Land* provides five guiding principles for sustainable land management: (i) keeping farmers and other land managers on the land; (ii) food production is vital – implying continued support for the economic activities of farmers; (iii) build a prosperous and resilient Welsh land-management industry; (iv) provide future support which encompasses the provision of additional public goods from land: clean air, water and flood management, better habitats, public health and education; and (v) all land managers should be able to access new schemes.

Thirdly, and linked to the first two characteristics, the policy documents propose a dual or twin support system. Unlike the English proposals it stipulates two new 'pillars' of support: The Economic Resilience Scheme and the Public Goods Scheme. The former focusing, though not exclusively, on the production of food and timber, will support the economic resilience of land-based businesses in the sub-areas of (i) increasing market potential, (ii) improving productivity, (iii) diversification, (iv) effective risk management, and (v) knowledge exchange, skills and education. This incentivises rural multifunctionality and diversification, a circular economy and high-quality products and processes.

A key source and motivation for these differences derive from the continuing strong political and cultural significance of family farming in Wales compared with England. Wales has steadily lost farms as has England. Indeed, this is a 'silent revolution' that is affecting our agri-food infrastructures across England and Wales. England lost 48 per cent of its farms between 2005 and 2013, whilst Wales lost 32 per cent. Much of this loss went unnoticed because farms and land are often amalgamated, often with farm buildings remaining, but converted to residential use. Much more land is now leased to larger farm-holding companies and larger farm businesses than has ever previously been the case since the end of the Middle Ages. In addition, food processing, especially the smaller independent abattoir sector, had been in secular decline.[42]

Both the Westminster and Welsh governments recognise that Brexit, and especially with the transition of support away from Pillar One payments in the CAP, will continue to undermine the economic resilience of the small and medium family farming sector. This is of much more political concern in Cardiff than in London. Despite the decline in farms and farm businesses, Wales is still dominated by small family-run businesses. In 2016 there were 21,200 farms in Wales that were classified as 'small' or 'very small' (with a turnover of less than £125,000) out of a total of 24,500. Many of those were disproportionately reliant on CAP Pillar One funding. In particular, extensive beef and sheep farm incomes are, on average, heavily reliant on Basic Payments schemes (BPS, Pillar One) and the Glastir agri-environmental scheme (Pillar Two). Nonetheless research has shown that small farms have a positive local economic multiplier when it comes to buying inputs to their businesses and in selling their products.[43] When average farm income is compared to total household family income on farms, however, this reliance upon farm subsidies is less clear. It is the large and very large farmers who have claimed the largest proportions of BPS subsidy, and that are most reliant upon it with regard to household family income. Small, part-time and even median-sized (up to £30,000 per annum) businesses are just less than half reliant on farm income as a component of total household income.[44]

In short many, if not most, small- and medium-sized Welsh family farmers have diversified family household incomes, much of which is both earned and spent in the local rural economy. Add to this the significance of the Welsh language to family farming in many parts of rural Wales, and one can see how future policies to promote multi-functional land and smaller and diversified family-based businesses is and should remain a central plank of future Welsh rural and agricultural policy. In addition, these policy directions tend to meet the wider 'future generations' and SMNR principles. This is a very different model than that currently advocated in England, despite similar conditions in much of its upland and mixed farming regions. DEFRA sees the Brexit transition as an opportunity to facilitate the prevailing and structural adjustments (that is, continuing farm exit), which it assumes is needed in farming once the BPS has been tapered or terminated, by adding the option for 'lump sum' end-of-scheme payments. Some assume that this can be expected to boost aggregated and conventional measures of efficiency and farm productivity, as well as usher in a new round of farm-based mechanisation and automation.[45]

A wider and more pro-active debate needs to be had in Wales, as in England, on what the remaining and hopefully more resilient farmers should be practising on their farms. This connects to the wider 'future generations' and SMNR goals. There are strong grounds for public investments in more diversified systems of agri-ecology, organic horticulture, permaculture and agri-forestry/woodland in Wales, which could sustainably deliver broader and wider 'productivity' gains and goals.[46] In order to address this wider agenda, it is necessary to integrate our 'agriculture' and farming policies with those wider ecological, health and rural development policies.

Conclusions: the new challenges for Welsh politics and policy: a new Welsh stripe and clear red/green water?

The onset and continuance of disruptive governance for Wales severely challenges the rather more consensual, if wrangling, politics of Welsh Labour versus Westminster which Rhodri Morgan's autobiography depicts. Multi-level governance has at best lost coherence, and at worst has become institutionally degraded and partially dismantled as a result of Brexit and the further centralisation of the English state. With the benefit of hindsight, the Welsh Labour/Blair/Brownite coalition did not foresee the political rise of disruptive governance. What is crucial now is that the Welsh Parliament and government politicians create the capacity to design bold plans and policies that will proactively embed and deliver the WBFGA framework already established but so far only partially implemented.

At the same time, whilst we may reminisce about the first phase of devolution (1998–2011) as one that pragmatically achieved expanding Welsh powers of decision-making, in the policy fields of agri-food, environment and rural development, the fact is that Wales has not really made the most of these powers. The development of the WBFGA, and Environment Act, as well as the new assemblage of public sector structures (public service boards, well-being plans, area statements, state of nature reporting, Office of the Future Generations Commissioner, etc.), and one might say the new environmental ethics embodied in the WBFGA's statutory seven principles and five ways of working, have indeed been a national and internationally recognised achievement.

However, as we see in these related SD policy fields, the challenge is in aligning underlying policy development and traction with these legislative tools. Local authorities, amongst other public bodies, are charged with producing well-being plans and activating public service boards to deliver on the enormous challenges set by the seven principles of the WBFGA and five ways of working, and to report accordingly. This is a major and almost unachievable duty for financially struggling public bodies in the context of a decade of public sector austerity cuts.[47]

There is no doubt that despite these caveats the SD agenda in Wales will continue to play a significant role in shaping environmental sustainability in Wales. A success might be seen in the stopping of the M4 relief road for the time being, or the recent innovative transport strategy *Llwybr Newydd: New Path*,[48] and not least the overall acceptance by economic development politics that de-carbonisation, green growth and the foundational and 'circular' economy is part of the future for Wales.[49]

However, rather paradoxically, we seem to see a rather less innovative and some might say timid political leadership in Welsh Labour on many of these issues, just at the time when it needs to contend with neo-liberalist (English) nationalism as the new Whitehall norm. In the agri-food, rural development and wider environmental agenda, Welsh Labour needs to widen its constituency interests and create bolder and distinctive sustainable visions for Wales in these policy fields.

The Senedd elections of May 2021 gave a critical opportunity for Wales to forge a new set of relationships with Whitehall at the same time as enact more distinctive real and restorative domestic SD policy. This requires the creation of more coherent political alliances going forward and it needs new leadership equivalent to that which created innovation in the first phase of devolution. It needs to recognise that 'the environment' and the Wales SD agenda has made some progress on the statute books, but not enough in real policy development which addresses and affects the unequal and vulnerable businesses and people of Wales. SD needs to become re-politicised, and seen not just as a convenient technical annexe to more autonomous territorial policy development in a post-Brexit UK. This will mean embracing real 'green growth' and innovation, prioritising and investing in Wales green assets, not least in the food, rural and energy sectors, innovating in green public procurement and re-vitalising its local communities.

We can conclude then with some concerted suggestions for development that would more clearly embed the ambitions and visions of SD in Wales, at a time of continuing disruptive governance, and the public and political need to maintain the Well-being of Future Generations mechanisms with underlying and effective policy developments.

The UK and Wales in particular will need to forge a new constitutional settlement, for which a constitutional convention could serve to resolve how internal UK distribution mechanisms and devolved competences will be organised, especially given the new UK internal market, and the significant differences and needs of the four nations.

There is a critical need to integrate agriculture and agri-food, environment and rural development policy in Wales, as bodies like the Food, Farming and Countryside Commission, WWF Cymru and Food Policy Alliance Cymru have advocated.[50] A more sustainable and long-term replacement for the Barnett formula needs to be developed that allocates funding for the regions across the UK based upon their diverse needs. In the meantime, WG is currently taking forward the shorter-term priority of pressing the UK Government to ensure that Wales is 'not a penny worse off' post-Brexit, with regard to both the EU CAP and European regional development funding mechanisms.[51]

Of all the devolved nations, Wales currently faces heightened party-political-led compromises with regard to both the future re-gearing of agricultural, and especially regional and rural development, policies. Welsh politicians will have to fight hard in Westminster to gain anything like the (largely preferential and historically ring-fenced) proportions of funding that came directly from Brussels. Notwithstanding the actual amounts coming now from the Treasury, there are also many unanswered questions about both the programming periods for such funds, and the subsequent allocation of such funds.

So far, the challenges of institutional changes at the heart of government administration, on a new devolved basis, have yet to be addressed. Rather, and worryingly, we have witnessed little more than attempts at 'muddling through'.[52] Yet recent committee reports both in Cardiff and Westminster have stated that the post-Brexit UK Government will need to foster close and reciprocal cooperation with the devolved authorities. This is particularly, but not exclusively, important for the future of the agri-food food system, and therefore also for environment and regional development policies. As the Institute of Government report recently explained:

Failure to cooperate could have an impact on the UK internal market and its ability to meet international obligations and trade objectives. For instance setting minimum environmental standards and rules for subsiding farming is likely to be necessary to create 'a level playing field' across the UK. Likewise, to minimise compliance costs there is a case for uniform chemicals and food labelling regulations. Concluding trade deals with third parties that include 'level playing' field provisions might also limit freedom to vary agricultural subsidy regimes or food standards regulations. Joint working will be necessary to meet the ambitious targets set by international obligations, such as the UN Framework Convention on Climate Change. Cooperation will also be required to manage common resources such as fisheries stocks and waterways, and mitigate against shared threats.[53]

There is therefore a profound governmental challenge both in UK and Welsh governments to build sufficient capacities and new institutional arrangements that can build and then operate these devolved and UK framework structures. So far there has been a conspicuous lack of attention to these fundamental challenges or the need for consultative two-way interchanges, which will enable third parties (like NGOs) to have a voice in their developments.[54]

Wales has developed some of the leading integrating governance innovations in the fields of environmental and sustainability policy since the devolution settlement in 1997, and especially with the passing of the groundbreaking Future Generations and Environment Acts of 2015 and 2016. These statutory frameworks provide a strong devolved basis to build policies for what we have termed here the 'great UK food transformation'. Post-Brexit they will require a strong cooperative and consultative set of institutional arrangements and practices to be developed between Cardiff and Whitehall, and with the other devolved countries, such that new UK-wide frameworks can be dovetailed to the needs of all corners of the post-Brexit UK. This is indeed the paradoxical public policy challenge that this uncertain and disruptive period of governance creates.

Here we have particularly focused on Wales–UK relations as it experiences a rather unique period of disruptive governance, with the uncertainties of Brexit. In this sense, whilst concentrating only on the

Welsh–UK context, it also speaks to many of the concerns and opportunities Brexit might bring to other UK regions, not least the English regions – so far denied any concerted regional autonomy. The analysis and recommendations have demonstrated the need to find collective hope and energy in exploring the real paradoxes that this disruptive governance also creates. These are opportunities to re-set and redesign former sectoral, fragmented and unevenly devolved policies and competences in ways that meet now the wider SD and climate change goals our international, as well as national, public commitments demand. That is why we have to convince politicians, policy makers, amongst many other stakeholders, that even more profoundly than in the case of Britain in 1947, a combination of severe austerity and food insecurity led to the assemblage of explicit state commitments to create national planning, food and farming policies for all. That is what present and future generations will expect of today's governments, and that is what is embedded in Wales's WBFGA.

Thus far the speed and direction of policy and governance in this realm is insufficient; we need to re-educate our politicians that with political will in the public interest many of the severe and interlinked problems in our environmental, food and farming systems can be corrected and ameliorated, and that, indeed, food systems play a critical and proactive role in delivering the wider macro-economic and SD goals. Brexit (and now COVID-19) and the onset of disruptive governance has indeed, for good or ill, shone a new head beam onto this policy arena which for too long has been taken for granted, and has been allowed to develop in largely unsustainable and wasteful ways at great cost to the public and the public purse. Wales now holds the opportunity to structurally re-locate the environment and food policy arena much more centrally into the body politic of the nation, across the whole of Wales and for all its people, and in ways that celebrate its rich and more democratically devolved diversity. This is what the onset of disruptive governance is in part telling us, and why its critical analysis both in the UK and beyond is of vital importance in harnessing and linking both food-systems thinking with an enlivened debate about participative and devolved forms of effective democratic governance. This imagines a new 'resettlement' in Wales, one that places nature and its food-systems thinking at the heart of its continuing democratic ambitions.

Notes

1. Rhodri Morgan, *Rhodri: A Political Life in Wales and Westminster* (Cardiff: University of Wales Press, 2017).

2. Ron Davies, *Devolution: A Process Not an Event*, address to the IWA Gregynog Seminar, 9–10 January 1999, Gregynog Papers, 2/2 (4 February 1999), 1–16sh. These words were first uttered by Ron Davies, the Secretary of State for Wales, in the early hours of 19 September 1997, after the devolution referendum result had been declared.

3. Jane Davidson, *#Futuregen: Lessons from a Small Country* (Vermont and London: Chelsea Green Publishing, 2020).

4. M. Chisholm, 'The Development Commission's employment programmes in Rural England', in M. Healey and B. Ilbery (eds), *The Industrialisation of the Countryside* (Norwich: Geo Books, 1985), pp. 279–93. It is important to recognise that these institutions had all generated cross-party support even during the Thatcher years of deregulation. The Rural Development Commission received additional powers in 1983 to designate and fund assisted rural areas.

5. The Well-being of Future Generations (Wales) Act 2015 covered wider areas than just environmental sustainability, with seven guiding principles: a prosperous Wales, resilience, health, equality, community cohesion, vibrant culture and language, global responsibilities. It also introduced five specific 'ways of working': to adopt a long-term perspective, take an integrated approach, involve citizens, collaborate, and provide a preventative approach. It placed a legal obligation on all public bodies, including the WG, to 'carry out sustainable development', including a requirement to set and publish 'well-being objectives' and to take 'all reasonable steps' to meet these objectives, and to report on progress annually. It created an independent Future Generations Commissioner and office to oversee and independently monitor progress.

6. John Osmond, *The National Assembly Agenda: A Handbook for the First Four Years* (Cardiff: IWA, 1998).

7. There were some leading academics (like Ron Edwards), environmental business interests (like Rod Aspinwall) and leading NGOs (RSPB, WWF) who convened important early meetings with successive Welsh politicians (such as Sue Essex) to create a collective vision for Welsh SD as devolution was occurring in the mid- to late 1990s.

8. NAW, *Learning to live differently: the first sustainable development scheme of the National Assembly for Wales; 'One Wales: One Planet' The Sustainable Development Scheme* (Cardiff: NAW, 2009).

9. Nikhil Seth, *Speech to the United Nations Development Programme (2015)*, quoted in Davidson, *#Futuregen: Lessons from a Small Country*, p. 1.

10. Rhodri Morgan was very supportive of SD and launched 'One Wales: One Planet' in May 2009 at the Hay Literature Festival arguing that: 'Our scheme for sustainable development gives Wales the opportunity to show leadership and ambition, and to learn from the past. It gives us the opportunity to show how we are playing our full role as a global citizen within the context of the

UN MDGs' (quoted in Davidson, *#Futuregen: Lessons from a Small Country*, p. 54).

11. Davidson, *#Futuregen: Lessons from a Small Country*, p. 109.

12. Alan Netherwood and Andy Flynn, 'A shift in governance, policy and delivery for future generations? Well-being planning in Wales', Discussion Paper, School of Geography and Planning, Cardiff University (July 2020).

13. The National Biodiversity Network, *State of Nature Report* (Nottingham: The National Biodiversity Network, 2019); National Resources Wales, *State of Natural Resources Report* (Cardiff: National Resources Wales, 2020).

14. It is important to point out that this concept is by no means restricted and indeed applicable well beyond the UK Brexit conditions. Most notably and built upon a rise of populist nationalism we can see wider geo-political variants of this disruptive governance in the ensuing North Atlantic Free Trade Alliance's reorganisation of trade; G20 resolutions on significantly reforming the World Trade Organization and its rule-making powers; US-China trade re-organisation and disputes, and EU-Russian trade embargoes and especially Ukrainian relations. In this sense there are wider and multiple-layered levels of disruption to which a Brexit UK (and Wales) will be further exposed, whatever the actual shape of the Brexit 'deal'.

15. T. K. Marsden, A. Moragues-Faus and R. Sonnino, 'Reproducing vulnerability in agro-food systems: tracing the links between governance, financialisation and vulnerability in Europe post 2007–8', *Journal of Agrarian Change* (2018), 1–19.

16. T. K. Marsden, P. Hebinck and E. Mathias, 'Re-building food systems: embedding assemblages, infrastructures and reflexive governance for food systems transformation in Europe', *Journal of Food Security* 10/6 (2019), 1301–9.

17. There is clearly a strong and scientifically sound set of arguments developed by many agri-food experts for adopting a normative systems perspective for food, based upon a wealth of knowledge, and indeed linked to wider sustainability and UN SD goals. The point is that disruptive governance needs to at least side-step, marginalise, fragment this science very much as fossil energy supporters challenge and attack recent IPCC climate change evidence. This is, as history shows most recently with EXXON and earlier strategies in the tobacco industry, a political strategy which attempts to question the status of overwhelming scientific evidence. This is another critical element of disruptive governance to diminish public science.

18. See, for instance, Royal Society of Arts, 'Our Common Ground: Report of the Food, Farming and Countryside Commission (October 2018), as one of many reasoned accounts of food system integrated thinking.

19. Stefan Sjoblom et al. (eds), *Sustainability and Short-term Policies: improving governance in spatial policy interventions* (UK: Routledge, 2016).

20. Tim Lang, Erik Millstone and Terry Marsden, 'A Food Brexit: time to get real – A Brexit Briefing', SPRU University of Sussex, Cardiff University and City University (July 2017).

21. For instance, Cabinet Office Strategy Unit, *Food Matters: Towards a strategy for the 21st Century* (London: Cabinet Office Strategy Unit, 2008).

22. IPCC, 'Global Warming of 1.5°C: A summary for Policymakers of IPCC Special Report on Global Warming of 1.5°C approved by governments', Geneva (8 October 2018).

23. Department of Exiting the EU, *Environmental Protections and the EU Bill, Factsheet 8: Environmental Principles* (London: UK Government, 2018).

24. See WWF Cymru and Sustainable Places Research Institute, 'A Welsh Food System Fit for Future Generations', Cardiff University (2020).

25. C. Burns et al., 'Environmental Policy in a devolved United Kingdom: challenges and opportunities after Brexit', ESRC Briefing Paper (October 2018); Mark Drakeford's statement before the House of Commons Select Committee on Welsh Affairs that the current UK governance arrangements are 'broken'. House of Commons Select Committee on Welsh Affairs, HC1255 (4 March 2021).

26. R. Cowell et al., *Wales: Challenges and opportunities for post-Brexit environmental governance* (Swindon: Economic and Social Research Council, 2018).

27. The Barnett formula allocates UK Government funding to the devolved regions as a block grant. The annual Welsh budget for 2018–19 was £15.5 billion. This is allocated with respect to population and some assessment of needs. It is largely up to the WG how it allocates its block grant. EU funding alternatively, for both regional development and agriculture, is a ring-fenced component. Because these are allocated on a needs basis as disadvantaged regions, and because Wales has qualified as the most disadvantaged region in the UK for these funds it has historically received a higher proportion of them. Measured on a per-capita basis, for instance, structural regional development funds have been more than double those of any other part of the UK. Again, with agricultural EU funding, given Wales's Less Favoured Area status it has received higher proportions of these funds as subsidies. Once these preferential allocation systems for Wales come to an end with Brexit, a key question is how the UK Government will allocate public funds.

28. P. Dews, 'The Idea of Hope', *New Left Review* (July/August 2018), 91–131.

29. A. Douglas-Scott, 'Without map or compass', *London Review of Books* (2–5 May 2018).

30. UK Government, *Frameworks Analysis: Breakdown of areas of EU Law that intersect with devolved competences in Scotland, Wales and Northern Ireland* (London: Cabinet Office, July 2018); also Institute for Government, 'Devolution after Brexit: managing the environment, agriculture and fisheries' (April 2018); also House of Lords, *The Impact of Brexit on Devolved Competences* (London: House of Lords Committee for European Affairs, 2018).

31. Maddy Thimont Jack et al., *Devolution after Brexit* (London: Institute of Government, 2018).

32. DEFRA, *Health and Harmony: The Future for Food, Farming and the Environment in a Green Brexit*, Cm 9577 (London: HMSO, 2018).

33. Tim Lang, 'The new Agriculture Bill has no vision for food', Inside Track blog, Green Alliance (September 2018).

34. Interestingly this is re-enforced by DEFRA categorising agriculture as providing public goods, and food as part of private goods provision. This of course is a

convenient use of a narrow set of economistic assumptions which allows farming and food to be unrealistically separated in policy terms. It creates a boundary where systems thinking and integration of the provision of both public and private goods is really needed.

35. Well-being of Future Generations (Wales) Act 2015; Environment (Wales) Act 2016.

36. Terry Marsden, *Agri-food and rural development: sustainable place making* (London: Bloomsbury, 2017); Angelina Sanderson Bellamy and Terry Marsden, *A Welsh Food System Fit for Future Generations: A report by the Sustainable Places Research Institute at Cardiff University*, commissioned by WWF Cymru (Cardiff: Cardiff University, 2020).

37. See Public Policy Institute for Wales, *The implications of Brexit for Agriculture, rural areas and land use in Wales* (Cardiff: Public Policy Institute for Wales, 2018); Sanderson Bellamy and Marsden, *A Welsh Food System Fit for Future Generations*; Michael Woods, *After Brexit: 10 key questions for rural policy in Wales* (Newcastle/Aberystwyth: Newcastle University/Aberystwyth University, 2018).

38. At the time of writing (February 2021) this is not how the prosperity fund is being designed. The Internal Market Act (UK) proposes central UK Treasury allocation of prosperity funding which bypasses the WG. Currently 'transitional funding', following the former CAP model, is continuing but becoming more contested, especially around what constitutes rural development funding. These disputes are likely to continue. Wales could face both reductions in former EU-type funding and more UK competition for those funds. In addition, it could also face less devolved authority in which to allocate them.

39. WG, *Brexit and our Land: securing the future of Welsh farming* (Cardiff: WG, 2018); Agriculture White Paper (WG, December 2020).

40. The WG is also in the process of revising the Welsh Food Strategy and Action Plan, which formerly was heavily reliant upon regional development and rural development EU funding.

41. WG, *Brexit and our Land*.

42. See *Welsh Agricultural Statistics* (Cardiff: WG, 2018), and WG's food action plan, *Towards Sustainable Growth: Action Plan for the food and drink industry 2014–2020* (Cardiff: WG, 2014).

43. Welsh Rural Observatory Report, *Impacts of CAP reform* (Aberystwyth: Welsh Rural Observatory Report, 2013).

44. DEFRA, *Farm Business Survey* (London: DEFRA, 2017).

45. Policy Exchange, *Report on the Future of Farming* (London: Policy Exchange, 2017), argues that it is advantageous that the average age of the farming population is in the late fifties, as this will facilitate faster structural adjustment in the sector.

46. Woodland Trust, *Policy statement* (Cardiff: Woodland Trust, 2018); see also WG, *Woodlands for Wales. The Welsh Government strategy for Woodlands and Trees* (Cardiff: WG, 2018); Woodland Trust, *Manifesto for the 2021 Welsh Parliament Elections* (Cardiff: Woodland Trust, 2021).

47. Netherwood and Flynn, 'A shift in governance, policy and delivery'.

48. WG, *Llwybr Newydd: New Path: Wales Transport strategy* (Cardiff: WG, 2020).
49. See the recent policies developed on the Circular economy and waste, March 2021: WG, 'Recycling, Waste and the Circular Economy', WG statement, 2 March 2021.
50. See, for instance, the new consensus developing around the Food Policy Alliance Cymru manifesto: *Our Priorities for a Food System Fit for Future Generations* (Cardiff: Food Policy Alliance Cymru, 2021).
51. NAW, *Preparations for replacing EU Funding for Wales* (Cardiff: NAW, 2018), p. 20.
52. Burns, 'Environmental Policy in a devolved United Kingdom'; Cowell, *Wales: Challenges and opportunities for post-Brexit environmental governance.*
53. Institute of Government, *Devolution after Brexit: managing the environment, agriculture and fisheries* (London: Institute of Government, 2018); House of Lords Constitution Committee, 'United Kingdom Internal Market Bill', 17th report session 2019–21, HL Paper 151 (2020), p. 9.
54. House of Lords Constitution Committee, 'United Kingdom Internal Market Bill'.

Select bibliography

Davidson, J., *#Futuregen: Lessons from a small country* (Vermont and London, Chelsea Green Publishing, 2020).

Lang, Tim, Erik Millstone and Terry Marsden, 'A Food Brexit: time to get real – A Brexit Briefing', SPRU University of Sussex, Cardiff University and City University (July 2017).

Marsden, T. K. (ed.), *The Sage Handbook of Nature*, 3 vols (London and New York: Sage, 2018).

Marsden, T. K., C. Lamine and S. Schneider, *A Research Agenda for Global Rural Development* (Cheltenham: Edward Elgar, 2020).

Morgan, Rhodri, *Rhodri: A Political Life in Wales and Westminster* (Cardiff: University of Wales Press, 2017).

Netherwood, Alan and Andy Flynn, 'A shift in governance, policy and delivery for future generations? Well-being planning in Wales', Discussion paper, School of Geography and Planning, Cardiff University (July 2020).

Osmond, John, *The National Assembly Agenda: A Handbook for the first four years* (Cardiff: IWA, 1998),

Sanderson Bellamy, Angelina and Terry Marsden, *A Welsh Food System Fit for Future Generations: A report by the Sustainable Places Research Institute at Cardiff University, commissioned by WWF Cymru* (Cardiff: Cardiff University, 2020).

Well-being of Future Generations (Wales) Act, (Cardiff: WG, 2015).

Acknowledgements

The author would like to thank the support and editorial guidance provided by the two editors, Aled Eirug and Jane Williams; and for the valuable comments provided on earlier drafts by Andrew Flynn and Jane Davidson.

6

CIVIL SOCIETY, EQUALITIES AND INCLUSION

Elin Royles and Paul Chaney

Introduction

'Civil society', 'equality' and 'inclusiveness' were central to the discourse of 'new politics' in the campaign for devolution to Wales. They encapsulated a rejection of the pre-existing arrangements for governing Wales, the Westminster culture, and conveyed the aspirations that devolution would address the perceived 'democratic deficit', accountability gap and crisis of representation in Wales.[1] In doing so, they contributed to the high expectations that the establishment of a national Welsh Government (WG) would change the political culture. Indeed, as part of Labour's radical constitutional reform and modernisation agenda, the main argument for devolution to Wales was to promote open, transparent and accountable governance and a more participative democracy.

In many respects, civil society, equality and inclusiveness were largely imported into the Welsh discussion of devolution from other parts of the UK to make the case for an elected assembly in Wales, influenced by the 'Third Way' stress on deepening and widening democracy, and the discussion surrounding devolution in Scotland. However, they quickly developed as intrinsic to the distinctiveness of devolved government in Wales. They are critical to understanding the impact of Welsh devolution over the first two decades and, in keeping with the aims of this volume, are instructive to exploring whether devolution can be understood as social democracy with a Welsh stripe. Consequently, this chapter examines the implications of devolved government in Wales for civil society, the equalities agenda and inclusion.

With regards to its structure, this introduction sets the context by outlining the expectations and arguments. The next section examines whether devolved government has enabled more participative structures of governance. The chapter then analyses the extent to which organisations have contributed to generating a distinctive policy agenda in Wales, focusing on equality of opportunity. We then examine the extent to which organisations have contributed to legitimising devolved government and then draw on the evidence regarding the implications of civil society relations with devolved governmental institutions for Welsh democracy. Key arguments emerging from the analysis in this chapter are the continuing need for open governance arrangements and vibrant civil society engagement with devolved institutions in order to develop the distinctive equalities agenda that has emerged over the past two decades. We also highlight key ongoing challenges in realising the vision of social democracy with a Welsh stripe; particularly addressing the variable progress in the equalities policy agenda (across and between policy areas and protected characteristics) and the need for sustained efforts to enable a critical, diverse and independent civil society as an essential ingredient of a revitalised and healthy Welsh democracy.

Civil society, equality and inclusiveness: the expectations

Reflecting their association with the discourse of 'new politics', the three terms – civil society, equality and inclusiveness – reflected the aspirations surrounding devolution and the aim of 'revitalising democracy'.[2] The rhetoric often encompassed a range of inter-related meanings that subsequently influenced the principles and operation of the National Assembly as established in 1999. Chaney and Fevre trace the proliferation and evolution of meanings associated with 'inclusiveness' during 1994 to 1999. We focus here on those interrelated meanings associated with civil society and equality.[3]

From its beginnings as a codeword for proportional representation and cross-party discussions, in 1997, under the influence of the 'Third Way', 'inclusiveness' was conflated with widening and promoting the engagement of different social groups in government, and a more pluralist political culture.[4] Consequently, key aspects included achieving greater descriptive representation of elected representatives, given the low number of females elected from Wales to Westminster and in local government, and the under-representation of ethnic minorities and people with disabilities.[5] Key gender campaigners were unsuccessful in their efforts to call for a legal requirement for the twinning of all constituencies. Instead, the government encouraged political parties to address gender representation within party mechanisms.

Following the close 1997 referendum result, 'inclusiveness' entailed a new emphasis on an active civil society mobilising a more participative democracy in Wales. Efforts to involve civil society organisations departed from the ways in which the devolution debate had been largely internalised within the Labour Party and the contribution of civil society sidelined, including in the context of an attempt to establish a Welsh Constitutional Convention at the beginning of the 1990s.[6] There is a distinct contrast between the way in which civil society in Wales was viewed as a 'fragile plant' and being conceived as the main beneficiary and motor of the new participative political culture in post-devolution Wales.[7]

The meanings associated with inclusiveness expanded considerably as a result of the National Assembly Advisory Group (NAAG), established by the Secretary of State for Wales in December 1997. To the fore came inclusiveness as a more open conduct of politics. The White Paper proposed that the Assembly would be 'a modern, progressive and inclusive democratic institution', that would 'operate under maximum openness and public accountability'.[8] NAAG recommendations also reaffirmed associations between 'inclusiveness' and promoting equality, tackling the marginalisation and disadvantages of 'minority' groups and in line with the earlier 'Third Way' emphasis on promoting participation in government.[9]

A final aspect to inclusiveness was developing a stronger civic sense of Welsh identity and the associated need to secure the legitimacy of devolution in Wales.[10] The 1997 Welsh referendum result indicated that elements of the population, particularly those born outside Wales, felt excluded from Welsh society and the low turnout raised concerns regarding the Assembly's legitimacy. Ron Davies's approach to nurturing a civic sense of identity was to devise 'new ways of incorporating people into the political process, and in turn affording them with a sense of ownership, that we can create a genuinely inclusive Wales'.[11] Consequently, civil society was an important vehicle to encourage participation to contribute to legitimising devolved government and to strengthening a civic-based sense of identification with Wales.

In many respects, these ideas and aspirations had a considerable influence on the National Assembly's design: first, more open and participative structures of government that would enable civil society engagement, particularly in policy-making, were reflected in the arrangements. In addition, as part of the Assembly's corporate body structure on its inception, the committees specified in the 1998 Act were envisaged as central to developing a more open and transparent style of politics and were to enhance partnership by consulting and receiving representations from external actors during policy reviews and policy development. Further routes to promote greater participation in government were the requirements to establish formal partnerships with the voluntary sector, business and local government. Of greatest relevance here, Section 114 of the Government of Wales Act required a voluntary sector scheme outlining how the Assembly aimed to promote the interests of voluntary organisations, and assist and consult with organisations on matters that affect them. As a result, 'the notion of partnership and inclusiveness permeated the work of the Assembly as a whole'.[12]

In addition, an early initiative was the development and funding of existing and new Assembly sponsored structures in response to the weaknesses of networks and structures to promote minority groups' engagement. They were to facilitate the engagement of under-represented groups related to race, gender, disability and sexuality. They included the Wales Women's National Coalition (WWNC), Disability Wales, the Black Voluntary Sector Network Wales (BVSNW), Minority Ethnic Women's Network (MEWN Cymru), All Wales Ethnic Minority Association (AWEMA), LGB Forum Cymru/Stonewall Cymru and Transgender Wales.[13] These pioneering structures were to be umbrella organisations to represent their respective interest groups, coordinate responses to consultations and promote activism.

The emphasis on promoting equality led to an equality statutory duty in the Government of Wales Act 1998 (subsequently replicated in the Government of Wales Act 2006). Gender equality campaigners led the lobby for the inclusion of, and indeed drafted, the equality clauses of the Act.[14] Sections 48 and 120 of the Government of Wales Act 1998 placed a duty on the Assembly to conform to the principle of equality of opportunity. Section 120 states: 'the Assembly shall make appropriate arrangements with a view to securing that its functions are exercised with due regard to the principle that there should be equality of opportunity for all people'. NAAG also recommended the establishment of a standing equal opportunities committee with a remit to include gender, race and disability at a minimum.[15] The statutory equality duty is unique amongst devolution statutes and is particularly significant owing to being 'singular in its non-prescriptive phrasing and all-embracing scope. It is an *imperative* that applies to *all* people and *all* functions of government.'[16]

The extent to which these ideas were institutionalised within the Assembly's structures supports Ron Davies's assertion that inclusiveness was 'an essential foundation stone for the whole enterprise', and that the extent to which devolved government would promote inclusive governance was equated with the success of the devolution project.[17] As Chaney, Hall and Dicks argued: 'the Assembly can expect to be held to account, by a range of commentators as well as the general population of Wales, on the extent to which it actually delivers government that is appreciably inclusive and open'.[18]

Two final issues need to be highlighted before moving onto our analysis. First, is the extent of change envisaged from the pre-1999 administrative devolution arrangements. The Welsh Office was seen as 'male-dominated, exclusive, centralizing and anti-democratic', that resulted in closed policy-making between civil servants and government ministers.[19] It led to a poor record on equality of opportunity and a lack of involvement opportunities for most civil society organisations.[20] Secondly, there were early concerns and indications regarding the relevance of the neo-corporatism literature to the Welsh case.[21] Chief amongst the issues was that the nature of partnership practices could result in more exclusive relations with some organisations, creating questions regarding the 'representativeness' of organisations, the impact upon the relative autonomy of organisations and the privileging of some groups over others.[22] The hype regarding generating a more participative democracy was therefore overshadowed quite early on by concerns regarding the potentially negative democratic consequences of some of the mechanisms being put in place to generate a more participative political culture in Wales.

Structures of governance

The remainder of this chapter now examines the evidence regarding the impact of devolution on civil society, equality and inclusion, turning first to the nature of structures of governance. In this respect, devolved government has been a major advancement in creating more open and participative structures.

A cornerstone of enabling a more participative governance model has been the commitment to open government. From the Assembly's establishment, it has been apparent in the accessibility to proceedings, documents and consultations online. Indeed, Rawlings argued that the Assembly was a 'world leader' in the 'modalities of democratic govern-ance in the new information age'.[23] In addition, there was a broader commitment to accessibility in terms of ease of contact and engage-ment with Assembly Members, also extending to civil servants. In the early years of devolution, one civil society representative explained: 'Devolution has given us other opportunities not specifically Welsh ones and to generally push the issue quite hard and get more access than on a parliamentary level.'[24] These trends have continued and lay a basis for organisations to engage with devolved institutions, resulting in greater levels of accessibility than at Westminster and within the UK Government context.

Beyond this, ongoing changes in the constitutional arrangements over the last two decades of devolution have inevitably had a direct impact on civil society's engagement with governance structures. A con-tributory aspect in the 1999–2006 period was the shift in the locus of decision-making as the corporate body principle was rejected and accompanied by developments towards a more parliamentary style of government, eventually legally enshrined in the Government of Wales Act 2006. The shift towards executive decision-making clarified the separation of powers in Wales. Assembly committees' policy-making influence declined and the role and influence of opposition parties simi-larly changed as the legislature veered towards holding government to account. The other significant aspect is the comparatively remarkable number of models of devolved government seen in Wales since 1999. Devolved government has shifted from the initial 1998 model of sec-ondary legislative powers constraining the Assembly's ability to act on its own initiative and limited influence on the primary legislative process at Westminster, to two interim sets of constitutional arrangements con-tained in the Government of Wales Act 2006 which afforded enhanced legislative powers in complex and piecemeal ways. The latest arrange-ment is the Wales Act 2017 that introduced a reserved powers model of devolution and the ability to legislate in over twenty policy areas alongside initial steps in fiscal devolution from 2014.

The overall impacts of constitutional developments on civil society are twofold. First, it has made influencing policy-making within government a greater imperative via formal and informal contacts with the governing parties and with civil servants. Alongside such developments, the Assembly (now Senedd) has developed its processes of facilitating the engagement of civil society in its work of scrutinising policy and holding government to account. This has included outreach and education teams encouraging participation in its activities and a range of initiatives in order to encourage a greater diversity in those giving evidence to its committees. Secondly, the rapidly evolving constitutional arrangements (necessitated by the flawed 1998 Government of Wales Act) have presented a challenge, requiring civil society organisations to keep abreast of the changing ways to engage and influence the legislative and policy processes in Wales.

Turning specifically to the equalities dimension, in order to promote the participation of groups associated with the equalities agenda with government, successive governments have invested significant funding to support the capacity development of policy networks representing women, Black and ethnic minority communities and disabled people; extended support for forums and networks around equality and to individual organisations, particularly in relation to 'disadvantaged groups'; and supported individual equality projects. For instance, during 2010–12, £6.65 million was dedicated to supporting twenty-five ethnic minority organisations.[25] Through these developments, groups sought to promote and facilitate activism and voluntary activity, and worked to channel grassroots views into the policy process as part of influencing policy-making.

Similarly, the statutory partnership requirements that resulted in establishing the Voluntary (subsequently Third) Sector Partnership Council composed of sectoral representatives. It enables organisations to lobby and consult government and established twice-yearly ministerial meetings with representatives of the relevant networks of voluntary organisations. Evidence points to the Council acting as a significant nexus in promoting equalities in the work of government. Moreover, since its creation in 2007, earlier analysis revealed that the Assembly (now Senedd) Petitions Committee was serving as a significant vehicle for organisations and others to promote the equality agenda. Half of its first meetings considered petitions with an equalities dimension. An indication of increased capacity is that in addition to the engagement outlined here, equalities organisations also routinely engage with WG in policy consultations.[26]

Overall, given the low starting point of equality organisations in 1999, there have been significant strides to support their capacity development. The extent of government support, including through state-sponsored policy networks relating to equality policies whose range also entailed alliance or umbrella bodies representing a range of networks, is critical to understanding the extent of efforts to promote non-governmental organisations' (NGOs) capacity to access and engage with governance structures, particularly with respect to policy-making. Many of these mechanisms provided unprecedented involvement and formalised the position of equality groups who had previously lacked access to government in the pre-1999 period. For instance, they resulted in 'systematic participation by ethnic minority communities across the breadth of government decision-making for the first time'.[27]

Therefore, significant efforts have been invested in achieving inclusiveness with regards to a more open conduct of politics and more participative structures of governance to facilitate civil society engagement. Whereas many developments resulted from the aspirations for more inclusive governance being built into the design of the devolved institutions, many developments have depended on a significant amount of funding, particularly in relation to capacity development and policy networks. Underlying such investment is the political commitment to promote the participation of 'minority' groups and the equality agenda in government.

Key aspects of this political commitment can be explained by the Assembly's record on diversity and the descriptive representation of elected representatives. Certainly, the National Assembly is more representative than either the Welsh Office or Westminster, and there have been dramatic increases in gender equality within the legislature as the number of female elected Assembly Members has been consistently above 40 per cent. Women have also held influential positions in the WG cabinet and as Assembly committee chairs. Such progress is largely as a result of measures and action by some political parties. At the same time, Assembly elections have largely underlined the marginalisation of ethnic minority groups, a situation that was somewhat better for disabled people.[28] The fact that it was not until 2007 that the first black or ethnic minority candidate was elected to the Assembly largely reinforced a sense of exclusiveness and marginalisation. Such circumstances created a clear impetus for elected politicians to seek to ensure that these voices were heard through civil society organisations.

Policy contribution

Here we consider the extent to which civil society equalities organisations' claims-making has contributed to the post-devolution public policy agenda. First, we examine the wider, systemic approach to policy- and law-making in Wales and the extent to which this enables (or frustrates) civil society equalities claims on government. Secondly, we refer to selected examples of policy and law and consider whether they exhibit territorial distinctiveness, promote citizens' rights, and were shaped by co-working or engagement between civil society groups and WG.

A systemic approach to equalities, policy- and law-making?

As noted, from the outset, compared to governance under the Welsh Office, the National Assembly took a more proactive, broad-based approach to engaging civil society and promoting equality in its policy work. This was not only reflected in new institutional structures such as the cross-party Committee on Equality of Opportunity and the Third Sector Scheme, but also WG's Mainstreaming Equality Strategy.[29] Mainstreaming is an ambitious, holistic approach to promoting equality of opportunity. Its adoption by government in Wales reveals international influences on the devolved approach to equalities, particularly as it forms an integral part of the United Nations' Beijing Declaration and Platform for Action.[30] Its adoption also reflects the influence of EU policies on Wales (mainstreaming became an official policy of the European Union and its member states under the terms of the Amsterdam Treaty of 1997).[31] Whilst, internationally the initial focus has been on gender, in some contexts, such as Wales, generic mainstreaming has emerged that relates to the full breadth of protected characteristics – such as disability, sexual orientation, age and ethnicity. Mainstreaming involves 'the (re)organisation, improvement, development and evaluation of policy processes, so that an equality perspective is incorporated in all policies at all levels and at all stages, by the actors normally involved in policy-making'.[32] WG's strategy was unambiguous: 'the key to delivering the equality and diversity vision is the principle of mainstreaming'.[33] Targeting civil society engagement, it continued: 'good communication with relevant stakeholders is vital to successful policy making ... [officials need to] facilitate effective engagement and consultation'.[34]

Earlier studies have described the impact of these developments.[35] In line with the previous section, for example:

> The views of policy actors working for equalities NGOs indicate that the impact of constitutional reform ... has led to greater 'system openness' and increased policy focus on promoting equality ... [resulting in] discontinuity with past practices by changing the power dynamics of the policy process by making it more accessible to hitherto marginalised groups.[36]

Yet, crucially, this work also identified a number of shortcomings including government failure to invest adequate resources in mainstreaming, to roll-out training to officials in the promotion of equalities, and its faltering political commitment and leadership. In the early years of devolution the result was 'institutional decoupling' on equalities, whereby government espoused one thing but practised another.[37] The overall result was that the Welsh experience demonstrated how

> the potential gains afforded by early adoption of mainstreaming by government in new legislative settings purposively designed to foster the engagement of exogenous interests can be negated by failings in political leadership to secure the full range of prerequisites prescribed by mainstreaming theory.[38]

A further systemic failing that continues to the present day is the lack of a fully integrated approach to equalities and human rights in WG policy-making. At the time of writing, WG does not have a human rights strategy.[39] Furthermore, as noted, the political priority that successive administrations have attached to promoting equalities has waxed and waned. For much of the second decade of devolution the commitment to equalities mainstreaming largely disappeared from policy documents. More recently it has re-appeared and the wider equalities agenda appears to have gathered new momentum. In part, this stemmed from the review of gender equality practices announced by First Minister Carwyn Jones in 2018. Its purpose was to ensure that the WG becomes a 'feminist government'. The resulting report acknowledges the scale of the challenge: 'Despite decades of EU, UK and Wales inspired legislation and policy, systemic gender intersectional inequalities persist.'[40] Notably, the language used in the WG's 'Advancing Gender Equality in Wales Plan' in 2020 evokes Rhodri Morgan's 'clear red water' speech of 2002 when he said 'Equality of provision must be underpinned by equality of access, and equality of opportunity. But most importantly of all, we match the emphasis on opportunity with what has been described as the fundamentally socialist aim of equality of outcome.'[41]

Strikingly, almost two decades on, WG's plan alludes to, 'Shifting how we consider impacts and development of policy and programmes focus on equality of outcome and not just equality of opportunity ... the government aims to create the conditions for equality of outcome for all.'[42] In this regard the Welsh approach to equalities is distinctive. What is less clear, however, is the way the government intends to resolve the conceptual tension between equality of opportunity and equality of outcome – specifically, which outcomes are being referred to? Whilst equal outcomes in terms of access to public services is an established part of the prevailing political discourse of successive Welsh Labour governments, equal outcomes in relation to areas such as household income suggests radical redistributive policies (only partially achievable under Senedd tax-varying powers at the time of writing).

Notwithstanding such issues, a further notable aspect of the commitments in the government's new plan for equalities is the re-affirmation of 'moving toward an evidence-based, mainstreaming model'.[43] The plan continues:

> This type of policy model relies on a robust evidence-base and analytical capacity and capability. Work is needed to bolster both of these across Welsh Government, and with external bodies and organisations. It will mean ... focus[ing] on assessing and mitigating negative impacts and investing in both the policy profession and research and statistical capacity.[44]

Despite earlier setbacks and ongoing challenges, the latest strategy is further evidence that devolution in Wales has led to the political reprioritisation of equalities in public policy.[45] Since 1999 many of the major policies and strategies issued by successive governments refer to the promotion of equalities as a crosscutting theme, underpinned by engagement with civil society. These developments resonate with the literature on mainstreaming equality, specifically, the need to engage with the groups targeted by the policies.[46] Over the past two decades, the majority of key strategies have been founded on consultation with those outside government. The systematic and diverse ways in which equalities considerations are now embedded in the language of policy-making is also noteworthy. Once again it underlines the shift that has taken place in public administration in the wake of devolution. Thus, the latest government equalities plan states the goal of being 'people-focused and collaborative, ensuring that all communities are meaningfully engaged in its work'.[47]

Examples of equalities policy and law

Earlier analysis of the political rhetoric of Rhodri Morgan quotes him as saying, 'I think the key lesson is that devolution has to mean what it says. There's not a one size fits all. We are talking variable geometry UK here.'[48] It also notes his eschewing what he labelled 'the English model' of public services reform; instead preferring his administration's 'Welsh way'.[49] Equalities policies provide evidence of the foregoing, namely a distinctively Welsh approach. In the wake of devolution, national Welsh strategies now exist for the first time on matters such as refugees and asylum seekers, and domestic abuse.[50] In areas of shared policy responsibility with Westminster (on issues such as child welfare, youth justice and older people's services) there is some evidence of WG pursuing a more advanced approach than central government. Examples include: the Rights of Children and Young Persons (Wales) Measure 2011 that imports 'due regard' to the requirements of the United Nations Convention on the Rights of the Child (UNCRC) into the exercise of Welsh ministerial functions; the statutory offices of the Children's and Older Peoples' Commissioners; and the Violence against Women, Domestic Abuse and Sexual Violence (Wales) Act 2015. The general result is policy that is specifically tailored to the socio-economic and cultural specificities of Wales, rather than the pre-existing 'one-size-fits-all' approach evident in earlier Whitehall policies.

To explore this further we now consider the extent to which these key policies were shaped by co-working or engagement between civil society groups and WG. In the case of children's rights an earlier study concludes:

> Strong links between government and NGOs have supported the historical commitment to children's rights in Wales … Devolution brought a new compulsion not only to act on this commitment but also to accelerate positive partnership working between government and the NGO sector.[51]

This account reveals how over the past two decades the Wales UNCRC monitoring group, made up of NGOs and academics, 'has developed a constructive, collaborative yet critical collective voice. This has contributed to significant changes to strategic policy-making for children in Wales, and to Wales becoming the first country within the UK to incorporate the UNCRC (within devolved limitations) into its domestic law.'[52] Participants' accounts show how the monitoring group shaped the development of the CRC measure through legislative scrutiny stages in the Welsh Parliament. One Assembly Member noted, 'I will say that I think that this is a historic piece of legislation and I pay tribute to all those involved … I pay particular tribute to the UNCRC Monitoring Group, which I think gave high quality evidence.'[53] Whilst another key account describes how the NGO community 'transformed itself during this period into an effective and cohesive coalition … in favour of a strong and cohesive law'. This resulted in:

> A creative conflict of ideas in which the overwhelming preference of politicians, professionals, children's organisations and children themselves won out over the conservative inclinations of the civil servants, who had managed to embrace and persuade departmental Ministers of the need for caution … We should draw from this process, however, the lesson that evidence and expertise are powerful weapons, especially when presented cogently, bravely and by well-placed members of civil society.[54]

In the case of policy on older people, earlier research describes the origins of the section 126 duty on local authorities to safeguard older people at risk of abuse, as set out in the Social Services and Well-being (Wales) Act 2014.[55] Specifically, they chart how it emerged from older people's organisations' lobbying to address the limited reference to domestic abuse of older people in the government's domestic abuse strategy.[56] Allied to this, earlier work highlighted the way that older people's policies have been shaped by capacity building amongst civil society organisations. Specifically, a series of older people's networks that received state support as part of the overarching WG older people's strategies, including the National Partnership Forum for Older People and Better Government for Older People Cymru.[57]

In similar fashion, civil society organisations' policy demands shaped WG's national strategy on violence against women, domestic abuse and sexual violence, 2016–21.[58] In consequence, WG promised to '*co-produce with key stakeholders* ... how we will deliver the actions within the Strategy'.[59] The resulting delivery plan demonstrates the ongoing role of civil society organisations in meeting equality policy objectives.[60] For example, it undertakes to, 'Work with stakeholders to develop a model for sustainable funding for the provision of specialist violence against women, domestic abuse and sexual violence services to underpin the delivery of this Strategy'.[61]

Rhodri Morgan's clear red water speech also alluded to how 'The creation of a new set of citizenship rights has been a key theme in the first four years of the Assembly – a set of rights, which are, as far as possible: free at the point of use; universal, and unconditional.'[62] At this juncture it is apposite to consider whether post-devolution equalities policies evidence territorial distinctiveness and citizens' rights. The answer is affirmative. Whilst prior to 2011 the National Assembly's absence of thoroughgoing primary legislative powers hampered the realisation of a new set of rights, recent years have seen significant activity. For example, it is not just the Rights of Children and Young Persons (Wales) Measure 2011 that has incorporated United Nations human rights treaty obligations into Welsh law. Other examples include the Section 7 duty in the Social Services and Well-being (Wales) Act 2014 ('A person exercising functions under this Act ... must have due regard to the United Nations Principles for Older Persons'). In similar fashion, under the provisions of the Additional Learning Needs and Education Tribunal (Wales) Act 2018, citizens have the right to education policy and tribunal services that uphold the United Nations Convention on the Rights of Persons with Disabilities. Moreover, under the terms of the Well-being of Future Generations (Wales) Act 2015, citizens in Wales have the right to policy and law that has due regard to the interests of future generations. The significance of these developments is that they are territorially distinctive to Wales, universal to all citizens and enforceable through the courts in Wales.

To sum up the policy contribution that devolution has made to equalities and engaging civil society, as the foregoing reveals, there is evidence of major discontinuity with pre-1999 governance practices, notably the often exclusive, top-down governing style of the Welsh Office. There continues to be significant political capital invested in institutionalising a systemic approach to engaging civil society in developing policies that promote equality. However, it is also the case that over the past two decades progress has faltered. Nevertheless, impactful policies can be identified in areas such as gender equality, children's and older people's rights. However, civil society groups associated with other protected characteristics have not secured as many policy gains and nor have they appeared as engaged in the devolved policy process.

WG's recent re-affirmation of mainstreaming as its overarching conceptual approach to equalities is to be welcomed on the proviso that lessons have been learned by ministers and officials from the failures and shortcomings of the first mainstreaming strategy in the early years of devolved governance. Inequality and discrimination have been a scourge throughout human existence. Thus, it was always unreasonable to think that devolved governance would overturn this in two short decades. Such a sentiment is evident in a recent ministerial statement: 'We have been striving for equality for generations and we recognise to take [this] forward ... a long-term plan for change and sustained commitment will be required.' Jane Hutt MS continues,

> Our implementation plan will not only ensure that we are able to monitor and review progress but will also allow us to maintain focus and momentum. We now need everyone to be engaged if we're to achieve the level of change we all want to see.[63]

Legitimisation of devolved government

A further implication is the contribution of civil society to legitimising devolved government, including their input to advocating more enhanced devolved powers to Wales.

Undoubtedly, as discussed above, civil society engagement with Welsh devolved institutions has had a substantive impact on policy and can also be recognised as the 'territorialization of policy communities'.[64] In this respect, Wales reflects a broader trend in the UK and beyond, in the development of a strong territorial dimension to interest representation with groups reorganising as interlocutors in the context of 'spaces for interest articulation and representation'.[65] The proliferation of equalities-related organisations in Wales is an instructive example of such a development, to the extent that they can be labelled as the largest potential interest grouping in the third sector.[66] With regards to the legitimisation of the devolved government dimension, the significant engagement of organisations in policy work has contributed to shifting from 'devolution on a shoestring' to enabling the development of a distinctively Welsh approach through policies tailored to the specificities of Wales.[67]

In parallel, civil society organisations (CSOs) have contributed to legitimising devolved government in Wales through their increasing focus on influencing and engaging with the governing institutions in Wales. This has often meant increasing their capacity to develop, inform and deliver policies specifically designed for Wales. For those organisations who were part of UK-wide organisations, such steps have involved restructuring, and processes of negotiating the level of autonomy of their office in Wales have varied with many coming to increasingly view themselves as Welsh-based organisations. Therefore, the organisational shift amongst civil society towards a stronger Welsh outlook and interaction with Welsh political institutions is a distinct contribution to the promotion of a civic sense of Welsh identity.

Another layer to civil society's contribution to legitimising devolution is advocating for further self-rule to Wales. Surveys have demonstrated the distinct shift in public attitudes post-1999 from the low public endorsement of devolution in the 1997 referendum, its acceptance as the appropriate form of government for Wales, to significant public supporting for extending devolved autonomy (Tables 6.1 and 6.2). There is also evidence of increased legitimacy with regards to Wales's devolved institutions when considering patterns of public trust in the devolved systems compared to the UK Government and other institutions within the political system.

In this context, based on their experience of engaging with the devolved governmental institutions, organisations have been proactive

Table 6.1: Constitutional preferences in Wales, 1997–2011[68]

Constitutional preferences	1997	1999	2001	2003	2006	2007	2009	2011
Independence	13	10	12	13	11	12	15	13
Parliament	18	28	37	36	40	42	34	34
Assembly	25	33	25	25	24	26	27	28
No elected body	37	24	23	20	20	16	17	18
Don't know	7	5	4	5	5	5	6	8
Number of respondents	686	1,256	1,085	988	1,000	884	1,078	2,359

Table 6.2: Constitutional preferences in Wales, 2014–20[69]

Constitutional preferences	March 2014	Sept 2014	2015	2016	2017	2018	2019	2020
Independence	5	3	6	6	6	7	7	11
More powers	37	49	40	43	44	44	46	43
Remain as present	28	26	33	30	29	28	27	25
Fewer powers	3	2	4	3	3	4	3	2
Abolish assembly	23	12	13	13	13	12	13	14
None/don't know	3	2	4	3	4	–	3	5

advocates for greater self-rule in Welsh constitution-building processes. For instance, during the early years of devolved government, they highlighted the limitations in the National Assembly's powers and advocated amending the Government of Wales Act 1998, partly as the complexity and lack of clarity of the Assembly's legislative competences detrimentally affected some organisations.[70] For others, engagement opportunities and responses to their policy demands provided an impetus to call for greater devolved powers. The main channels through which organisations have influenced constitution-building are through the reviews and inquiries conducted into the devolved arrangements, including the three most significant: the Richard Commission, the All-Wales Convention and the Silk Commission. Whereas the majority of organisations advocated based on their particular policy areas and experience of the constitutional arrangements at the time, other organisations such as Cymru Yfory were set up specifically to campaign for more enhanced constitutional arrangements, in their case making the intellectual case for moving towards primary law-making powers and thus to securing a positive result in the 2011 referendum.

Democracy, civil society and devolved governmental institutions

From the vantage point of two decades of devolved government, the early indications of the negative implications of civil society relations with devolved institutions for Welsh democracy have not only proven to be valid but have been exacerbated over time. Whereas the complexities of the Welsh constitutional arrangements have been a contributory factor, the emerging most significant factor is the continuing electoral dominance of Welsh Labour and its prolonged period as the main party in government since 1999.

Analysis of civil society's engagement with devolved institutions during the first term of devolved government highlighted the potentially negative democratic implications arising from some organisations having closer and more exclusive relations with devolved institutions. Of particular concern were the increasing power inequalities between professionalised organisations with well-developed lobbying capabilities, both formally and informally, and those with limited resources. In addition to some organisations having the advantage of being better equipped to be represented in the political process than others, there was evidence that devolved institutions exacerbated existing inequalities. More exclusive relations were forged with some organisations, particularly through receipt of Welsh Government funding and support for policy networks. Whereas the aims of empowering civil society and building partnerships were genuine, rather than promote inclusive governance in the form of broad civil society involvement, the devolved government's engagement methods lacked adequate recognition of the risks of creating more exclusive relations that could result in issues regarding the representativeness of organisations, increasing inequalities within civil society with repercussions for the relative autonomy of organisations, including challenging their propensity to scrutinise government as expected in a vibrant democracy.[71]

After over a decade of devolved government, analysis of the capacity of civil society to scrutinise the Welsh executive and legislature concluded that greater commitment was needed to realise a vibrant and engaged civil society.[72] The previously identified impact of the complexities and evolution of the Welsh constitutional arrangements contributed to a division between well-organised and well-resourced organisations who had developed the capacity to be more professional and well positioned in positively and actively engaging by influencing and scrutinising devolved institutions and others that felt 'disengaged, disillusioned and disregarded by the political and public sector institutions in Wales, either because they feel situated outside of the "go-to" organisations or lack the right knowledge about how to engage'.[73] A track record of influencing and engaging with particular parties was also a valuable asset. Of particular concern were assertions of 'institutional lethargy' on the part of WG in its approach to broadening the participation of civil society in policy development and delivery beyond the 'usual suspects'.[74] Its established relationships and funding support for some organisations placed them in a dominant position, with other organisations finding it challenging to be heard or secure funding. The effect was that only a limited number of organisations who depended on WG funding felt able to criticise government as part of their role in advising and scrutinising government.[75]

Moreover, later work has highlighted the significant implications of electoral politics and the lack of change in the governing party on the strategies of civil society organisations associated with the equalities agenda.[76] It underlines the distortive impact of single party dominance in the Welsh case on civil society policy engagement. Though sub-state elections have created moderate change in the Welsh party system, the first two decades of devolved government suggests only limited evidence of Wales transitioning into more multi-party politics. Instead, Wales's one-party dominance, initially associated with the Liberal Party, has continued in Labour's 'essentially uninterrupted dominance over Welsh politics'.[77]

The consequences of one-party dominance for civil society organisations and their policy demands are wide-ranging and provide a backdrop to understanding the challenges faced by some civil society groups who have found it difficult to successfully advocate their policy demands and engage in the policy process. First, the Welsh political context creates a tendency for some elected politicians to be in post for extended periods, leading to examples of acting as 'veto players' in response to some equality organisations' policy demands. Some organisations felt concerns of uncertainty and mistrust in engaging with elected representatives, particularly as they were conceived as prioritising party interests over a policy demand. As a consequence, organisations strategically target and develop relations with other ministers and backbenchers in order to address challenges arising from the concentration of power. Secondly, continued one-party dominance can lead to embedding power relations in policy-making. Therefore, equality organisations utilised a range of ways in order to gain influence and be heard, including working in 'defensive' coordinated ways to avoid being sidelined. Rather than challenge government, they narrowed their focus on framing their demands in language and approaches that align with Welsh Labour's political and ideological agenda. Thirdly, another implication is the party politicisation of engagement to the extent that criticism of the government by CSOs is understood as criticism of the Labour Party itself. Fourthly, given the extent to which WG have funded policy networks, a particularly significant aspect is that the closeness of organisations to government heightens political patronage, risks eroding organisational autonomy, compromising their independence and their willingness to criticise and hold government to account. Indeed, there were examples of 'social control' as interviewees referred to 'toning down' or avoiding criticism of government for fear that some CSO managers – who were also members of the dominant party, convey their comments to ministers'.[78] Fifthly, more informal, often intra-party, processes and networks were extremely important in engagement with government. By often bypassing formal political channels and processes, they ran the risk of marginalising some organisations unable to access such informal channels, were not transparent and hindered accountability. A further implication of one-party dominance identified in Wales is in creating insider and outsider organisations, thus running the risk of heightening tension and mistrust between equalities organisations.

A particularly problematic angle to the findings was the self-sustaining impact of these tendencies. One-party dominance reduces the value of organisational efforts to engage with and build alliances with opposition parties, thus potentially further reinforcing Labour's dominant position to the detriment of opposition parties.[79] Over time, as opposition parties are viewed as lacking potential influence and power,

particularly as a party of government, such patterns of declining engagement with opposition parties perpetuates one-party dominance.

Conclusions

Civil society, equality and inclusiveness remain central to devolution
in Wales. They are integral to understanding progress towards securing
effective devolved governance over the first two decades and are likely
to be pivotal in Wales's future constitutional journey. As if building a
devolved system of governance with a deeply flawed legal blueprint in
1999 and weak public support was not hard enough; early promises of a
'new politics' founded upon civil society engagement, equality and inclusiveness raised public expectations to new, perhaps unrealistic, levels. At
the same time, chronic (and enduring) failings on the part of mass media
to report devolved politics to civil society in Wales meant that the future
development of Welsh devolution was always likely to be challenging.[80]

From civil society being depicted as a 'fragile plant' over the past two
decades, civil society organisations have flourished and contributed to
legitimising devolved government in Wales through engaging with and
influencing Welsh governing institutions and being energetic exponents
of greater self-rule. Developing their capacity in this respect has often
contributed to the development of a distinctive Welsh approach to policy
areas such as equalities policies. Overall, a stronger Welsh outlook amongst
civil society alongside their interaction with Welsh political institutions
is a distinct contribution to promoting a civic sense of Welsh identity.

With regard to the implications of civil society relations for Welsh
democracy, some of the early indications of the negative implications
of civil society relations with devolved institutions were not only well
grounded but have become more acute over time. This includes issues
around civil society organisations' 'representativeness' and autonomy in
dealings with the devolved state. Indeed, some of the negative repercussions of these relations represent a profound challenge for our 'social
democracy with a Welsh stripe' and have a potentially significant impact
on the democratic health of the polity. Research has recommended a
series of actions for civil society organisations in Wales to redress these
challenges, in ways that seek to compensate for the circumstances created
by one-party dominance and to try to enable organisations to contribute
to holding government to account. They include acting in proactive

ways in order to challenge existing power relations in policy-making; to develop their demands in ways that facilitate broad-based, cross-party engagement; to purposefully engage with weaker opposition parties; and to use their capacities to build coalitions to address any threat to civil society's independence. Equally, governing institutions and key political parties have a responsibility to be more aware and sensitive to practices and cultures that have a negative impact on the autonomy of civil society. They have the potential to shift their outlook in order to broaden civil society engagement with government and to respect civil society's right to actively challenge government policy.

Despite the flaws and setbacks, from an equalities perspective, devolution has transformed governance in Wales for the better. Indeed it has created a new and increasingly distinctive mode of Welsh governance (rather than 'governance in Wales'). At the outset of devolution, civil society organisations spoke of being passed back and forwards between Whitehall and the Welsh Office with neither willing to assume responsibility for equality matters. Devolution has changed this, and a distinctive equalities agenda has emerged.

This is a significant achievement that, to a large degree, has its origins in Welsh Labour's co-working with other parties and interests in the 1990s and 2000s, and its vision of social democracy with a red stripe. In the face of scepticism and sometimes hostility from Labour at Westminster, the work of Rhodri Morgan and colleagues in putting devolution on a sustainable basis with the Government of Wales Act 2006 has been a key part of the story to date. Devolution has institutionalised (that is, embedded – often by legal means, in Welsh structures and processes of governance) the promotion of equalities and the engagement of civil society. This has been achieved through the investment of significant levels of political capital and instances of cross-party working. There are notable examples of positive equality policy advances and a step-change in civil society engagement. However, progress has been variable and much remains to be done – including greater strategic coordination of the equalities, human rights, Welsh language and socio-economic equalities agendas. As elected devolution in Wales reaches its first quarter century, broad-based engagement and scrutiny of government by a critical, diverse and independent civil society holds the key to better realising the twin goals of inclusive governance and social democracy underpinned by equality and social justice.

Notes

1. Ron Davies, *Devolution: A Process Not an Event* (Cardiff: IWA, 1999).
2. Elin Royles, *Revitalizing Democracy: Devolution and Civil Society in Wales* (Cardiff: University of Wales Press, 2007).
3. Paul Chaney and Ralph Fevre, 'Ron Davies and the Cult of Inclusiveness: Devolution and Participation in Wales', *Contemporary Wales*, 14 (2001), 21–49.
4. Chaney and Fevre, 'Ron Davies and the Cult of Inclusiveness', 26.
5. Paul Chaney, Fiona MacKay and Laura McAllister, *Women, Politics and Constitutional Change* (Cardiff: University of Wales Press, 2007).
6. R. Wyn Jones and Bethan Lewis, 'The Wales Labour Party and Welsh Civil Society: Aspects of the Constitutional Debate in Wales', paper presented to PSA Annual Conference, University of Keele (1998).
7. R. Wyn Jones and L. Paterson, 'Does civil society drive constitutional change? The cases of Scotland and Wales', in B. Taylor and K. Thomson (eds), *Scotland and Wales: Nations Again?* (Cardiff: University of Wales Press, 1999), p. 176; P. Chaney and R. Fevre, 'Is There a Demand for Descriptive Representation? Evidence from the UK's Devolution Programme', *Political Studies*, 50 (2002), 897–915, 899.
8. Welsh Office, *A Voice for Wales* (London: Stationery Office, 1997), p. 28.
9. Chaney and Fevre, 'Ron Davies and the Cult of Inclusiveness', 29.
10. Chaney and Fevre, 'Ron Davies and the Cult of Inclusiveness', 30.
11. Davies, *Devolution*, p. 8.
12. E. Royles, 'Objective One', in J. Osmond and J. B. Jones (eds), *The Birth of Welsh Democracy: The First Term of the National Assembly for Wales* (Cardiff: IWA, 2003), p. 138.
13. P. Chaney and R. Fevre, 'Inclusive Governance and "Minority" Groups: The Role of the Third Sector in Wales', *VOLUNTAS: International Journal of Third Sector Research*, 12/2 (2001), 131–56, 139.
14. Colin Williams, 'Equalities and Social Justice in a Devolved Wales', in Colin Williams (ed.), *Social Policy for Social Welfare Practice in a Devolved Wales* (Birmingham: Venture Press, 2011).
15. National Assembly Advisory Group, *Report to the Secretary of State for Wales* (Cardiff: NAAG, 1998), p. 36.
16. P. Chaney, 'The post-devolution equality agenda: the case of the Welsh Assembly's statutory duty to promote equality of opportunity', *Policy and Politics*, 32/1 (2004), 63–77, 68.
17. Davies, *Devolution*, p. 7.
18. P. Chaney, T. Hall and B. Dicks, 'Inclusive Governance? The Case of "Minority" and voluntary sector groups and the National Assembly for Wales', *Contemporary Wales*, 13 (2000), 182–212, 205.
19. P. Chaney, 'Women and Constitutional Change in Wales', *Regional and Federal Studies*, 14/2 (2004), 281–303, 281.

20. P. Chaney, 'The Post-Devolution Equality Agenda: The Case of Welsh Assembly's Statutory Duty to Promote Equality of Opportunity', *Policy and Politics*, 32/1 (2004), 37–52, 42.
21. F. L. Wilson, 'Neo-corporatism and the rise of new social movements', in R. Dalton and M. Kuechler (eds), *Challenging the Political Order: New Social and Political Movements in Western Democracies* (Cambridge: Polity Press, 1990).
22. Chaney and Fevre, 'Ron Davies and the Cult of Inclusiveness', 38.
23. Richard Rawlings, *Delineating Wales: Constitutional, Legal and Administrative Aspects of National Devolution* (Cardiff: University of Wales Press, 2003), p. 114.
24. Quoted in Royles, *Revitalizing Democracy*, p. 116.
25. Paul Chaney, 'Exploring the Pathologies of One-Party-Dominance on Third Sector Public Policy Engagement in Liberal Democracies: Evidence from Meso-Government in the UK', *VOLUNTAS: International Journal of Voluntary and Nonprofit Organizations*, 26 (2015), 1460–84, 1465.
26. Paul Chaney, *Equality and Public Policy* (Cardiff: University of Wales Press, 2011), pp. 239–40.
27. P. Chaney and C. Williams, 'Getting Involved: Civic and Political Life in Wales', in Colin Williams, Neil Evans and Paul O'Leary (eds), *A Tolerant Nation? Exploring Ethnic Diversity in Wales* (Cardiff: University of Wales Press, 2003), p. 209.
28. Chaney, 'The Post-Devolution Equality Agenda', 73.
29. NAW, *Report on Mainstreaming Equality in the Work of the Assembly*, papers of the Cross-party Equality of Opportunity Committee, March 2004 EOC(2) 03–04 (p07 – Annex A) (Cardiff: NAW, 2004); WAG, *Mainstreaming Strategy* (Cardiff: WAG, 2006).
30. Article 79: 'In addressing unequal access to and inadequate educational opportunities, Governments and other actors should promote an active and visible policy of mainstreaming a gender perspective into all policies and programmes, so that, before decisions are taken, an analysis is made of the effects on women and men, respectively.' *https://www.un.org/en/events/pastevents/pdfs/Beijing_Declaration_and_Platform_for_Action.pdf* (accessed 3 May 2021).
31. R. Minto and A. Parken, 'The European Union and Regional gender equality agendas: Wales in the shadow of Brexit', *Regional Studies*, 55/9 (2020), 1550–60.
32. Council of Europe (CoE), *Gender mainstreaming: conceptual framework, methodology and presentation of good practices final report of activities of the Group of Specialists on Mainstreaming* (EG-S-MS) (Strasbourg: Directorate General of Human Rights, CoE, 2004), p. 7.
33. WAG, *Mainstreaming Strategy*, p. 7.
34. WAG, *Mainstreaming Strategy*, p. 10.
35. P. Chaney, 'New legislative settings and the application of the participative-democratic model of mainstreaming equality in public policy making: evidence from the UK's devolution programme', *Policy Studies*, 33/5 (2012), 455–76.
36. Chaney, 'New legislative settings and the application of the participative-democratic model of mainstreaming equality in public policy making: evidence from the UK's devolution programme', 470.

37. P. Chaney, 'A Case of Institutional Decoupling: Equality and Public Policy in Post Devolution Wales', *Scottish Affairs*, 56 (2006), 22–34.

38. Chaney, 'Older People, Equality and Territorial Justice', 122.

39. P. Chaney, 'Human Rights and Social Welfare Pathologies: Civil Society Perspectives on Contemporary Practice across UK Jurisdictions', *International Journal of Human Rights* (2020).

40. Natasha Davies and Cerys Furlong, *Deeds Not Words: Review of Gender Equality in Wales (Phase Two)* (Cardiff: Chwarae Teg, 2019), p. 5.

41. WG, *Advancing Gender Equality in Wales Plan* (Cardiff: WG, 2020). Available at: *https://gov.wales/sites/default/files/publications/2020-03/advancing-gender-equality-plan.pdf* (accessed 22 February 2021); Rhodri Morgan, 'Clear red water', Rhodri Morgan's speech to the National Centre for Public Policy, Swansea (11 December 2002). Available at: *https://www.sochealth.co.uk/the-socialist-health-association/sha-country-and-branch-organisation/sha-wales/clear-red-water/* (accessed 22 February 2021).

42. WG, *Advancing Gender Equality in Wales Plan* (Cardiff: WG, 2020), p. 3.

43. WG, 'Welsh Government accepts "Deeds Not Words" Gender Review Report', WG press release (26 November 2019).

44. WG, 'Welsh Government accepts "Deeds Not Words" Gender Review Report'; Alison Parken, Natasha Davies, Rachel Minto and Polly Trenow, *Improving Well-being and Equality Outcomes: Aligning processes, supporting implementation and taking new opportunities, and Equality Mainstreaming: Policy Development Model* (Cardiff: Report for WG, 2019). Available at: *https://www.researchgate.net/publication/335993400_Equality_Mainstreaming_Policy_Development_Model* (accessed 22 February 2021).

45. WG, *Advancing Gender Equality in Wales Plan*.

46. T. Barnett Donaghy, 'Mainstreaming: Northern Ireland's participative democratic approach', *Policy and Politics*, 32/1 (2003), 49–62.

47. WG, *Advancing Gender Equality in Wales Plan*, p. 5

48. BBC News, *Panorama: losing control* [transcript], BBC News (28 January 2000).

49. Rhodri Morgan, 'Delivering the Connections: From Vision to Action' [speech], NAW, Cardiff (2005); D. S. Moon, 'Rhetoric and policy learning: On Rhodri Morgan's "Clear Red Water" and "Made in Wales" health policies', *Public Policy and Administration*, 28/3 (2012), 306–23.

50. WG, *Refugee and asylum seeker plan – Nation of Sanctuary* (Cardiff: WG, 2019); P. Chaney, 'Examining Political Parties' Record on Refugees and Asylum Seekers in UK Party Manifestos 1964–2019: The Rise of Territorial Approaches to Welfare?', *Journal of Immigrant & Refugee Studies* (2020); WG, *National Strategy on Violence against Women, Domestic Abuse and Sexual Violence: Cross Government Delivery Framework 2018–2021* (Cardiff: WG, 2018); S. Wydall et al., 'Domestic Abuse and Elder Abuse in Wales: A Tale of Two Initiatives', *The British Journal of Social Work*, 48/4 (2018), 962–81.

51. Trudy Aspinwall and Rhian Croke, 'Policy advocacy communities: The collective voice of children's NGOs in Wales', in Jane Williams (ed.), *The United Nations Convention on the Rights of the Child in Wales* (Cardiff: University of Wales Press,

2013), p. 35. See also Rhian Croke and Anne Crowley, *Righting the Wrongs: The Reality of Children's Rights in Wales* (Cardiff: Save the Children, 2006).

52. Aspinwall and Croke, 'Policy advocacy communities', p. 46.
53. Andrew Davies AM quoted in Wales UNCRC Monitoring Group, *Report to the United Nations Committee on the Rights of the Child* (Cardiff: Wales UNCRC Monitoring Group, 2015), p. 5.
54. M. Sullivan and H. M. Jones, 'Made to Measure: cooperation and conflict in the making of a policy', in Jane Williams (ed.), *The United Nations Convention on the Rights of the Child in Wales* (Cardiff: University of Wales Press, 2013), p. 32.
55. Wydall et al., 'Domestic Abuse and Elder Abuse in Wales', 965.
56. WAG, *Tackling Domestic Abuse: The All-Wales National Strategy* (Cardiff: WAG, 2005).
57. Chaney, 'Older People, Equality and Territorial Justice', 120.
58. Amanda Robinson et al., *The Welsh Government's proposed 'Ending Violence against Women and Domestic Abuse (Wales) Bill': Recommendations from the Task & Finish Group* (Cardiff: Task and Finish Group, 2012).
59. WG, *Violence against women, domestic abuse and sexual violence: national strategy 2016 to 2021* (Cardiff: WG, 2016), p. 3.
60. WG, *National Strategy on Violence against Women, Domestic Abuse and Sexual Violence*.
61. WG, *National Strategy on Violence against Women, Domestic Abuse and Sexual Violence*, p. 28.
62. Morgan, 'Clear red water'.
63. WG, *National Strategy on Violence against Women, Domestic Abuse and Sexual Violence*, p. 1.
64. M. Keating, P. Cairney and E. Hepburn, 'Territorial policy communities and devolution in the UK', *Cambridge Journal of Regions, Economy and Society*, 2/1 (2009), 51–6.
65. Keating, Cairney and Hepburn, 'Territorial policy communities and devolution in the UK', 52.
66. Chaney, *Equality and Public Policy*, p. 217.
67. Rawlings, *Delineating Wales*, p. 159.
68. R. Scully and R. Wyn Jones, 'The public legitimacy of the National Assembly for Wales', *Journal of Legislative Studies*, 21/4 (2015), 515–33.
69. ICM–BBC Wales St David's Day polls. Available at: *https://www.icmunlimited.com/our-work/bbc-wales-st-davids-day-poll-2020/* (accessed 6 May 2021).
70. See Royles, *Revitalizing Democracy*.
71. Royles, *Revitalising Democracy*.
72. R. Rumbul, 'The scrutiny capacity of civil society in Wales', in J. Osmond and S. Upton (eds), *A Stable, Sustainable Settlement for Wales* (Cardiff: UK's Changing Union Project, 2012). Available at: *http://www.law.cardiff.ac.uk/ukcu/papers/05/A%20Stable,%20Sustainable%20Settlement%20for%20Wales-%20UKCU%20Research%20Papers.pdf* (accessed 22 February 2021).
73. Rumbul, 'The scrutiny capacity of civil society in Wales', p. 141.

74. Rumbul, 'The scrutiny capacity of civil society in Wales', p. 137.
75. Rumbul, 'The scrutiny capacity of civil society in Wales', p. 139.
76. Chaney, 'Exploring the Pathologies of One-Party-Dominance'.
77. Roger Awan-Scully, *The History of One-Party Dominance in Wales. Part 3 1999–2011: Hegemony Under Challenge?* Elections in Wales blog (2013). Available at: *https://blogs.cardiff.ac.uk/electionsinwales/2013/10/15/the-history-of-one-party-dominance-in-wales-part-3-1999-2011-hegemony-under-challenge/* (accessed 21 January 2021).
78. Chaney, 'Exploring the Pathologies of One-Party-Dominance', 138.
79. P. Chaney, 'How does single party dominance influence civil society organisations' engagement strategies? Exploratory analysis of participative mainstreaming in a "regional" European polity', *Public Policy and Administration*, 31/2 (2016), 122–46, 132.
80. S. Cushion, J. Lewis and C. Groves, 'Reflecting the Four Nations? An analysis of reporting devolution on UK network news media', *Journalism Studies*, 10/5 (2009), 655–71; BBC Trust, *The BBC Trust Impartiality Report: BBC Network News and Current Affairs Coverage of the Four UK Nations* (London: BBC Trust, 2008); BBC Trust, *BBC Trust Impartiality Review: Network News and Current Affairs Coverage of the Four UK Nations: 2015 and 2016 Follow-up to 2008 Review* (London: BBC Trust, 2016).

Select bibliography

Chaney, Paul and Ralph Fevre, 'Ron Davies and the Cult of Inclusiveness: Devolution and Participation in Wales', *Contemporary Wales*, 14 (2001), 21–49.

Chaney, Paul, *Equality and Public Policy* (Cardiff: University of Wales Press, 2011).

Chaney, Paul, 'Exploring the Pathologies of One-Party-Dominance on Third Sector Public Policy Engagement in Liberal Democracies: Evidence from Meso-Government in the UK', *VOLUNTAS: International Journal of Voluntary and Nonprofit Organizations*, 26 (2015), 1460–84, 1465.

Chaney, Paul, Fiona MacKay and Laura McAllister, *Women, Politics and Constitutional Change* (Cardiff: University of Wales Press, 2007).

Keating, M., P. Cairney and E. Hepburn, 'Territorial policy communities and devolution in the UK', *Cambridge Journal of Regions, Economy and Society*, 2/1 (2009), 51–6.

Royles, Elin, *Revitalizing Democracy: Devolution and Civil Society in Wales* (Cardiff: University of Wales Press, 2007).

Williams, Colin (ed.), *Social Policy for Social Welfare Practice in a Devolved Wales* (Birmingham: Venture Press, 2011).

Williams, Colin, Neil Evans and Paul O'Leary (eds), *A Tolerant Nation? Exploring Ethnic Diversity in Wales* (Cardiff: University of Wales Press, 2003).

Williams, Jane (ed.), *The United Nations Convention on the Rights of the Child in Wales* (Cardiff: University of Wales Press, 2013).

Wydall, S. et al., 'Domestic Abuse and Elder Abuse in Wales: A Tale of Two Initiatives', *The British Journal of Social Work*, 48/4 (2018), 962–81.

7

THREADS IN POLICY ON CHILDREN AND YOUNG PEOPLE: RIGHTS AND WELL-BEING

Jane Williams

Introduction

Speaking at a 'Happy 30th Birthday UNCRC' event organised by the Welsh children's organisation, Children in Wales, on International Children's Day, 20 November 2019, the First Minister of Wales, Mark Drakeford, said 'the Welsh Government has sought to embed the idea of children's rights in the way that government in Wales has developed over the last 20 years'. 'It was', he said, 'a thread connecting all the five administrations that we have now had here in the devolution era.'[1] He described a steady progression through all five administrations and paid tribute to the influence of Rhodri Morgan in establishing this thread.

This chapter traces the impact of the United Nations Convention on the Rights of the Child (UNCRC) on post-devolution policy and considers the extent to which this supports the notion of social democracy with a Welsh stripe, both as a part of the legacy of Rhodri Morgan and as a broader, consistent theme over twenty-three years of devolution. It begins by explaining why adherence to the UNCRC is consistent with social democracy understood in terms of progression via democratic, parliamentary means towards realisation of the goals of equality, welfare and social citizenship. It then presents an analysis of the evolution of the children's rights agenda in Wales and whether the 'idea of children's rights' has become successfully embedded in a Welsh way of government, specifically in the context of greater prominence of the concept of well-being. It notes that despite the promise of both agendas, there remain persistent and even deepening inequalities and welfare concerns for children in Wales, and that devolved governmental action to address these concerns is in some ways constrained by the parameters of devolved powers. It concludes that a Welsh way is, however, clearly discernible in the recognition of children as social citizens with their own rights not only to equality and welfare but also to be part of the conversation about policies that may help to realise those goals.

Underpinning ideologies

This volume poses the question whether post-devolution public policy in Wales can be characterised as social democracy with a Welsh stripe. It is therefore important to consider why special adherence in Wales to children's rights as set out in the UNCRC might support such characterisation.

The UNCRC is one of the UN's specialised human rights treaties. The founding phase of the post-Second World War international human rights system coincided with the period that is sometimes described as a 'golden age' of social democracy.[2] These two phenomena do not explicitly share an ideological underpinning. The rights set out in the Universal Declaration of Human Rights, which laid the cornerstone for all subsequent human rights treaties, were agreed by a 'culturally, philosophically and religiously diverse' committee of thinkers convened by UNESCO in 1947, who found it remarkably easy to agree the content of the rights without attempting to reach a common ideological justification.[3]

> It is related that at one of the meetings … someone expressed astonishment that certain champions of violently opposed ideologies had agreed on a list of those rights. 'Yes,' they said, 'we agree about the rights *but on condition that no one asks us why.*' That 'why' is where the argument begins.[4]

The argument about the philosophical justification for human rights continues in theoretical discourse, with claims from libertarian theories of personal autonomy, from concepts of natural law or a conception of public trust, among others, as well as that all theories are flawed and unnecessary for understanding rights.[5] It is not necessary here to interrogate these various claims since, for present purposes, what matters is what human rights require, and specifically what a particular human rights treaty – the UNCRC – requires, rather than why, and the extent to which state action to fulfil those requirements corresponds with an agenda for social democracy. However, it is important to note that the UNCRC, whilst in part the progeny of the Universal Declaration on Human Rights, also has a pre-history of its own,[6] featuring early child labour, child protection and social welfare legislation and the efforts of twentieth-century champions for children. Perhaps best known amongst the latter is Eglantyne Jebb, who, with her sister Dorothy Buxton, founded Save the Children International in response to the wreckage of children's lives caused by the First World War. Jebb wrote the Geneva Declaration of the Rights of the Child which was adopted by the League of Nations in 1924, thereby providing a foothold for children's rights in the terrain of intergovernmental organisations.[7] Other champions were Janusz Korczak, the Polish-Jewish educator and doctor who pioneered a form of children's democracy in the running of his orphanages, and the educator Maria Montessori, whose child-centred approaches designed initially for disabled children influenced modern mainstream classroom settings as well as being the foundation for the Montessori schools.

None of these champions was identified politically with socialism, or social democracy, as such. In his life's work and its heroic, tragic end, Korczak personified kindness to children.[8] Intellectually, he was interested in the moral agency of children and, in practical terms, creating micro-environments in which this could be recognised and understood. Montessori's work was dedicated to understanding children's experiences and perspectives to unlock their potential through education, and Jebb's was directed at establishing that saving children from destitution and neglect was a matter of governmental obligation rather than charity. The text of the UNCRC represents the collective legacy of these figures together with some ten years of deliberation within the UN involving both non-governmental and governmental protagonists. Forty-two substantive articles lay down requirements for recognition, protection, respect for and fulfilment of civil, political, economic, social and cultural rights, and specify standards and actions, all directed to progression towards the general goals found in the preamble which include, along with peace and security, equality and welfare. The text is, in effect, a charter for social justice for children.

At least at the high level of general aspiration, there is commonality between children's rights and social democracy. Anthony Crosland, Labour politician and prominent socialist thinker of the mid-twentieth century, postulated a distillation of the intellectual influences on British socialism which included amongst others the philosophy of natural law, one of the theoretical justifications for human rights. Crosland argued that ultimately the objects of social democratic political effort must be equality and welfare, which are also claimed amongst the general goals of the UNCRC as set out in its preamble.[9] Conversely, it is unthinkable, given the structural context of the UNCRC, that its realisation in practice should be other than by peaceful, democratic methods of reform within the states' parties. And *social* democracy aims to create a fairer distribution of goods, services and resources, without which there cannot be realisation of the rights of the child as required by the UNCRC.

Sullivan and Jones, writing in 2013, argued that the ideology underpinning the Welsh initiatives on children's rights lay squarely within Crosland's vision for post-war social democracy, with rights-based public services as key to achieving equality of opportunity and citizen involvement a necessity in shaping policy priorities. This they saw as 'consistent with the underpinning philosophy of Labour in the Assembly ... and expressed most clearly in Morgan's "clear red water" lecture at Swansea in 2002'.[10] Yet these principles were not, at least in relation to children, the sole property of Labour, but shared across the political parties. They could be seen 'as expressions of "Welsh" rather than "Labour"' ideals.[11] Dafydd Elis-Thomas, speaking as a Plaid Cymru AM in one of several debates in the push for abolition of the defence of reasonable punishment,[12] exemplified this:

> What is happening here today is entirely consistent with the way in which Welsh legislation is developing in terms of its treatment of children. This is the clear argument for me: children are not children, but citizens of Wales. They receive public services that have been provided by the Welsh Government and Welsh Ministers, and they go through educational systems that have been put in place for them. They also receive, in difficult family circumstances, the support of social services. Therefore, they are full citizens. Children are not citizens in the making, some

sub-species of citizen, or citizens that are to be treated differently, either ethically or legally, to other citizens.[13]

The notion of social citizenship is central to post-Second World War discourse on social democracy,[14] but such discourse does not, at least until recently,[15] consider children as social citizens in their own right. The UNCRC, by contrast, asserts the status of children as citizens from birth: citizen-subjects in the quest for social justice, not merely the appendages of fully fledged adult citizen-subjects.[16] A Welsh way that privileges adherence to the UNCRC and asserts children's social citizenship is not only evidence of social democracy with a Welsh stripe, but also represents advancement in the concept of social citizenship to include everyone, from birth.

Telling the story of children's rights in Wales

At the 'Happy 30th Birthday UNCRC' event, the First Minister presented selected highlights in the story of children's rights from each of the five devolved administrations so far: from the first Assembly (1999–2003), Wales was the first country in the UK to create the post of Children's Commissioner with a general remit to protect the rights and interests of children;[17] from the second (2003–7), the Assembly's plenary resolution adopting the UNCRC as overall policy framework on children and young people;[18] from the third (2007–11), the enactment of the Rights of Children and Young Persons (Wales) Measure 2011, which imposed a legal duty on Welsh Ministers, when exercising their functions, to have due regard to the requirements of the UNCRC and its optional protocols as ratified by the UK; in the fourth Assembly (2011–16), the inclusion of education for children's rights in new curricula for education to age sixteen;[19] and in the fifth (2016–21), legislation to end the defence of reasonable punishment[20] and to extend the franchise to 16- and 17-year-olds in elections to the Senedd.[21]

Had time permitted, the First Minister could have added further examples. The UNCRC was explicitly the underpinning for early Welsh devolved administrations' strategies on local partnerships for children and young people's services, youth services, youth offending and child poverty.[22] In 2004, an overarching policy document, *Rights to Action*, set out seven core aims which were presented as a direct translation of the UNCRC.[23] The first Assembly funded a youth-led charity, Funky Dragon, to act as a children and young people's Assembly for Wales, encouraged direct dialogue between the organisation's grand council of young people and the Assembly Cabinet, and lauded the young people's work on reporting to the UN Committee on the Rights of the Child.[24] The Children and Families (Wales) Measure 2010 required local authorities to make arrangements to ensure that children could participate in decisions that might affect them, introduced aims and tools for the eradication of child poverty, and introduced a world-first 'play sufficiency duty'. With the enactment the following year of the Rights of Children and Young Persons (Wales) Measure, imposing a general duty on Welsh Ministers, when exercising any of their functions, to have due regard to the requirements of the UNCRC, Wales appeared to be at the cutting edge of innovation towards implementation of the UNCRC. By the time Rhodri Morgan stepped down as First Minister, the story of children's rights in Wales was one of coherent and consistent progression of an agenda explicitly connected to the international law on the rights of the child. This was, and is, remarkable, and begs inquiry as to why it happened.

Why children's rights in Wales?

Mark Drakeford, writing with Ian Butler when both were special advisers to Welsh Ministers, explored why children's rights came to prominence in the first decade of Welsh devolution.[25] They argued that there were three main factors: policy, people and politics.

As to policy, children and young people were a group in relation to which the new Assembly had a relatively complete set of powers, including across health, education and social services. This stood in contrast to some fields of policy in which the original transfer of powers model of Welsh devolution meant that developing coherent policies for implementation in Wales was more challenging. In relation to children and young people, something wide-ranging, coherent and, crucially, distinctive from England, could be done.

As to the people, key figures in the newly elected Assembly had a background of experience or interest in working with children and young people. Within the Labour group, First Secretary Alun Michael was a former youth worker and, with other Labour colleagues, notably Jane

Davidson who served as Education Minister until 2007, enthusiastically supported the establishment of Funky Dragon. The first Health and Social Services Secretary, later to become Minister for Education, Lifelong Learning and Skills, was Jane Hutt, a former chair of a local authority's children's committee and head of the childcare organisation Chwarae Teg. Within Plaid Cymru, Helen Mary Jones, formerly a teacher and leader of Barnardo's youth justice project, emerged as 'a formidable voice for children's issues'.[26] Within the Welsh Conservatives, David Melding had promoted the work of UNICEF and had organised the first conference in Wales on the UNCRC in 1989. Within the Liberal Democrats, Kirsty Williams, who became Education Minister in the fifth Assembly, had a background in further education and had, in the Assembly's 2004 debate on children's policy, moved an amendment urging abolition of the defence of reasonable punishment, building on an earlier motion brought by Labour Assembly Member Christine Chapman, who also had an earlier career in education. Rhodri Morgan, the prime political mover of the Rights of Children and Young Persons (Wales) Measure 2011, was personally committed to the principles of children's rights and had also the influence of his wife Julie Morgan, who both as Member of Parliament and later Assembly Member, was a constant campaigner on children's issues. Thus, in all the political parties represented in the Assembly, there were people who would naturally be drawn to an agenda for children's rights.

This in turn helps to explain the politics of children's rights in newly devolved Welsh policy-making. The backdrop to the early Assembly administrations was the wafer-thin referendum mandate for Welsh devolution in 1997. There was an urgent political need to demonstrate that there was a point to Welsh devolution. Difference and distinctiveness in policy could help to do this, but the early administrations operated in successive minority or coalition arrangements with inherent challenges for taking forward big policy change. However, on children's rights there was a relatively high level of cross-party consensus, which meant that in this field something bold and distinctive could be done. Importantly, it could stand in positive contrast to action on children's rights elsewhere, especially at the UK Government level and by comparison to England.

In England, under Prime Minister Tony Blair's New Labour administration, children's rights had had a promising start, but then faltered. The 2001 consultation paper, *Building a Strategy for Children and Young*

People, contained a set of principles 'developed to take into account the UN Convention on the Rights of the Child' (para. 2.3) and an associated framework for monitoring outcomes.[27] However, this was not followed through in subsequent UK Government strategy documents, notably in *Every child matters*, which followed the Laming Inquiry into the death of Victoria Climbié and provided the foundation for the Children Act 2004 as it applies to England.[28] The Children Act 2004 was focused on structural change and managerial controls aimed at promoting 'well-being', defined in terms of five outcomes, making no reference to rights. *Youth Matters* continued this approach.[29] During the parliamentary passage of the Children Act 2004 it became clear that the UK Government had made a deliberate policy choice to eschew children's rights as an explicit part of the policy and legislative framework.[30] From that point, the contrast with Wales became clear. In Wales, the 'principal aim' of the Children's Commissioner in exercising their function was to 'safeguard and promote the rights of children' and they were under a statutory duty, when exercising their function, to have regard to the UNCRC.[31] In England, the Commissioner's 'general function' was merely to 'promote awareness of the views and interests of children', and they were required to have regard to the UNCRC merely when 'considering what constitutes the interests of children'.[32] In Wales, it was *Rights to Action*, rather than *Every child matters*, which provided the guiding framework for implementation of the Children Act 2004. Here were examples of policy differentiation, and of Wales seizing the opportunity to establish a Welsh way of embracing children's rights.

It is also significant that, during the first decade of Welsh devolution, there was considerable organisational strength in civil society advocacy for children's rights. From 2001, two leading charities, Save the Children and Children in Wales, collaborated to develop an NGO alliance that would galvanise Welsh NGO monitoring and reporting under the UNCRC and work as a critical friend to government. Save the Children provided a chair and secretariat for this alliance, known as the Wales UNCRC Monitoring Group. Members included NGOs: Action for Children, Barnardo's Cymru, Children in Wales, Funky Dragon, Nacro Cymru, NSPCC Wales, Save the Children and Play Wales; legal and medical experts from Aberystwyth, Cardiff and Swansea universities and, as observers, officials representing Welsh Government (WG), the Equalities and Human Rights Commission, Children's Commissioner for Wales and the Welsh Local Government Association. This civil society group produced an interim report on UNCRC implementation,[33] engaged with children's organisations, child rights activists in Wales, the UK and internationally, and enjoyed proximity to WG. This meant that:

> when the opportunity arose in 2009 to create a general legislative measure of implementation for Wales, it was in a context of established dynamics involving policy advisers, politicians, officials, external activists and NGOs, with the Group playing a significant part variously as coordinator, facilitator, partner, lobbyist and conduit to the UN system itself.[34]

In summary, promotion of child rights-aligned policies played to strengths within the Assembly at a time when Welsh devolution was often seen as the weaker sibling of devolution elsewhere in the UK. It provided an opportunity to demonstrate that Welsh devolution enabled distinct, principled policy developed through collaboration and consensus, not only between political parties but also with voluntary and statutory sectors and with children and young people themselves. And it offered positive exposure on the world stage: an opportunity to present Welsh innovation in policy and law reform in favourable contrast to other countries in the UK, especially England, and the world.

Un-telling the story? Changing priorities and the rise of well-being

As shown above, there were, during the first decade of Welsh devolution, various conditions which cumulatively facilitated the stitching of a thread marked 'UNCRC' into Welsh devolved policy- and law-making. However, by the time Rhodri Morgan stepped down as First Minister and Carwyn Jones took over, those conditions were already changing.

First, the structure and powers of Welsh devolution were evolving, and this subtly but significantly changed the relationship between WG and civil society child rights activists. The Government of Wales Act 2006 separated WG and the Assembly into a more conventional model of distinct executive and legislative bodies. Amongst the detail of the consequential provisions, responsibility for funding and governance arrangements for both the Children's Commissioner for Wales and Funky Dragon were transferred to the executive, not the legislature.

This was odd, because both functions, one statutory and one discretionary, were purposed towards holding the executive to account, which would have been better aligned with the purpose of the parliamentary function in the evolving Welsh constitution. The statutory scrutineer, the Children's Commissioner, fared better in this situation than the non-statutory one. In a response to the Shooter review on the role and functions of the Children's Commissioner for Wales, which recommended transfer of responsibility for the Commissioner to the National Assembly for Wales (NAW),[35] the Commissioner acknowledged that 'in practice, there has not been inappropriate interference compromising the role of the Commissioner', but stated also that there was a 'fundamental conflict of interest that cannot be ignored'.[36] Repeated calls for the resolution of this conflict have been consistently rejected by WG. In January 2020, responding to a recommendation of the Children, Young People and Education Committee, the Deputy Minister for Health and Social Services stated that the current arrangement, on balance, was 'working well'.[37]

Funky Dragon, the recipient of discretionary funding from WG, fared less well. The organisation experienced diminishing engagement with its paymaster and increasing tension about who should be setting the young people's agenda. In 2013, Funky Dragon ceased operations following what was in effect a switch of funding to another charity, Children in Wales, to establish a consultative platform for young people called Young Wales. Unconvinced that this could fulfil the ambition for a young people's Assembly, the Funky Dragon trustees continued as a voluntary body to campaign, ultimately successfully, for a Welsh Youth Parliament aligned to the Senedd rather than Welsh Ministers.[38] This ended the regressive position wherein from 2014 to 2018 Wales had no national democratic platform for under 18-year-olds.

Secondly, new avenues emerged to demonstrate the impact of Welsh devolution both through domestic law-making and through international engagement. In March 2011, a referendum returned a vote in favour of further extension of Welsh law-making powers. Going into the Assembly elections in May 2011, Carwyn Jones, who had taken over as First Minister following Rhodri Morgan's retirement in December 2009, captured the significance of the referendum result, saying 'Today an old nation came of age'.[39] The fourth Assembly would have power to enact primary legislation known as 'Acts' over a more coherent set of policy 'fields', signifying the maturity of the Assembly as a parliament closer to, if not yet at, par with its UK and Scottish counterparts. For Carwyn Jones, using the new law-making powers and pushing for further powers were high political priorities, along with building the international presence of WG. The first thing he did as the new First Minister, even before finalising his first Cabinet, was attend a conference on climate change in Copenhagen.[40] In the May 2011 elections, Welsh Labour increased its representation and he was able to form a non-coalition government to deliver Welsh Labour's election manifesto. With a suite of new powers, growing opportunities for international engagement and a working majority in the Assembly, there was scope for policy differentiation and distinctiveness across more fields, including those attracting less cross-party consensus than the agenda on children's rights had done in the first three terms.

Thirdly, key ministers changed. Leighton Andrews, who had spearheaded Carwyn Jones's leadership campaign, had been appointed Minister for Children, Education and Lifelong Learning in Jones's first Cabinet under the One Wales government. In the fourth Assembly, Andrews continued in that role, with Huw Lewis, who would later succeed to the full portfolio, as Deputy Minister for Children. This was clearly an important portfolio for driving forward the children's rights agenda but, as revealed in Andrews's personal memoir of office, he was sceptical of children's rights as a policy objective and saw them as pertinent only insofar as instrumental to his primary mission of improving performance.

> I came to learn that, if pursued as a collective approach, the children's rights agenda was a powerful tool in challenging vested interests within education in the drive to raise standards. However, too often it was described in highly individualistic terms. I was worried that it was too often emphasizing a naïve Rousseau-esque natural development model of childcare and early years learning, which some might see as 'anything goes', leaving children to develop as they saw fit rather than being challenged consistently to grow and progress.[41]

Andrews was not alone in his child rights scepticism. As related by Sullivan and Jones, the 2011 Measure represented a narrowly won victory for 'a coalition of forces from both within the Assembly and from wider civil society' over 'a coalition of civil service and departmental Ministers unenthusiastic about change'.[42] The challenge now was to implement the duty of due regard imposed on Welsh Ministers by the Measure in a way that went beyond a mere tick-box exercise. The Welsh Labour manifesto of 2011 promised to ensure that the 'Rights Measure' that had been enacted in March 2011 would be 'given full effect in government policies and programmes', but enthusiasm for the agenda amongst the Cabinet ministers now occupying key portfolios to drive forward that ambition did not match that of their predecessors.[43] This augured badly for effective implementation of the Rights Measure since its central implementation mechanism was an administrative scheme to be made, periodically reported upon and reviewed by Welsh Ministers. Such a mechanism is inherently susceptible to becoming a tick-box exercise unless there is internal discipline driven by political leadership.

By 2014, the main focus of the statutory scheme was child rights impact assessment, a tool regarded by the UN Committee on the Rights of the Child as an implied obligation on states parties to the UNCRC derived from the general duty to implement in Article 4.[44] Child rights impact assessments (CRIAs) are supposed to help establish the evidential base for decision-making, mainstream and embed children's rights in policy process, and provide a basis for subsequent evaluation.[45] Wales's record of conducting CRIAs compares favourably with that of the UK Government: between 2010 and 2017 the latter conducted just five CRIAs, whereas in Wales, 260 were carried out between 2012 and 2018.[46] However, both an evaluation of WG CRIAs in 2015 and a study of integration of the UNCRC in Wales in 2018 found that while CRIAs had raised awareness of children's rights, the quality of examination was often poor, inconsistent and not reflective of detailed understanding of the requirements of the UNCRC.[47] Significantly in terms of the resource-allocative implications of a social democratic and children's rights agenda, CRIAs were done worst, and often not at all, in relation to budgetary and resource-allocative decisions.[48] Ten years on from the enactment of the Measure, the evidence suggests that WG CRIAs have too much of the appearance of a tick-box exercise.

Fourthly, the deployment of 'well-being' as a legislative concept began to obscure and even subsume children's rights, and human rights in general. As mentioned above, the UK Government had, back in 2004, chosen 'well-being' as the legislative concept rather than children's rights in the Children Act 2004. Ten years on, in Wales, a similar trajectory began to manifest, albeit in Wales well-being has risen, more confusingly, alongside and sometimes, variably, intertwined with rights, rather than instead of rights. The Social Services and Well-being (Wales) Act 2014 appeared progressive in terms of human rights protection, extending, in section 7, human rights 'due regard' duties to 'persons having functions under this Act'. This meant, amongst other things, that the duty to have due regard to the UNCRC now applied not only to Welsh Ministers in exercise of their functions but also to local statutory decision makers and service providers in relation to specified categories of vulnerable children and young people. However, the same 2014 Act also contained seeds of regression in terms of human rights implementation by relegating rights, or 'having access to rights and entitlements', to just one aspect of 'well-being', and differentiating between children's and adults' well-being in a way that implies that only adults', and not children's, well-being may include having control over day-to-day life or participation in work.[49] Despite the progressive appearance of section 7, the general trend set by the 2014 Act was towards absorption of rights, with their internationally recognised, normative value, into the more malleable and less enforceable concept of well-being.

Reluctance to embed rights within service-delivery frameworks was further evidenced when, in the following year, the Welsh Minister for Health and Social Services resisted calls for an extension of the UNCRC due regard duty to persons (including both public and private sector care providers as well as statutory inspectors) having functions under what became the Regulation and Inspection of Social Care (Wales) Act 2015. The Minister argued that the Bill provided 'effective rights' via reporting, regulation and inspection against well-being outcomes, and that in the context of the Bill, this was preferable to what he termed the 'declaratory rights' of the UNCRC.[50] By implication, the latter were relevant only at the high level of strategic decision-making and not at the interface between social citizen and provider of welfare services. This position chimes with the concern of the internal opponents of the Rights Measure during its pre-legislative and legislative stages, about floods of individual legal claims based on international human rights standards.[51] Taken together, these two Acts on important aspects of state provision for children's (and others') welfare deploy the concept of well-being as a buffer against that perceived spectre.

Alongside the rise of well-being in Welsh social care law, it also emerged as the key legislative concept in the bigger policy area of sustainability. The Well-being of Future Generations (Wales) Act 2015 has been praised as a world-leading, radical response to the UN Sustainable Development Goals (SDGs).[52] It is interesting to note that the UN's work on international development, wherein sit the SDGs, and on human rights, wherein sit children's rights, have been described as disconnected, and that increasingly this is recognised as problematic. Kilkelly criticises the SDGs' failure to adopt the language of human rights as 'a missed opportunity', and Alston has referred to the two agendas as 'ships passing in the night'.[53] McInemey-Lankford observes that, 'the relationship between human rights and development is arguably defined more by its distinctions and disconnects than by its points of convergence, despite substantial evidence of the potential for mutual reinforcement'.[54] Slightly more optimistically, Vandenhole suggests that a children's rights approach to sustainable development is still 'very much under construction'.[55]

In the second decade of devolution, the disjuncture between the two agendas at international level was replicated in Wales.[56] Unlike children's rights, sustainable development was written into Welsh devolution from the start and was supported from early on by a central policy unit.[57] By 2009, under Jane Davidson as Welsh Minister for Environment, Sustainability and Housing, the third statutory sustainability scheme, titled One Wales One Planet, declared sustainable development to be 'the central organising principle' of WG. In her personal account, *#futuregen*, Jane Davidson describes the journey from that point to the commitment to legislation in the Welsh Labour election manifesto of 2011, and how well-being became the concept of choice to underpin actions aimed at achieving the goal of 'sustainable Wales'.[58] Just as at the international level, human rights do not feature prominently, in fact hardly at all, in that conversation. The text of the Well-being of Future Generations (Wales) Act 2015 contains no references either to human rights or to children's rights.

Unsurprisingly, that situation attracted criticism from children's rights advocates. The 'missed opportunity' and worse, regressive impact on human rights, is borne out by research by Bangor University School of Law, which reported feelings amongst research participants that the focus on well-being in the legislation 'as the cornerstone to good administration has led to the marginalisation of other foundations, e.g., human rights, equality, and specifically, principles of administrative justice' that had been developed for Wales.[59]

Despite the above, it would be wrong to see the second decade of Welsh devolution as one in which children's rights disappeared from devolved Welsh public policy. The abolition of the defence of reasonable chastisement, the inauguration of the Welsh Youth Parliament and the lowering of the voting age to 16 for elections to the Senedd are all progressive measures in terms of UNCRC implementation.[60] The thread marked UNCRC was not discontinued; rather, other priorities, such as Leighton Andrews's drive to raise educational standards and the well-being agendas in social care and sustainability, emerged without sufficient attention being given to the mutuality between children's rights and the realisation of policy goals in those fields.

Towards alignment of children's rights and well-being

Croke et al., in a detailed case study of the parallel developments of children's rights and sustainability agendas in Wales,[61] note early steps taken jointly by the Children's Commissioner for Wales and the Future Generations Commissioner towards a framework for alignment of implementation.[62] Croke et al.'s conclusion is that charting a path towards such alignment requires further strengthening of public sector obligations and enforcement mechanisms on children's rights, and the development of a children's rights approach to sustainable development, including recognition of the crucial contribution of children themselves. The first part of this requirement, strengthening public sector obligations and enforcement mechanisms, would require legislation for which there is now a precedent in the UNCRC (Incorporation) (Scotland) Bill 2021, which would make it unlawful for any public authority to act incompatibly with the Convention and confer a right of individual action for breach of that duty. Similar legislative progression was recommended also by the Senedd's Children, Young People and Education Committee following its inquiry during 2020 into the impact of the Rights of Children and Young Persons (Wales) Measure,[63] but WG declined to act on this recommendation, at least pending further review.[64] The second part of the requirement identified by Croke et al. – recognition of children's crucial contribution to development of a child rights approach to sustainable development – would not require further legislation. It would simply require upscaling of practices of engagement with the young, to which both the Children's Commissioner for Wales and the Future Generations Commissioner, as well as WG, Senedd and many public bodies in Wales are committed, not least because of the innovations in children's rights that have been described in this chapter.

There remains a danger, however, that in efforts to integrate rights and sustainability, with the latter re-conceptualised as the well-being of future generations and associated well-being goals, children themselves are re-conceptualised, away from the UNCRC's concept of children as 'citizens now', so clearly evoked by Dafydd Elis-Thomas,[65] towards being included in the conversation because they somehow represent future generations. An example of this is the remark in the Future Generations Report 2020 that it was 'particularly encouraging' to see how public service boards, established under the Well-being of Future Generations (Wales) Act, 'are increasingly involving children and young people in their work, *providing a voice to future generations*'.[66]

Striving to promote the well-being of future generations should not occlude opportunity for children in the here and now, and focus on the prescribed well-being goals should not occlude progression in realisation of children's human rights. In another example from the same report, 'Investing in children's well-being' is illustrated by reference to new school buildings deploying sustainable technologies without explaining (as would surely be possible) how this is for the benefit of children attending the school. Nor is there any mention of current schoolchildren being involved or even consulted, which would be a manifestation of respect for their rights under Article 12 UNCRC as well as of 'involvement' as one of the 'ways of working' prescribed by the Future Generations Commissioner.[67] Nor is there recognition of how the new, eco-conscious 'uplifting learning spaces' may help realise the rights of children now or in the future (for example, in relation to play space (Article 31 UNCRC) or the aims of education (Article 29 UNCRC)).

These admittedly granular examples illustrate both the opportunity to align sustainability and rights in implementation of Wales's innovative agendas on each, and the ease with which the opportunity may be missed, even with the best of intentions.

The impact on children's lives in Wales

This chapter has explored how the idea of children's rights has become embedded in government in Wales, and its contribution to the establishment of a Welsh stripe in social democracy. It has therefore dwelled upon the supply side of ideas rather than their impact on the ultimate consumers of their product: children in Wales. Turning to that impact, it must be said that at the end of two decades of devolution, data on the key indicators of equality and welfare of children in Wales do not suggest significant improvement.

Throughout the devolution era, Wales has continued to have the highest percentage rates in the UK of relative income poverty for all age groups.[68] Of all age groups, children are most likely to be in relative income poverty and children in lone parent and larger families, some BAME families, workless households and in households with a disabled adult or child are disproportionately affected.[69] Pre-COVID-19 data covering the periods 2015–18 show 29 per cent of children in Wales living in relative income poverty, and by reference to multiple indicators, children in poor families were on average living further below the poverty line and experiencing poorer outcomes in 2018 than in 2013.[70] The impact of COVID-19 has yet to be fully appreciated, but evidence suggests that it has worsened and will continue to worsen the situation, specifically exacerbating pre-existing inequalities.[71] Wales saw the largest rise in unemployment within the UK during the pandemic in 2020.[72] Yet parental employment does not necessarily lift children in Wales out of poverty: two-thirds of children in poverty live in households where at least one parent is working.

As discussed elsewhere in this volume, in educational outcomes, Wales is, at the end of two decades of devolution, moving up the table of PISA rankings, nearing the international average in math, science and reading although still below the other three UK countries.[73] But it remains the case that pupils in receipt of free school meals scored lower and school exclusions, which increased in a 4-year period from 2015, disproportionately affect children from poorer backgrounds, additional learning needs and some protected characteristics and the rate of permanent exclusions doubled between 2014/15 and 2017/18 and has continued to increase.[74] A sobering statistic is that at the end of the 'well-being' decade in Welsh policy, pupils in Wales were less satisfied with their lives than the OECD average, more likely to feel miserable and worried, and less likely to feel joyful, cheerful or proud.[75]

In a 10-year period to 2019, Wales saw an overall increase of 37 per cent in the number of children taken into local authority care, with abuse or neglect being the reason in some two-thirds of those cases.[76] It cannot be concluded that this represents an increase in abuse and neglect: it might equally be the result of better detection and appropriate action taken by social services. However, research suggests that increased socio-economic stress on households is associated with higher likelihood of children coming into the looked-after system: children from the most deprived 10 per cent of areas are sixteen times more likely to be taken into local authority care than those from the least deprived 10 per cent.[77] Children from the most deprived backgrounds fare similarly worse in terms of health outcomes, although robust analysis is hampered by the lack of adequately disaggregated official data on children's (as opposed to general population) health and on the health of children in different groups.[78]

Many of the levers for poverty reduction are not within WG's control. In 2019, a UN Special Rapporteur report on extreme poverty and human rights in the UK was highly critical of the UK Government's austerity measures, especially with regards to changes to the benefits system which lie outside devolved powers. WG was not spared criticism, however. The Special Rapporteur saw as problematic a shift of focus from interventions targeted directly at reducing poverty, with associated performance targets and progress indicators, to a focus on increasing economic prosperity and employment as the gateway to poverty reduction.[79] Whether influenced by this criticism or not, WG's child poverty income maximisation action plan 2020–1, published in November 2020, reasserts the centrality of children's rights and child poverty. It sets out a suite of actions that WG took during the COVID-19 pandemic to date, together with further actions to be worked on: actions aimed at increasing benefits take-up; progression of a range of support, including free school meals, pupil development grant, free period products and free access to cultural and leisure activities; better public transport access for young people and various forms of discretionary financial assistance and debt and financial advice services. Importantly, the plan includes milestones and data collection to inform future policy and maximise impact on the alleviation of child poverty in Wales in the context of emergent thinking about reconstruction following the crises generated by COVID-19.

If there has been little improvement, by reference to the available data, on equalities and welfare for children in Wales post-devolution, the same is not true of their recognition as social citizens with a right to be part of the conversation about what needs to change. As well as, and no doubt encouraged by, the statutory duties under the Children and Families (Wales) Measure 2010 and the Rights of Children and Young Persons (Wales) Measure 2011, there are increasing examples of proactive efforts at all levels of governance to involve children in policy and decision-making. The office of the Children's Commissioner for Wales has institutionalised practices of engagement with its network of ambassadors in schools and community groups and supports a youth advisory panel to advise and provide internal scrutiny on the Commissioner's work. Senedd committees increasingly strive to include children's evidence in their inquiries on relevant topics and the Welsh Youth Parliament has institutional resource for its operations from the Senedd. WG does, increasingly if not consistently, try to draw children's 'voices' into some, at least, of its policy-making, whether via its support for Young Wales[80] or activities tailored to specific policy proposals.[81] At local authority level and amongst other public bodies in Wales, there is a plethora of child rights charters, normally focusing on participation, and participatory platforms such as youth forums and youth representation on service boards.

Wales is not unique in progression of children's participation in policy-making and the democratic life of the country during the past two decades. A study on child participation in EU democratic and political life, commissioned by the European Commission and published in 2021, documents many structures and institutions established in European countries dedicated to that aim, with myriad examples of their practices and recommendations for their improvement, in the context of a refreshed EU-wide strategy on the rights of the child.[82] However, the way in which this has been formalised in legislation and institutional practices in post-devolution Wales is unusual and is the consequence of deliberate policy choices that were made possible by devolution.

Conclusion

Children's rights are a clearly discernible ideological theme in devolved policy and law-making in Wales, and one that is consistent with the characterisation of social democracy with a Welsh stripe. In the first decade of

Welsh devolution, remarkable steps were taken towards integration of the requirements of the UNCRC in the business of government, but later, priority given to children's rights varied according to other conditions relating to the people, powers and politics of devolved governance and its interaction with civil society organisations. Nonetheless, significant specific, child rights compliant reforms continued, notably the equalisation of children's protection from assault under the criminal law and the extension of the franchise to 16- and 17-year-olds. It is not yet clear how an agenda for practical implementation of the UNCRC fits with the decision-making paradigms set by the legislation on well-being of future generations, but this challenge is shared with the international community in relation to human rights generally and the SDGs. At the end of the second decade of Welsh devolution, the thread of children's rights remains firmly stitched into the framework for decision-making, but its prominence compared to other political priorities remains variable. How future Welsh governments factor children's rights into the crucial decisions that will be made to respond to the major issues of the day: recovery from the COVID-19 pandemic, transitions following Brexit and action on climate change, will be a test of its commitment to this aspect of Rhodri Morgan's political legacy.

Notes

1. UNRC – the United Nations Convention on the Rights of the Child; a recording can be found on the Facebook page for Children's Rights Wales: *https:// www.facebook.com/2525319394194623/videos/401382797433186* (accessed 26 March 2021).
2. B. Jackson, 'Social Democracy', in M. Freeden and M. Stears (eds), *Oxford Handbook of Political Ideologies* (Oxford: Oxford University Press, 2013), p. 352.
3. John Macready, *Hannah Arendt and the Fragility of Human Dignity* (USA: Lexington Books, 2018), p. 4.
4. Jacques Maritain, 'Introduction', in *Human Rights: Comments and Interpretations*, UNESCO PHS/3:01, Paris (25 July 1948), quoted in Macready, *Hannah Arendt and the Fragility of Human Dignity*, p. 5.
5. D. Frydrych, 'The Case against the Theories of Rights', *Oxford Journal of Legal Studies*, 40/1 (2020), 320–46.
6. B. Milne, 'From Chattels to Citizens? Eighty Years of Eglantyne Jebb's Legacy to Children and Beyond', in A. Invernizzi and J. Williams (eds), *Children and Citizenship* (London: Sage, 2008), pp. 44–54.
7. Geneva Declaration on the Rights of the Child, adopted 26 November 1924, League of Nations.

8. Refusing offers of escape for himself, Korczak accompanied the children in his care when they were forcibly removed from the Warsaw ghetto to the death camp at Treblinka, where all were murdered. For a biography of Korczak, see Betty Jean Lifton, *King of Children: A Biography of Janusz Korczak* (London: Farrar, Straus and Giroux, 1988).

9. Jackson, 'Social Democracy', p. 356.

10. M. Sullivan and H. M. Jones, 'Made to measure: cooperation and conflict in the making of a policy', in J. Williams (ed.), *The United Nations Convention on the Rights of the Child in Wales* (Cardiff: University of Wales Press, 2013), p. 23.

11. Sullivan and Jones, 'Made to Measure', p. 25.

12. Reasonable chastisement is a common law defence to assault when committed against a child by a person with parental authority. It is abolished in Wales with effect from 21 March 2022 under the Children (Abolition of Defence of Reasonable Punishment) (Wales) Act 2020.

13. Record of Proceedings, NAW, 19 October 2011, quoted in Sullivan and Jones, 'Made to Measure', p. 26.

14. T. H. Marshall, *Citizenship and Social Class* (Cambridge: Cambridge University Press, 1950).

15. For example, R. Lister, 'Unpacking Children's Citizenship', in A. Invernizzi and J. Williams (eds), *Children and Citizenship* (London: Sage, 2008), pp. 9–19.

16. J. Doek, 'Citizen Child: A Struggle for Recognition', foreword to A. Invernizzi and J. Williams (eds), *Children and Citizenship* (London: Sage, 2008), pp. xii–xvi.

17. Care Standards Act 2002; Children's Commissioner for Wales Act 2001.

18. Record of Proceedings, NAW, 14 January 2004.

19. A recommendation contained in the Donaldson Report, *Successful Futures: An Independent Review of Curriculum and Assessment Arrangements in Wales* (Cardiff: WG, 2015).

20. Children (Abolition of Defence of Reasonable Punishment) (Wales) Act 2020.

21. Senedd and Elections (Wales) Act 2020.

22. NAW, *Children and Young People: A Framework for Partnership* (Cardiff: NAW, 2000); NAW, *Extending Entitlement: Supporting Young People in Wales* (Cardiff: NAW, 2000); WAG and Youth Justice Board, *All-Wales Youth Offending Strategy* (Cardiff: WAG, 2004); WAG, *A Fair Future for our Children: The Strategy of the Welsh Assembly Government for Tackling Child Poverty* (Cardiff: WAG, 2005).

23. WAG, *Children and Young People: Rights to Action* (Cardiff: WAG, 2004).

24. Funky Dragon, 'Our Rights, Our Story: Funky Dragon's Report to the United Nations Convention on the Rights of the Child', in A. Invernizzi and J. Williams (eds), *The Human Rights of Children, From Visions to Implementation* (Farnham: Ashgate, 2011), pp. 328–31.

25. I. Butler and M. Drakeford, 'Children's rights as a policy framework in Wales', in J. Williams (ed.), *The UNCRC in Wales* (Cardiff: University of Wales Press, 2013), pp. 9–20.

26. Butler and Drakeford, 'Children's rights as a policy framework in Wales', p. 10.

27. HM Treasury, 'Building a Strategy for Children and Young People', Children and Young People's Unit (2001).

28. HM Treasury, *Every child matters*, Cm. 5860 (London: The Stationery Office, 2003); Lord Laming, *The Victoria Climbié Inquiry Report*, Cm. 5730 (London: The Stationery Office, 2003).

29. Department for Education and Skills, *Youth Matters*, Cm. 6629 (London: The Stationery Office, 2005).

30. See the debate on government amendments to remove 'rights' from the text of the Bill as had been inserted by the House of Lords during committee stage: Hansard, 10 November 2004, vol. 666, col. 934–61.

31. Section 2, Children's Commissioner for Wales Act 2001, amending section 72 Care Standards Act 2000; Children's Commissioner for Wales Regulations 2001, S.I. 2001/2787, Reg. 22.

32. Children Act 2004 s. 2(11).

33. Rhian Croke and Anne Crowley, *Righting the Wrongs: The Reality of Children's Rights in Wales* (Cardiff: Save the Children UK, 2006).

34. T. Aspinwall and R. Croke, 'Policy advocacy communities: the collective voice of children's NGOs in Wales', in Jane Williams (ed.), *The UNCRC in Wales* (Cardiff: University of Wales Press, 2013), p. 39.

35. Michael Shooter, *Review of the role and functions of the Children's Commissioner for Wales* (Cardiff: WG, 2014), Recommendation 6.

36. Sally Holland, *Paper on the Children's Commissioner for Wales' position on the recommendations from the Independent Review into the Role and Functions of the Children's Commissioner for Wales* (Swansea: Children's Commissioner for Wales, 2015), p. 3.

37. Record of Proceedings, Senedd, 20 January 2021, column 220.

38. Rhian Croke and Jane Williams, *Our Rights, Our Parliament: The Story of the Campaign for the Children and Young People's Assembly for Wales 2014–2018*. Available at: *https://childrenslegalcentre.wales/resources/our-rights-our-parliament/* (accessed 6 April 2021).

39. BBC News, 'Welsh referendum: Voters give emphatic Yes on powers', 4 March 2011.

40. Carwyn Jones, *Not Just Politics* (London: Headline Accent, 2020), p. 116.

41. Leighton Andrews, *Ministering to Education* (Cardigan: Parthian Books, 2014), p. 82.

42. Sullivan and Jones, 'Made to Measure', p. 33.

43. Welsh Labour, *Standing Up for Wales: Welsh Labour Manifesto 2011* (Cardiff: Welsh Labour, 2011), p. 58.

44. WG, *Children's Rights Scheme: Arrangements for having due regard to the United Nations Convention on the Rights of the Child (UNCRC) when Welsh Ministers exercise any of their functions* (Cardiff: WG, 2014); UN Committee on the Rights of the Child, *General measures of implementation of the Convention on the Rights of the Child*, General Comment no. 5 (2003), CRC/GC/2003/5, para. 45.

45. S. Hoffman, 'Ex ante children's rights impact assessment of economic policy', *International Journal of Human Rights*, 24 (2020), 1333–52.

46. Hoffman, 'Ex ante children's rights impact assessments', p. 1343.

47. Lisa Payne, *Child Rights Impact Assessment (CRIA): A review of comparative practice across the UK* (London: UNICEF-UK, 2017); Simon Hoffman and Sean O'Neill, *The Impact of Legal Integration of the UN Convention on the Rights of the Child in Wales* (Cardiff: Equalities and Human Rights Commission, 2018), p. 24.

48. Simon Hoffman and C. Morse, *Evaluation of the Welsh Government's Child Rights impact Assessment Procedure under the Children's Rights Scheme pursuant to the Rights of Children and Young Persons' (Wales) Measure 2011* (Swansea: Wales Observatory on Human Rights of Children and Young People, 2015), p. 4; Hoffman and O'Neill, *The Impact of Legal Integration*.

49. Social Services and Well-being (Wales) Act 2014, section 2.

50. Minutes of Proceedings, Health and Social Care Committee, NAW, 3 June 2015.

51. Sullivan and Jones, 'Made to Measure' pp. 26–7.

52. Jane Davidson, *#futuregen: Lessons from a Small Country* (London: Chelsea Green Publishing, 2020), p. i.

53. U. Kilkelly, 'The Health Rights of Children', in J. Todres and M. King (eds), *The Oxford Handbook of Children's Rights Law* (Oxford: Oxford University Press, 2020); P. Alston, 'Ships Passing in the Night: The Current State of the Human Rights and Development Debate Seen through the Lens of the Millennium Development Goals', *Human Rights Quarterly*, 27 (2005), 755–829.

54. S. McInemey-Lankford, 'Human Rights and Development: A Comment on Challenges and Opportunities from a Legal Perspective', *Journal of Human Rights Practice*, 1/1 (2009), 51–82.

55. W. Vandenhole, 'Children's Rights and Sustainable Development from a "Law and Development" Perspective', in C. Fenton-Glyn, *Children's Rights and Sustainable Development* (Cambridge: Cambridge University Press, 2019), p. 29.

56. R. Croke et al., 'Integrating Sustainable Development and Children's Rights: A Case Study on Wales', *Social Sciences*, 10/100 (2021).

57. Section 121, Government of Wales Act 1998; section 79, Government of Wales Act 2006.

58. Davidson, *#futuregen*, pp. 46–52.

59. Bangor Law School, Public Law Research Group, *Response to the Senedd Public Accounts Committee Inquiry into Barriers to the Successful Implementation of the Well-Being of Future Generations (Wales) Act 2015*. Available at: *https://business.senedd.wales/documents/s500005886/FGA47%20Bangor%20Law%20School%20Public%20Law%20Research%20Group.pdf* (accessed 1 April 2021).

60. Children (Abolition of Defence of Reasonable Punishment) (Wales) Act 2020; *https://youthparliament.senedd.wales* (accessed 15 April 2021); Senedd and Elections (Wales) Act 2020.

61. Croke et al., 'Integrating Sustainable Development and Children's Rights'.

62. Children's Commissioner for Wales and Future Generations Commissioner, *The Right Way: A Wales Future Fit for Children* (2017). Available at: *https://www.childrensrightsplanning.wales/wp-content/uploads/2018/06/CCFW-FGCW-Report-_English_ 01.pdf* (accessed 21 December 2020)

63. Welsh Parliament Children, Young People and Education Committee, *Children's rights in Wales* (Cardiff: Senedd Commission, 2020), Recommendation 15.
64. Record of Proceedings, Senedd, 20 January 2021, para. 219.
65. Record of Proceedings, NAW, 19 October 2011.
66. Future Generations Commissioner, *The Future Generations Report 2020* (Cardiff: Future Generations Commissioner, 2020), p. 85; emphasis added.
67. *The Future Generations Report 2020*, p. 69.
68. Statistics Wales, *Percentage of all individuals, children, working-age adults and pensioners living in relative income poverty for the UK, UK countries and regions of England between 1994–95 to 1996–97 and 2017–18 to 2019–20*. Available at: *https://statswales.gov.wales/Catalogue/Community-Safety-and-Social-Inclusion/Poverty/householdbelowaverageincome-by-year* (accessed 15 April 2021).
69. Peter Matejic, *Poverty in Wales 2020* (Cardiff: Joseph Rowntree Foundation, 2020). Available at: *https://www.jrf.org.uk/report/poverty-wales-2020* (accessed 15 April 2021).
70. Tom Lee, *Dragged Deeper: How families are falling further and further below the poverty line* (London: Child Poverty Action Group, 2020).
71. Welsh Parliament Children, Young People and Education Committee, *Impact of COVID-19 on children and young people* (Cardiff: Senedd Commission, 2020).
72. Bevan Foundation, *Reducing the impact of Coronavirus on Poverty in Wales* (Merthyr Tydfil: Bevan Foundation, 2020).
73. See Chapter 3 in this volume.
74. WG, *Permanent and fixed term exclusions from schools* (Cardiff: WG, 2019).
75. Juliet Sizmur et al., *Achievement of 15-Year-Olds in Wales: PISA 2018 National Report* (Slough: National Foundation for Educational Research), p. 77.
76. WG, *Experimental Statistics: Children looked after by local authorities, 2018–19* (Cardiff: WG and Statistics for Wales, 2019), SFR 106/2019.
77. Child Welfare Inequalities Project, *Identifying and Understanding Inequalities in Child Welfare Intervention Rates: comparative studies in four UK countries* (London: Nuffield Foundation, 2017).
78. Wales UNCRC Monitoring Group, *Wales Civil Society Report to the United Nations Committee on the Rights of the Child to inform their List of Issues Prior to Reporting* (Cardiff: Children in Wales, 2020), p. 28. Available at: *https://www.childreninwales.org.uk/application/files/6116/1676/8681/All-Presentations-launch-of-report-event-10.12.20-compressed.pdf* (accessed 27 January 2022).
79. Philip Alston, *Report of the Special Rapporteur on extreme poverty and human rights* (Geneva: United Nations Human Rights Council, 2019), A/HRC/41/39/Add.1.
80. Hosted by Children in Wales and funded by WG: *childreninwales.org.uk*.
81. For example, the consultation process leading to WG's *Beyond Recycling Strategy* (2021) included children and young people as a stakeholder group.
82. European Commission, *Study on child participation in EU democratic and political life* (RAND Europe and Eurochild, 2021); *EU strategy on the rights of the child*, Communication from the Commission to the European Parliament, the Council, the European Economic and Social Committee and the Committee of the Regions, Brussels (March 2021). COM (2021), 142.

Select bibliography

Croke, R. et al., 'Integrating Sustainable Development and Children's Rights: A Case Study on Wales', *Social Sciences*, 10/100 (2021).

Fenton-Glyn, C. (ed.), *Children's Rights and Sustainable Development* (Cambridge: Cambridge University Press, 2019).

Hoffman, S., 'Ex ante children's rights impact assessment of economic policy', *International Journal of Human Rights*, 24 (2020), 1333–52.

Invernizzi, A. and J. Williams, *Children and Citizenship* (London: Sage, 2008).

Invernizzi, A. and J. Williams (eds), *The Human Rights of Children, From Visions to Implementation* (Farnham: Ashgate, 2011).

Todres, J. and M. King, *The Oxford Handbook of Children's Rights Law* (Oxford: Oxford University Press, 2020).

Williams, J. (ed.), *The UNCRC in Wales* (Cardiff: University of Wales Press, 2013).

8

TOWARDS A MILLION SPEAKERS? WELSH LANGUAGE POLICY POST-DEVOLUTION

Huw Lewis and Elin Royles

Introduction

Across several European cases, the move towards greater regional autonomy seems to have had significant implications on efforts to maintain and revitalise regional or minority languages. For example, in locations such Catalonia, the Basque County, Galicia and Scotland, regionalisation has meant the creation of political and institutional contexts that are more conducive to the development of planned public policy interventions to support such languages.[1] To what extent has this also been the case in Wales? Over two decades have now passed since the advent of devolution and during that period the nature of the constitutional arrangements that set the parameters for how Wales is governed have been revised and reformed on several occasions. This chapter critically examines how policy-making in relation to the Welsh language has evolved during this period. After summarising some of the main developments during the years preceding devolution, the chapter then analyses key policy developments post-devolution, before assessing and unpacking the main features of the current Welsh approach to language revitalisation. In doing so, it is argued that it is important not to fall into the trap of assuming that 1999 represented some kind of 'year zero' for policy activity in relation to the Welsh language – while the post-devolution period has clearly witnessed several significant developments, it is also important to acknowledge elements of continuity from earlier

periods. Finally, the chapter concludes by highlighting persistent challenges associated with the effective implementation of language policy
and argues that it is this issue, as opposed to further rounds of legislative or institutional reform, that members of the Welsh language policy
community should prioritise over the coming years.

Welsh language promotion before devolution

Efforts to promote the Welsh language and to reverse the decline in numbers of speakers and levels of use witnessed since the second half of the
nineteenth century have a long history.[2] However, the 1960s marked a
step change in language revitalisation efforts with more concerted action
being taken, first by various civil society organisations and then, increasingly, by governmental institutions in Wales.[3]

Between the early 1960s and the late 1980s, a variety of policy interventions sought to support and promote the Welsh language. During
this period, both the UK Government, in the form of the Welsh Office,
as well as Welsh local government, showed an increasing willingness to
draw on a mixture of legislative, policy and financial instruments in order
to further the language's prospects.[4] Developments originally focused
on the public status of the language and issues of official bilingualism.[5]
However, important steps were also taken in fields such as broadcasting
and education.[6] Yet, overall, most policy reforms introduced during this
period tended to be piecemeal or ad hoc, usually stemming from periods
of sustained pressure by sections of the Welsh language movement, rather
than being the result of a systematic and planned approach to language
revitalisation by policy makers.[7]

To a large extent, this was also the case with the eventual introduction of the Welsh Language Act of 1993.[8] As with its 1967 predecessor,
the 1993 Act fell short of the expectations of many who had campaigned
for revised legislation throughout the 1980s. Among the main complaints were the fact that it did not include a 'purpose clause' declaring
the Welsh language an official language in Wales, and the fact that its
provisions were limited to the public sector and did not cover a number of key services offered by the private sector.[9] Nevertheless, more
recently, it has been argued that the passing of the 1993 Act 'was a
turning point in the history of Welsh language promotion'.[10] The legislation transformed the role played by the Welsh language within public

administration across Wales. The duty placed on public bodies to prepare Welsh language schemes that detailed how they would uphold the key principle of treating Welsh and English on the basis of equality led to a drastic increase in the status of Welsh across the public sector. Also, as Williams has demonstrated, it led to changes in the internal culture of many institutions, and 'created a discourse within institutions which had never previously been required to discuss the needs of Welsh speakers'.[11]

The broader significance of the Welsh Language Act of 1993 is the scope it afforded the Welsh Language Board to develop into being more than simply a narrow regulatory body. The Board came to interpret the brief of 'promoting and facilitating the use of the Welsh language' in more expansive terms.[12] Over time, it evolved into a fully fledged language promotion agency. This became increasingly apparent during the 1990s and the early 2000s as successive strategy documents published by the Board set targets that included the need to: i) increase the numbers of Welsh speakers; ii) provide more opportunities to use the language; iii) change habits in relation to language use; iv) strengthen Welsh as a community language.[13] In pursuing these objectives, the Board initiated a range of innovative programmes in areas such as language transfer within the family, community development, information and communication technology, and also language in business. It established itself as the 'principal agency for the promotion of Welsh' and the 'main determining influence on the contours of Welsh language policy' – thus during the 1990s it was possible to talk of explicit 'language planning' with regard to Welsh.[14]

The impact of devolution on Welsh language policy

Further development of the policy and planning infrastructure designed to promote the prospects of the Welsh language became possible with the establishment of the National Assembly for Wales (NAW) in 1999. Despite the ambiguities and weaknesses of the original devolution legislation, the Welsh language was clearly listed in the Government of Wales Act 1998 as one of the fields in which functions were being transferred, in its Schedule 2. The Act also stated that: 'The Assembly may do anything it considers appropriate to support the Welsh language.'[15] Moreover, as the legislative competence of the Assembly/Senedd expanded, the range of policy instruments that could be used in order to promote the language also increased. Overall, over the first two decades of devolution, one central theme evident in most national-level policy activity linked to the Welsh language is the effort to gradually build a strategic framework to effectively coordinate different aspects of language promotion. This section reviews key planks in this emerging framework: first, the series of national language strategies adopted by the Welsh Government (WG); secondly, reforms introduced in the field of Welsh-medium education planning; and finally, the impact of new language legislation and associated reforms to the institutional structure of language policy governance.

The emergence of national language strategies

Post-devolution, WG has followed the lead of several other European administrations by adopting a series of official strategy documents that outline its approach to Welsh language protection and promotion, and that provide an overarching framework for all other language promotion activity.[16] The preparation of the first of these key strategy documents, *Iaith Pawb* (Everyone's Language), was the main language policy activity during the first Assembly (1999–2003).[17] Indeed, the strategy's publication was another important milestone in the evolution of the Welsh language revitalisation effort. It represented the first time that government had declared unambiguously that its official policy objective was to see an increase in both the number and percentage of Welsh speakers and also an increase in its everyday use. Despite the numerous language initiatives undertaken since the 1960s, none of the previous activity could be described as constituting a comprehensive 'national plan' designed to coordinate Welsh language revitalisation.[18]

Given the significance of the strategy it is worth reflecting briefly on the political and institutional dynamics that led to its adoption. With Labour running a minority administration, Plaid Cymru used its influence to ensure that a plenary debate was held during July 2000 that considered the position of the Welsh language. The outcome of this was the approval of a motion that committed the Assembly to the ambitious objective of creating 'a bilingual Wales'.[19] The motion also called for the development of a 'coordinated and targeted strategy' and for 'comprehensive policy reviews' to be undertaken by the culture and education committees.[20] Subsequently, due to the Assembly's then corporate structure, these committee-led reviews, which were both chaired by Plaid AMs, and the detailed joint report which they produced fed directly into the process of formulating what eventually became *Iaith Pawb*. What this episode helps to underline is how the balance of power between parties within the Assembly/Senedd, and in particular the ability of Plaid Cymru to exert influence, has been, at certain junctures, a key factor that has prompted significant policy developments with regard to the Welsh language. Indeed, it is a theme that is relevant to other important post-devolution developments, such as the adoption of the first national Welsh-medium education strategy and the introduction of the 2011 Welsh Language (Wales) measure, which we discuss further below.

The general objectives and targets outlined in *Iaith Pawb* also seemed to reflect the sense that its publication would mark 'a radical departure' from earlier governmental initiatives.[21] The very first page stipulated that the strategy's general objective was the construction of a 'truly bilingual' society where 'people can choose to live their lives through the medium of either or both English or Welsh'.[22] It also set out a series of ambitious targets, which included ensuring an increase of 5 per cent by 2011 in the percentage of people in Wales able to speak Welsh from the 2001 baseline; and arresting the decline in the number of communities where Welsh is spoken by over 70 per cent of the population.[23] These objectives and targets were to be pursued through a variety of initiatives in areas such as language transmission within the family, early years education, the social use of Welsh within the community and the link between language use and economic development.

Yet, despite the far-reaching nature of many of its pronouncements, *Iaith Pawb* received some sustained criticism. In a particularly detailed analysis, Williams argued that while the strategy featured 'fine rhetoric which legitimizes government action' it was also 'characterized by ill-defined mechanisms', for example numerical targets to increase the overall percentage of Welsh speakers that had been set with 'little statistical or sociolinguistic thought' and, therefore, were merely aspirational in nature.[24] He also added that 'most of the remedial answers on offer are but slight extensions of existing programmes', reflecting an 'unconvincing political will' to implement the strategy in full.[25] Of particular concern was the lack of detail on the future place of Welsh within the statutory education sector; a key issue if some of the strategy's targets were to be achieved.[26] Finally, Williams highlighted financial resources and that, despite the additional money allocated, the strategy's 'declared aims do not square with the current relatively low investment'.[27]

Therefore, notwithstanding its historical significance, *Iaith Pawb* came to be seen as at best 'a work in progress', or a sign of good intent by a government that had yet to work out how to operationalise its general objectives.[28]

A process of revising WG's official language strategy began during 2010 and this eventually resulted in the publication of *A Living Language: A Language for Living* in 2012. In many ways, this strategy followed on from *Iaith Pawb*, particularly the types of interventions envisioned. However, the distinct difference was how general objectives and targets were presented in the 2012 strategy. First, statements professing a desire to create a truly bilingual Wales in which one could live life wholly in either English or Welsh had been removed and in their place were much vaguer declarations regarding a desire 'to see the Welsh language thriving in Wales'.[29] Secondly, the 2012 strategy did not set specific and measurable census-based targets akin to those included in *Iaith Pawb*. Rather, a set of more open-ended targets were established, including an increase in the number of people who both speak and use the language; an increase in opportunities for people to use Welsh; an increase in people's awareness of the value of Welsh; and the strengthening of the position of the Welsh language at community level.[30] At first glance, the decision to be less definitive on key objectives and targets weakened the strategy in comparison to its predecessor. Nevertheless, it all depends on how and why targets are set. As mentioned above, the 2003 targets – particularly the 5 per cent increase in Welsh speakers – were primarily statements of political ambition and were not based on detailed analysis of the available demographic and sociolinguistic evidence.[31] Moreover, as Williams reminds us, preparing long-term language promotion strategies is a highly speculative endeavour and as a result more open-ended statements may actually 'suit the vagaries of the situation and the dynamics of policy implementation where even medium-term trajectories are hard to guarantee as social fact'.[32]

By the time that WG launched its third and most recent national language strategy, *Cymraeg 2050*, numerical targets were back on the agenda. *Cymraeg 2050* is widely regarded as the most ambitious of the national language strategies published to date, primarily due to the eye-catching headline target: to reach 1 million Welsh speakers in Wales by 2050. In terms of its general structure, the strategy document opens with a declaration of WG's general vision:

The year 2050: The Welsh language is thriving, the numbers of speakers has reached a million, and it is used in every aspect of life. Among those who do not speak Welsh there is goodwill and a sense of ownership towards the language and a recognition by all of its contribution to the culture, society and economy of Wales.[33]

Based on this declaration, the strategy identifies a series of areas or themes that will require attention to achieve the desired vision by 2050. These are: i) increasing the number of Welsh speakers; ii) increasing the use of Welsh; and iii) creating favourable conditions – infrastructure and context.[34] The rest of the document focuses, in turn, on each of these themes and outlines 'targets' and 'aims' that specify areas of planned activity (see Table 8.1).

Unsurprisingly, much of the public debate surrounding the strategy focused on the target to increase the numbers of Welsh speakers to 1 million by 2050. On the one hand, some welcomed the political ambition demonstrated by the government in adopting such a target but warned that it needed to be matched with careful implementation and sufficient resources. On the other hand, others warned of the danger that an iconic target focused solely on increasing the absolute numbers of Welsh speakers could potentially distract attention and resources away from the equally important task of promoting greater use of the language across different socio-spatial domains. Moreover, some questioned the wisdom of adopting a target that was not informed by 'scientific' evidence or analysis, and expressed concern that language planning in Wales seemed increasingly to be matter of 'political positioning' rather than 'strategic long-term planning' or 'as wish fulfilment for language activists'.[35]

More recently, detailed analysis of the events that influenced *Cymraeg 2050* highlighted the non-linear and multi-stranded nature of the process. While work on drafting the strategy began during 2015, the 1 million speakers target only came onto the agenda quite late in the day.[36] Campaigning by Cymdeithas yr Iaith Gymraeg in 2016 had prompted Labour to publish an election manifesto that stated that its goal was 'to see one million people speaking the Welsh language'.[37] This wholly unexpected development prompted a radical rethink and resulted in a very different strategy from that originally envisaged. While such an approach may not meet the 'scientific' or 'strategic' planning norms

Table 8.1: Summary of strategic themes, targets and aims included in *Cymraeg 2050* [38]

Strategic themes	Increase the number of Welsh speakers	Increase the use of Welsh	Create favourable conditions – infrastructure and context
Targets	The number of Welsh speakers to reach 1 million by 2050	The percentage of the population that speak Welsh daily and can speak more than just a few words of Welsh to increase from 10 per cent (in 2013–15) to 20 per cent by 2050	
Aims	**Language transmission in the family:** expand support for families to transmit the language in the home **The early years:** expand Welsh-medium provision in the early years as an access point for Welsh-medium education **Statutory education:** create a statutory education system that increases the number of confident Welsh speakers **Post-compulsory education:** develop post-compulsory education provision which increases rates of progression and better supports the development of Welsh-language skills **The education workforce, resources and qualifications:** plan in order to increase the education and training workforce which can teach through the medium of Welsh	**The workplace:** increase the use of Welsh within the workplace across all sectors **Services:** increase the range of services offered to Welsh speakers, and an increase in use of Welsh-language services **Social use of Welsh:** embed positive language-use practices supported by formal and informal opportunities to use Welsh socially	**Community and economy:** support the socio-economic infrastructure of Welsh-speaking communities **Culture and media:** ensure that the Welsh language is safeguarded as an integral part of our contemporary culture **Wales and the wider world:** ensure that the Welsh language is an integral part of our efforts to enhance Wales's relationship with the wider world **Digital technology:** ensure that the Welsh language is at the heart of innovation in digital technology **Linguistic infrastructure:** ensure the continued development of Welsh-language infrastructure (dictionaries, terminology; the translation profession) **Language planning:** embed language planning and promotion nationally, regionally and locally

called for by certain commentators, many involved in the process of formulating *Cymraeg 2050*, as well as more recent efforts to implement the strategy, have drawn attention to the symbolic significance of the 1 million speakers target and its potential as a political tool that can instigate a response among reluctant policy actors in a way that more modest and incremental targets would not.[39] Indeed, language policy development is always an intensely political activity in which positioning and symbolism can play an important role alongside elements such as knowledge and expertise.

Strategic planning for Welsh-medium education
Alongside the general policy objectives established by different national language strategies, since 2010 important steps have been taken to expand the provision of Welsh-medium education. During this period, important initiatives have been undertaken right across the education sector, from the pre-school sector, through to the post-16 and higher-education sectors, where the establishment of the Coleg Cymraeg Cenedlaethol in 2011 was a key milestone. However, here we focus specifically on reforms introduced to strengthen the process of planning statutory Welsh-medium provision.

The first step was the publication of the first ever national Welsh-medium education strategy by the Labour-Plaid 'One Wales' Government.[40] This was seen as important, given criticism of WG's education department for not contributing in a sufficiently detailed manner to earlier language policy work.[41] Moreover, the strategy was seen as significant in signalling a new willingness by WG to set a clear direction for the development of Welsh-medium education, including clearer expectations on local education authorities. Despite the growth in Welsh-medium education since the early 1970s, criticisms highlighted the largely ad hoc and unstructured nature of the process, with local councils often inconsistent in how they responded to parental demand, and national government being too unwilling to provide clear leadership and strategic direction.[42] The new strategy sought to respond by setting a series of quite challenging targets that would require proactive work by both WG and local authorities in order 'to respond in a planned way to the growing demand for Welsh-medium education' and thus to enable 'an increase in the number of people of all ages and backgrounds who are fluent in Welsh'.[43]

The main instrument introduced to drive the desired increase in Welsh-medium provision was the requirement that each local authority produce a Welsh in Education Strategic Plan (WESP), operational from April 2012. The process of preparation was placed on a statutory footing following the passing of the School Standards and Organisation (Wales) Act 2013 with each WESP to be submitted for approval by WG Ministers, and plans expected to set out the local authority's proposals on how it will improve the provision of Welsh-medium education and their targets over the lifetime of the plan.

Over the past decade the WESPs process has been subject to sustained criticism by a series of stakeholders. A systematic review of the 2010–15 Welsh-medium education strategy concluded that, while placing the plans on a statutory basis had improved Welsh-medium education planning insofar as local authorities were now expected to work within a formal and structured process, there were serious questions regarding the 'quality' of the plans and the 'effectiveness' of local implementation.[44] Similar concerns were expressed in reviews of the WESPs system conducted by the National Assembly's Children, Young People and Education Committee and by Estyn.[45] The Committee's report observed that 'many of those stakeholders are disappointed by the lack of impact WESPs have had in practice. For them, the story of WESPs so far is one of a missed opportunity. More worryingly, there are growing concerns they are not fit for purpose.'[46]

These arguments were reinforced further by the conclusions of a 'rapid review' of the WESPs in 2017. The report emphasised the added political impetus to address the weaknesses of the WESPs given that WG's *Cymraeg 2050* strategy and its 1 million speakers target had established a general language policy objective far beyond what was envisaged when the WESPs were originally conceived.[47] Moreover, meeting such a target called for a wholesale transformation of the Welsh-medium education sector. For example, the trajectory prepared by WG, which outlined how the 1 million speakers target could be met by 2050, noted that the proportion of all learners in Welsh-medium education would need to increase from 22 per cent in 2017 to 30 per cent in 2031, and then increase again to 40 per cent by 2050.[48]

The outcome was a revised set of statutory regulations and guidelines relating to the preparation of WESPs that came into force in 2020. One of the significant reforms was the shift from 3-year cycles to longer

10-year plans, reflecting the calls for the WESP process to encourage more strategic forward planning. More importantly, however, the new regulations instructed local authorities to 'move away from a system of planning on the basis of measuring demand for Welsh-medium education', and towards an approach to 'systematically and proactively' expand the Welsh-medium sector.[49] This important change responded to a growing consensus that the earlier system had not led to the expected growth in provision, in part due to a 'reluctance' and 'slowness' to conduct the appropriate assessments and to respond effectively.[50] The revised regulations therefore shift towards an expectation that local authorities proactively 'create more Welsh-medium places'.[51] This work will be based on targets to be agreed with WG and that align with the overall national targets for Welsh-medium education from the 1 million speakers trajectory set out in *Cymraeg 2050*.

Overall, during the period since 2010, a mix of policy and legislation has been used to address previous weaknesses in the planning of Welsh-medium education by seeking to develop a national policy framework that is underpinned by consistent forward planning at local authority level. As noted, this process was given added impetus following the adoption of *Cymraeg 2050* and its 1 million speakers target, and this, in turn, has prompted recent revisions to the WESPs process. This latter move is significant: government in Wales has moved to a policy position that explicitly states that Welsh-medium education should be proactively expanded. It marks a further development in the post-devolution trend of WG being increasingly overt in its stated long-term language policy objectives.

Legislation and the institutional structure of language policy governance
Since 2010, there have been substantial reforms to the institutional structure of language policy governance in Wales. Central to this was the decision to abolish the Welsh Language Board as an arm's-length agency and to draw many of its functions into WG's civil service. This reform was originally proposed as early as 2004, and finally initiated with the passing of the Welsh Language (Wales) Measure (2011).[52]

The 2011 Measure was another language policy development instigated by the 'One Wales' Labour and Plaid Cymru coalition agreement. It responded to the fact that the preceding years had seen increasing calls for the earlier 1993 Act to be revised.[53] Given the evolution of the Welsh

devolution arrangements since 1999, this latest language law was passed
in Wales, rather than at Westminster. The 2011 Measure included a series
of significant provisions, both of a symbolic and procedural nature. First,
in contrast to earlier language legislation, the 2011 Measure included
a clause confirming Welsh as an official language in Wales. The 2011
Measure also introduced a new system of 'language standards' to replace
the previous language schemes in operation since 1993. The wisdom of
such a reform generated much debate.[54] The third key reform instigated
by the 2011 Measure was the aforementioned abolition of the Welsh
Language Board and the establishment of the post of a Welsh Language
Commissioner. Consequently, certain functions were transferred to the
Commissioner's office, primarily those relating to the regulation of Welsh
language service provision by public bodies in Wales. A number of the
board's other functions were transferred to WG, including responsibility for some of the broader promotional initiatives in areas such as
intergenerational transmission and social or informal language use that
the Board had instigated over the years. Reflecting on these changes,
Williams observes that 'the central political and policy message that one
can derive from the passage of the measure is that the Welsh Government
has taken unto itself the prime responsibility for Welsh language promotion'.[55] At the same time, the clause that sets out the principal aim for
the Welsh Language Commissioner states that it should endeavour 'to
promote and facilitate the use of the Welsh language'.[56] Consequently, a
certain degree of uncertainty arose regarding how the new institutional
regime would allow for an appropriate balance between the general task
of promoting the Welsh language (that is, creating more speakers and
encouraging wider social use) and the more technical task of regulating
compliance with statutory requirements stemming from the new system
of language standards. Indeed, certain voices within the Welsh language
policy community began to argue forcefully that the new structure for
language policy governance meant that too much emphasis was being
placed on maintaining the public status of the language and the regulation of bilingual public services at the expense of broader promotional
work, particularly that which focused on facilitating greater social use
of the language.[57]

 While such arguments were not shared by all stakeholders, they
provided the context that eventually led to WG publishing a White
Paper, *Striking the Right Balance*. It proposed to legislate in order to

make further reforms to the institutional arrangements that under-pinned Welsh language policy, including abolishing the role of the Welsh Language Commissioner and establishing a new arm's-length agency, a Welsh Language Commission that would combine responsibility for promotional and regulatory functions relating to the Welsh language. The White Paper argued that such reforms would 'strike the right balance between promoting and facilitating the use of the Welsh language and regulating Welsh language duties'.[58] Moreover, in a fore-word to the document Alun Davies, then minister with responsibility for the Welsh language, argued that there was a need 'to give new energy to our efforts to promote the language' through focusing less on rights and regulation and more on efforts to 'foster people's desire and confidence to learn and to use the language as a normal part of everyday life'.[59]

The White Paper's proposals generated a substantial amount of public discussion and sparked disagreement among different sections of the Welsh language policy community.[60] Citing this lack of consensus, in 2019, Eluned Morgan, who had by then assumed ministerial responsibility for the Welsh language, announced that the government would not proceed to introduce new legislation. An alternative way forward was announced which entailed establishing a dedicated language-planning unit – branded as *Prosiect 2050* – within WG's Welsh language division. This unit is tasked with driving forward the language-planning work required in order to make meaningful progress in relation to the long-term targets set out in the *Cymraeg 2050* strategy. In terms of policy responsibilities, the new *Prosiect 2050* unit leads on:

- language transmission and language use within families
- use of Welsh by children and young people
- use of Welsh by businesses
- Welsh and new technology
- spatial and area-based language planning: e.g. advising local language promotion strategies, or the linguistic impact of planning or economic development
- institutional language-planning capacity and awareness of bilingualism, particularly across the public sector
- marketing and communication
- research, data and evaluation.[61]

Significantly, an internal discussion paper prepared by civil servants that set out the arguments in favour of the new internal unit explicitly questioned the charge that post-2011 language-policy structures had placed too much of an emphasis on rights and regulation at the expense of language planning aimed at promoting greater social use of Welsh:

> Some stakeholders ... said that a missing component of the current policy delivery landscape were sufficient interventions rooted in language planning principles to address the fundamental issue of the use of the language in society ...Welsh Government activity to support the Welsh language following the abolition of the Welsh Language Board has also been rooted in [general language planning principles]. The *Cymraeg 2050* strategy was developed within a conceptual framework rooted in the social science of language planning – and the three themes of the *Cymraeg 2050* strategy ... demonstrate the interconnected nature of the various elements of language planning.[62]

A further issue raised in the paper is that recent experience suggests that a major benefit of a structure in which WG itself leads on language planning, as opposed to an external arm's-length body, is that it becomes easier 'to work across government departments to ensure that language planning principles are included in other policy areas'.[63] This is a significant point given that realising the objectives set out in the *Cymraeg 2050* strategy requires more effective mainstreaming of linguistic considerations across a range of WG departments. Moreover, this claim chimes with research findings that highlighted how movement in and around WG's offices in Cathays Park was a key factor in language policy development and facilitates efforts to engage policy makers from other policy divisions and areas of government activity.[64]

Unpacking the Welsh approach to language promotion

Back in 2014, Williams argued that 'in terms of policy and legislation, one can justifiably argue that the Welsh language has never been in such an advantageous position'.[65] Given the developments discussed in the previous section, this argument carries even more force six years later. Indeed, that it is now possible to credibly advance such an argument underlines the extent to which there has been a fundamental change in public policy-making with regard to the Welsh language over the past forty years or so. The largely piecemeal, ad hoc and often reluctant approach of earlier periods has given way to an increasingly systematic and planned approach in which an emphasis is placed on national-level strategies and explicit long-term objectives.

As suggested earlier, the origins of this process can be traced back to the mid-1990s and the early work of the Welsh Language Board. Yet this leads to the question of what, if anything, has been the distinctive impact of devolution on the evolution of Welsh language policy? As part of a broader discussion, Mitchell emphasises the importance of considering the long-term historical context when assessing the significance of the devolution reforms introduced across the UK at the end of the 1990s, given the 'path dependent' and ongoing influence of earlier periods.[66] This is particularly pertinent to policy relating to the Welsh language. In certain respects, the impact of devolution has not been fundamental and the general trajectory of language policy from the 1990s into the post-devolution period is marked by a degree of continuity, as opposed to a radical change in direction. Although highly significant in their own right, the trio of national language strategies adopted by WG since 2003 have in several respects been successors to the earlier strategies formulated by the Board before 1999. First, each strategy can be seen as a further step in the process of formalising a coordinated national approach to language revitalisation. Secondly, and more importantly, while each strategy has varied in terms of the targets that they have set, there has been relatively little deviation from the broad areas identified in the Board's original strategy as being those where policy interventions should be prioritised. In sum, it can be questioned whether the establishment of devolved government in itself represented a 'critical juncture' as far as the substance of language policy in Wales is concerned.[67]

The impact of devolution has been most pronounced with regard to the institutional structure underpinning language policy governance in Wales. Since 1999, devolved government has come to play an increasingly 'hands-on' role. Initially, this occurred in partnership with the Welsh Language Board. Yet the dissolution of the Welsh Language Board and the establishment of the post of the Welsh Language Commissioner meant that responsibility for coordinating and funding work focused on promoting greater acquisition and social use of the Welsh language was transferred to WG. Consequently, since 2012, competence over Welsh language promotion lies within government and with the establishment of the *Prosiect 2050* unit the language-planning capacity of government itself is set to increase further. Yet, even here, it is possible to view post-devolution developments as a continuation of a longer-term trend, rather than representing a wholly novel development. Indeed, from a longer-term perspective, the recent move by WG to shoulder more direct responsibility for language policy is a further step in the growing institutionalisation that has been a feature of language promotion in Wales since the early 1980s, when the Welsh Office began to accept the argument that maintaining the language would require a measure of proactive planning on the part of public officials.[68] Indeed, looking back even further, one of the overarching characteristics of Welsh revitalisation efforts since the 1960s has been a gradual shift in the locus of activity away from the language community working through different civil society organisations and towards public officials located within different governmental or quasi-governmental institutions.

To a large extent, this trajectory in which public officials have assumed a more prominent role in language promotion work reflects the trend amongst regional and minority languages across several parts of Europe.[69] For example, since the re-establishment of autonomy in Catalonia following the fall of the Franco regime in the 1970s, the Generalitat's Directorate-General for Language Policy has been central in language revitalisation, driving different legislative and policy initiatives in favour of Catalan.[70] By today, this powerful policy unit attached to the regional government's Ministry of Culture also encompasses a Sub-Directorate-General for Language Policy, which, in turn, oversees the work of a series of 'service' sections, including the Service for Fostering the Use of Catalan, the Language Resources Service, which aims to disseminate resources that facilitate acquisition and use of Catalan, and the Information, Dissemination and Studies Service, charged with informing public bodies and civil society groups about new activities or developments.[71] Similarly, in the Basque Autonomous Community, regional autonomy led to the establishment in the early 1980s of the Sub-Ministry for Language Policy, attached to the Basque Government's Ministry of Culture, and also the Basque language unit within the Ministry of Education, both of which have come to play leading roles in the coordination of policies aimed at promoting greater acquisition and use of Basque.[72]

Indeed, in the European context, the main exception to the trend described above (and operating within a state context) is Ireland. As Walsh argues, the evolution of Irish language policy since roughly the 1960s is characterised by an increasing withdrawal on the part of government.[73] This shift has been manifested by a series of developments, including the general narrowing of the overall objectives of the government's language revitalisation effort; the consistent emasculation of the central government department with responsibility for the Irish language and the Gaeltacht; and the increasing tendency for government to refrain from properly implementing and monitoring key language policy strategies. Indeed, as Ó Ceallaigh demonstrates, this process of governmental withdrawal gathered pace significantly since the 2008 economic crisis, as evidenced by disproportionate cuts in public funding experienced by governmental agencies associated with the promotion of Irish or with the Gaeltacht. During this more recent period the Gaeltacht Act of 2012 was introduced, which transferred operational responsibility for language promotion across Gaeltacht communities away from the executive governmental agency, Údarás na Gaeltachta, to a series of voluntary community committees.[74]

Nevertheless, while the influence of governmental actors over efforts to support and promote regional and minority languages has clearly increased in several parts of Europe, care is needed when considering how to describe the governance model that has emerged. In the Welsh context, at least, it is too simplistic to characterise the process as a simple shift from ground-up, grass-roots planning towards a rigid and hierarchical top-down approach. First, reflecting other policy areas, while WG ministers and civil servants play a more 'hands-on' role, the formulation and implementation of policy interventions aimed at promoting the Welsh language features a significant degree of engagement between a wide range of different actors. For example, recent analysis of the different organisations involved in policy work linked to pursuing the general objectives of *Cymraeg 2050* distinguished between eight different categories of actors: i) governments; ii) commissioners and regulators; iii) non-departmental public bodies; iv) publicly funded arm's-length bodies; v) public service broadcasters; vi) civil society organisations; vii) private sector companies; viii) private individuals (see Table 8.2 for examples of each type of actor).

Table 8.2: Who are the main actors involved in the governance of language revitalisation in Wales? [75]

Government	Commissioners and regulators	Non-departmental public bodies	Public service broadcasters	Publicly funded arms'-length bodies	Civil society/Third sector	Private sector	Key individuals
Welsh Government	Welsh Language Commissioner	Arts Council of Wales	BBC Cymru Wales (UK Gov.)	National Centre for Learning Welsh	Mudiad Meithrin	Contract research companies (e.g. Arad, OB3)	Individual members of governmental forums or advisory groups
Local government	Ofcom (UK Gov.)	National Library of Wales	S4C (UK Gov.)	Coleg Cymraeg Cenedlaethol	Mentrau Iaith Cymru	Iaith	Academic researchers
UK Government		National Museum Wales		Books Council of Wales	Individual Mentrau Iaith (× 23)		
					Urdd Gobaith Cymru		
					Yr Eisteddfod Genedlaethol		
					Cymdeithas Eisteddfodau Cymru		
					Merched y Wawr		
					Clybiau Ffermwyr Ifainc Cymru		
					Papurau Bro		

Note: Where UK Gov. is noted in brackets this denotes that the organisation is formally answerable to the UK Government rather than the Welsh Government.

Secondly, the practices of engagement between WG and these quasi-governmental and non-governmental actors resemble what is described in the public administration literature as 'interactive governance'. While traditional government-centred governance relies on the top-down imposition of authority, interactive governance assumes that the policy process features more open, direct and regular engagement between governmental and a range of other quasi-governmental or non-governmental actors, and a greater emphasis on the notion of governing through 'partnership'.[76] Several examples of practices associated with this model of governance are evident when considering the current approach to language revitalisation in Wales. These include WG's use of grant schemes, such as the Welsh Language Promotion Grant to enable civil society partners to undertake activities that align with and that seek to further the *Cymraeg 2050* strategy's key objectives; the use of formal contracts to enable government to co-deliver programmes such as *Cymraeg i Blant* and *Cymraeg Byd Busnes* with external organisations; and use of stakeholder forums such as the Promotion Group, or advisory boards such as the Welsh Language Partnership Council and the Welsh Technology Board that facilitate consultation on the part of government.

Overall, engagement and interaction with non-governmental actors through these channels focuses primarily on policy implementation. Nevertheless, there are instances where the influence of non-governmental actors is also evident at the formulation and adoption stage of the policy cycle. These include examples where policy formulation work was channelled through a multilateral process that saw government engaged in discussions with several stakeholders, as in the cases of the new policy on Welsh language transmission and the Welsh Technology Action Plan. In contrast, formulating and deciding on the policy targets that guide current activity in the area of Welsh-medium early years' provision resulted from bilateral negotiation between the government and Mudiad Meithrin.[77] In these cases, it appears that the development of policy objectives or programmes linked to the *Cymraeg 2050* strategy resulted from a relatively 'collaborative' process that featured 'two-way communication and influence'.[78]

Yet, while such examples point to a relatively interactive mode of governing in relation to language revitalisation in Wales, the type of relationships that emerge are not ones where government and its external partners stand on an equal footing. Moreover, the evidence does not suggest that non-governmental partners have the capacity to confront or dictate to government, as implied by 'network' perspectives on contemporary governance.[79] Indeed, recent research notes that an unwillingness amongst some key stakeholders to scrutinise or to question either the work of certain partners or the current role played by WG itself in relation to certain projects is a distinct weakness in the 'Welsh language sector'.[80] Consequently, WG retains both the ability and authority to set the terms of its interactions with external partners as part of its language promotion work. Based on its control of key financial resources, grants or contracts, as well as relevant organisational and administrative resources, government can decide when its interaction with other actors will be more directive and top-down and when it will allow its partners more autonomy to shape how they implement projects or activities linked to furthering the objectives of the *Cymraeg 2050* strategy. All of this seems to confirm Torfing, Peters and Sørensen's contention that even where there is an apparent embrace of more interactive modes of governing, 'public actors generally remain important for defining and shaping the arenas within which interactions may be occurring'.[81] More broadly, it suggests that any interaction with non-governmental actors as part of the governance of language revitalisation in Wales must be seen as taking place 'in the shadow of hierarchical authority'.[82]

A further point to acknowledge is the increasing relevance of multi-level governance to Welsh language policy-making. While regional-level actors and organisations may have been responsible for overseeing most of the recent activity in support of European regional or minority languages, these regional-level initiatives have rarely been conceived and developed in isolation. Rather, as in many other policy domains, initiatives seeking to promote such languages are likely to be influenced by political and institutional factors across several territorial levels – local, regional, state, continental and global. For example, even when the regional level has formal competence for policy relating to regional or minority languages, state-level structures (such as constitutional or financial arrangements) are still likely to exert significant influence on language revitalisation initiatives. Continental- or global-level structures are also potentially significant, with current evidence suggesting that their influence may be greater if a state adopts a more restrictive stance in relation to its regional or minority language(s).[83]

In the Welsh context these multi-level dynamics have influenced the formulation and implementation of language policy post-devolution in various ways.[84] For example, the earlier discussion on efforts to strengthen the process of planning statutory Welsh-medium education highlighted the significance of interactions between regional and local levels. Moreover, the influence of interactions between the regional and state levels were evident in the process of drafting the 2011 Welsh Language Measure. Despite the declared intention to introduce legislation that sought to accord official status to the Welsh language and establish a series of legal language rights, the nature of the UK's unwritten constitutional order meant that realising such objectives proved to be challenging and contentious. More broadly, institutional structures at the continental and global levels have also influenced policy-making with regard to the Welsh language post-devolution, particularly by informing the work of WG civil servants. For example, officials report that regular engagement with other European partners through networks such as the Network to Promote Linguistic Diversity (NPLD) has been an important source of policy ideas, including during the process of developing the *Cymraeg 2050* strategy.[85] Of course, looking to the future, it will be necessary to assess how the Brexit process impacts the ability of European-level structures to inform or influence the work of language policy practitioners across the UK. At this point, it is clear that the option of seeking to exploit mainstream EU-funding programmes to support projects that support language maintenance and revitalisation will no longer be possible. Yet, significantly, it does not seem that the important engagement, collaboration and information-sharing opportunities afforded by networks such as the NPLD will be closed off completely.

Conclusion: ambition, implementation and impact

Overall, looking back over the first two decades of devolution, one central theme evident in most national-level policy activity linked to the Welsh language is the effort to gradually build a strategic framework to effectively coordinate different aspects of language promotion. This chapter has reviewed some of the main elements in this framework, specifically the series of national language strategies adopted by WG; the reforms introduced in the area of Welsh-medium education; as well as the new language legislation and associated reforms to the institutional structure of language policy governance. It has also identified and assessed key features of the governance model that underpins the current Welsh approach to language revitalisation.

As part of the discussion, it was emphasised that it is important not to fall into the trap of assuming that devolution represented some kind of year zero for policy activity in relation to the Welsh language. Indeed, both in terms of the substance of policy initiatives and the nature of the actors that lead on their implementation, it was demonstrated that the trajectory of language policy between the pre- and post-devolution periods is marked by a certain degree of continuity, as opposed to a radical change in direction. At the same time, there is a clear sense that the consistency of policy activity associated with the language has increased over recent years. Moreover, it appears that the post-devolution period has seen a step change in the general sense of ambition conveyed in key policy publications. For example, we have become familiar with WG statements that profess an ambition to create 'a truly bilingual Wales', or a Wales where the 'Welsh language is thriving' and where 'it is used in every aspect of life'.[86] This transformative rhetoric has also been accompanied by a willingness to adopt language policy strategies that are centred on ever more ambitious targets. This began with the publication of *Iaith Pawb* in 2003. Yet all previous targets were dwarfed by the scale of those adopted in 2017 as part of the formulation of the most recent national language strategy, *Cymraeg 2050*. Along with the widely quoted headline target of 1 million Welsh speakers by 2050, this strategy commits WG to seeking a 10 per cent increase in levels of daily language use and roughly 20 per cent increase in the number of learners in Welsh-medium education.

However, this invites the obvious question of what has been the effect of all the post-devolution policy activity? To what extent has ambition been matched by effective implementation and impact? Examining some of the general statistical evidence that informs our understanding of the Welsh language's overall level of vitality, it must be concluded that the rhetoric of official strategies has not yet resulted in a fundamental transformation in the fortunes of the language. On the whole, when we consider the position of the Welsh language today, a series of different demographic, social, economic and linguistic trends tend to pull in different directions. These trends have been increasingly evident since about the 1970s and they have remained relatively consistent post-devolution. They include:

- a consistent decline in the language's traditional demographic strength across parts of west Wales, with striking signs of growth across many parts of the east and south-east
- a consistent growth in the numbers of Welsh speakers among younger age groups that does not seem to be maintained over time and reflected in later increases among older age groups
- a significant growth in the numbers that learn the language as a second language through education, and a parallel decline in the numbers that learn the language at home
- a decline in the numbers that claim that they speak the language daily, and an increase in the numbers that speak it occasionally
- a striking increase in the numbers that claim basic competence in the language, alongside a decline in the numbers that claim fluency.[87]

To a degree, it is unfair to point to some of these trends as clear evidence of policy failure on the part of WG and other relevant actors. Rather, it reminds us that seeking to arrest and reverse societal language shift is a particularly complex undertaking – or a particularly 'wicked problem' – especially in the contemporary period as societies have become increasingly individualistic, mobile and characterised by more networked forms of social interaction. Nevertheless, in the Welsh context, the continuing evidence of language shift has been accompanied by an acknowledgement that the development of a national-level language policy framework over the past two decades has not led to consistent and effective implementation of key strategies or initiatives. A series of independent evaluations have highlighted structural difficulties in ensuring effective coordination of efforts in support of the Welsh language across different policy departments, agencies, local authorities and third-sector organisations.[88] As discussed earlier, a particular challenge with regard to Welsh-medium education has been that of securing a meaningful commitment to national policy objectives among local authorities. However, arguably of more significance have been the difficulties in ensuring that national language policy objectives are integrated, understood and accepted right across WG. While every national language strategy since *Iaith Pawb* has included bold statements regarding the need to mainstream language policy considerations across all governmental departments and agencies, meaningful progress on this front has been very limited.[89] Of course, this is not a challenge that is unique to language policy. Yet in this context, general obstacles to effective mainstreaming are compounded by the fact that the Welsh Language Division represents a small and relatively low-status unit within WG and consequently is constrained in its ability to influence much larger and politically influential departments.

In summary, therefore, effective cross-government implementation is a key challenge for language policy in Wales post-devolution. As demonstrated, events over the past two decades have led to the formation of a relatively developed national-level policy framework in support of the Welsh language. However, effective coordination and implementation of language promotion initiatives across different policy departments, as well as across relevant agencies, local authorities and third-sector organisations, remains elusive. It is arguably this issue, as opposed to further rounds of legislative or institutional reform, that members of the Welsh language policy community should prioritise over the coming years.

Notes

1. Colin H. Williams, 'Language policy, territorialism and regional autonomy', in B. Spolsky (ed.), *The Cambridge Handbook of Language Policy* (Cambridge: Cambridge University Press, 2012), pp. 174–202.
2. See, for example, Marion Löffler, 'The Welsh Language Movement in the First Half of the Twentieth Century: An Exercise in Quiet Revolutions', in Geraint H. Jenkins and Mari A. Williams (eds), *Let's Do Our Best for the Ancient Tongue: The Welsh Language in the Twentieth Century* (Cardiff: University of Wales Press, 2000), pp. 173–205.
3. Rhys Jones and Huw Lewis, *New Geographies of Language: Language Culture and Politics in Wales* (Basingstoke: Palgrave Macmillan, 2019).
4. Elin Royles and Huw Lewis, 'Language policy in multi-level systems: a historical institutionalist analysis', *British Journal of Politics and International Relations*, 21/4 (2019), 709–27.
5. Gwilym Prys Davies, 'The legal status of the Welsh language in the twentieth century', in Geraint H. Jenkins and Mari A. Williams (eds), *Let's Do Our Best for the Ancient Tongue: The Welsh Language in the Twentieth Century* (Cardiff: University of Wales Press, 2000), pp. 207–38.
6. Robert Smith, 'Broadcasting and the Welsh Language', in Geraint H. Jenkins and Mari A. Williams (eds), *Let's Do Our Best for the Ancient Tongue: The Welsh Language in the Twentieth Century* (Cardiff: University of Wales Press, 2000); Colin Baker and Meirion Prys Jones, 'Welsh Language Education: A Strategy

for Revitalization', in Colin H. Williams (ed.), *Language Revitalization: Policy and Planning in Wales* (Cardiff: University of Wales Press, 2000), pp. 116–37.

7. See Andrew Edwards, Duncan Tanner and Patrick Carlin, 'The Conservative Governments and the Development of Welsh Language Policy in the 1980s and 1990s', *The Historical Journal*, 54 (2011), 529–51; Colin H. Williams, 'The Lighting Veil: Language Revitalization in Wales', *Review of Research in Education*, 38 (2014), 242–72.

8. Davies, 'The legal status of the Welsh language in the twentieth century', pp. 245–6; Edwards, Tanner and Carlin, 'The Conservative Governments and the Development of Welsh Language Policy in the 1980s and 1990s', 546–50.

9. Davies, 'The legal status of the Welsh language in the twentieth century', pp. 247–8.

10. Colin H. Williams, 'Cultural Rights and Democratization: Legislative Devolution and the Enactment of the Official Status of Welsh in Wales', in I. Urrutia, J. P. Massia and X. Irujo (eds), *Cultural Rights and Democratisation* (Clermont-Ferrand: Institut Universitaire Varenne, 2015), p. 185.

11. Williams, 'Cultural Rights and Democratization', p. 187.

12. Welsh Language Act 1993, Part 1, Section 3.

13. Williams, 'The Lighting Veil', 246; see also Welsh Language Board, *Strategic Review* (Cardiff: Welsh Language Board, 1995); Welsh Language Board, *A Strategy for the Welsh Language* (Cardiff: Welsh Language Board, 1996).

14. Williams, 'Cultural Rights and Democratization', p. 185.

15. Government of Wales Act 1998, Part II, Clause 32.

16. Colin H. Williams, *Official Language Strategies in a Comparative Perspective* (Cardiff: Network for the Promotion of Linguistic Diversity, 2013).

17. WAG, *Iaith Pawb: A National Action Plan for a Bilingual Wales* (Cardiff: WAG, 2003).

18. Colin H. Williams, '*Iaith Pawb*: The Doctrine of Plenary Inclusion', *Contemporary Wales*, 19 (2004), 2.

19. Given the corporate body structure of the National Assembly during the early years of devolution these types of plenary motions would commit the assembly as a whole to pursuing particular objectives.

20. Cynog Dafis, *Mab y Pregethwr* (Talybont: Y Lolfa, 2005), pp. 236 and 261–2.

21. Williams, '*Iaith Pawb*', 2.

22. WAG, *Iaith Pawb*, p. 1.

23. WAG, *Iaith Pawb*, p. 11.

24. Williams, '*Iaith Pawb*', 10, 14.

25. Williams, '*Iaith Pawb*', 10.

26. Williams, '*Iaith Pawb*', 16–19.

27. Williams, '*Iaith Pawb*', 6.

28. Williams, *Official Language Strategies in a Comparative Perspective*, p. 22.

29. WG, *A Living Language: A Language for Living – Welsh Language Strategy 2012–2017* (Cardiff: WG, 2012), p. 14.

30. WG, *A Living Language: A Language for Living*, p. 14.

31. Colin H. Williams, *Minority Language Promotion, Protection and Regulation: The Mask of Piety* (Basingstoke: Palgrave Macmillan, 2013), p. 203.
32. Williams, *Official Language Strategies in a Comparative Perspective*, p. 70.
33. WG, *Cymraeg 2050: A Million Welsh Speakers* (Cardiff: WG, 2017), p. 4.
34. WG, *Cymraeg 2050*, p. 4.
35. Diarmait Mac Giolla Chríost, 'Tilting at Linguistic Windmills – A Million Welsh Speakers', *Democratic Audit* (2017). Available at: *democraticaudit. com/2017/07/20/tilting-at-linguistic-windmills-a-million-Welsh-speakers* (accessed 5 May 2021); C. H. Williams, 'Policy Review: Wake me up in 2050! Formulating language policy in Wales', *Languages, Society and Policy* (2017), 6.
36. Jones and Lewis, *New Geographies of Language*, pp. 268–73.
37. Welsh Labour, *Together for Wales: Welsh Labour Manifesto 2016* (Cardiff: Welsh Labour, 2016), p. 20.
38. WG, *Cymraeg 2050*.
39. Jones and Lewis, *New Geographies of Language*.
40. WG, *Welsh-Medium Education Strategy* (Cardiff: WG, 2010).
41. Williams, '*Iaith Pawb*', 16.
42. Williams, 'The Lighting Veil', 254.
43. WG, *Welsh-Medium Education Strategy*, p. 4.
44. WG, *Evaluation of the Welsh-medium education strategy: final report* (Cardiff: WG, 2016).
45. NAW (2015) Children, Young People and Education Committee, *Inquiry into Welsh in Education Strategic Plans (WESPs)*; Estyn, *Local authority Welsh in Education Strategic Plans* (Cardiff: Estyn, 2016).
46. NAW, *Inquiry into Welsh in Education Strategic Plans*, p. 7.
47. WG, *Rapid review of the Welsh in Education Strategic Plans – 2017–20* (Cardiff: WG, 2017), p. 3.
48. WG, *Cymraeg 2050*, pp. 24–5.
49. WG, *Guidance on Welsh in Education Strategic Plans* (Cardiff: WG, 2019), p. 7.
50. WG, *Evaluation of the Welsh-medium education strategy*.
51. WG, *Guidance on Welsh in Education Strategic Plans*, p. 7.
52. See Colin H. Williams, 'Foras na Gaeilge and Bwrdd yr Iaith Gymraeg: Yoked but not yet shackled', *Irish Studies Review*, 17 (2009), 55–88.
53. Colin H. Williams, 'Deddfwriaeth Newydd a'r Gymraeg', *Contemporary Wales*, 19 (2007), 217–33.
54. See Diarmait Mac-Giolla Chríost, *The Welsh Language Commissioner in Context: Roles, Methods and Relationships* (Cardiff: University of Wales Press, 2016).
55. Williams, 'Cultural Rights and Democratization', p. 193.
56. Welsh Language Measure 2011, Clause 3.1; emphasis added.
57. See, for example, Dyfodol i'r Iaith, 'Angen newid cyfeiriad gyda'r Gymraeg: lansio manifesto Dyfodol i'r Iaith' (2015). Available at: *www.dyfodol.net/2015/09/29/ angen-newid-cyfeiriad-gydar-gymraeg-lansio-maniffesto-dyfodol-ir-iaith* (accessed 18 March 2021).
58. WG, *White Paper Consultation Document – Striking the Right Balance: Proposals for a Welsh Language Bill* (Cardiff: WG, 2017).

59. WG, *White Paper Consultation Document*, p. 2.
60. See, for example, Cymdeithas yr Iaith Gymraeg, 'Ymgynghori ar y Papur Gwyn: ymateb Cymdeithas yr Iaith Gymraeg' (Aberystwyth, 2017), and Dyfodol i'r Iaith, 'Ymateb Dyfodol i ymgynghoriad Papur Gwyn Bil y Gymraeg' (Carmarthen, 2017).
61. WG, *Discussion paper: arrangements for implementing Cymraeg 2050* (Cardiff: WG, 2019).
62. WG, *Discussion paper*, p. 5.
63. WG, *Discussion paper*, p. 6.
64. Jones and Lewis, *New Geographies of Language*, pp. 286–7.
65. Williams, 'The Lighting Veil', 257.
66. James Mitchell, *Devolution in the UK* (Manchester: Manchester University Press, 2009).
67. Royles and Lewis, *Language policy in multi-level systems*.
68. Edwards, Tanner and Carlin, 'The Conservative governments and the Development of Welsh Language Policy in the 1980s and 1990s'.
69. Williams, 'Language policy, territorialism and regional autonomy'.
70. Williams, *Minority Language Promotion, Protection and Regulation*.
71. Williams, 'Language policy, territorialism and regional autonomy', p. 200.
72. Williams, *Official Language Strategies in a Comparative Perspective*.
73. John Walsh, 'The governance of Irish in the neoliberal age: the retreat of the state under the guise of partnership', in Huw Lewis and Wilson McLeod (eds), *Language Revitalisation and Social Transformation* (Basingstoke: Palgrave Macmillan, 2021).
74. Ben Ó Ceallaigh, 'Neoliberal Globalisation and Language Minoritisation: Lessons from Ireland 2008–18', *Language and Communication*, 75 (2020) 103–16.
75. Huw Lewis, 'The governance of language revitalisation: the case of Wales', in Huw Lewis and Wilson McLeod (eds), *Language Revitalisation and Social Transformation* (Basingstoke: Palgrave Macmillan, 2021).
76. Jacob Torfing, Guy Peters and Eva Sørensen, *Interactive Governance: Advancing the Paradigm Interactive Governance: Advancing the Paradigm* (Oxford: Oxford University Press, 2019).
77. Lewis, 'The governance of language revitalisation'.
78. Chris Ansell and Alison Gash, 'Collaborative Governance in Theory and Practice', *Journal of Public Administration and Practice*, 18/4 (2008), 546.
79. Rod A. W. Rhodes, *Understanding Governance* (Buckingham: Open University Press, 1997); Rod A. W. Rhodes, 'Understanding Governance: Ten Years On', *Organisational Studies*, 28/8 (2007), 1243–64.
80. Lewis, 'The governance of language revitalisation'.
81. Torfing, Peters and Sørensen, *Interactive Governance*, p. 3.
82. F. W. Scharpf, 'Games real actors could play: positive and negative coordination in embedded negotiations', *Journal of Theoretical Politics*, 6 (2014), 41.
83. Huw Lewis and Elin Royles, 'Governance, complexity and multi-level LPP', in (Abingdon: Routledge, forthcoming).

84. Royles and Lewis, 'Language policy in multi-level systems'.
85. Jones and Lewis, *New Geographies of Language*, p. 278.
86. WAG, *Iaith Pawb*, p. 1; WG, *A Living Language*, p. 14; WG, *Cymraeg 2050*, p. 4.
87. See Welsh Language Commissioner, *The Position of the Welsh Language 2012–2015* (Cardiff: Welsh Language Commissioner, 2016).
88. Williams, 'Policy Review', p. 4.
89. Williams, '*Iaith Pawb*'; Williams, 'Deddfwriaeth Newydd a'r Gymraeg'; Williams, 'Policy Review'.

Select bibliography

Jenkins, Geraint H. and Mari A. Williams (eds), *Let's Do Our Best for the Ancient Tongue: The Welsh Language in the Twentieth Century* (Cardiff: University of Wales Press, 2000).

Jones, Rhys and Huw Lewis, *New Geographies of Language: Language Culture and Politics in Wales* (Basingstoke: Palgrave Macmillan, 2019).

Lewis, Huw and Wilson McLeod (eds), *Language Revitalisation and Social Transformation* (Basingstoke: Palgrave Macmillan, 2021).

Mac Giolla Chríost, Diarmait, *The Welsh Language Commissioner in Context: Roles, Methods and Relationships* (Cardiff: University of Wales Press, 2016).

Royles, Elin and Huw Lewis, 'Language policy in multi-level systems: a historical institutionalist analysis', *British Journal of Politics and International Relations*, 21/4 (2019), 709–27.

WAG, *Iaith Pawb: A National Action Plan for a Bilingual Wales* (Cardiff: WAG, 2003).

Welsh Language Commissioner, *The Position of the Welsh Language 2012–2015* (Cardiff: Welsh Language Commissioner, 2016). Available at: *https://www.welshlanguagecommissioner.wales/media/edji51vn/adroddiad-5-mlynedd-2012-15.pdf* (accessed 27 January 2022).

WG, *A Living Language: A Language for Living – Welsh Language Strategy 2012–2017* (Cardiff: WG, 2012).

WG, *Cymraeg 2050: A Million Welsh Speakers* (Cardiff: WG, 2017).

Williams, Colin H. (ed.), *Language Revitalization: Policy and Planning in Wales* (Cardiff: University of Wales Press, 2000).

Williams, Colin H., '*Iaith Pawb*: The Doctrine of Plenary Inclusion', *Contemporary Wales*, 17 (2004), 1–27.

Williams, Colin H., 'Deddfwriaeth Newydd a'r Gymraeg', *Contemporary Wales*, 19 (2007), 217–33.

Williams, Colin H., 'Language policy, territorialism and regional autonomy', in B. Spolsky (ed.), *The Cambridge Handbook of Language Policy* (Cambridge: Cambridge University Press, 2012).

Williams, Colin H., *Minority Language Promotion, Protection and Regulation: The Mask of Piety* (Basingstoke: Palgrave Macmillan, 2013).

Williams, Colin H., *Official Language Strategies in a Comparative Perspective* (Cardiff: Network for the Promotion of Linguistic Diversity, 2013).

9

WALES AND THE WORLD

Geraint Talfan Davies

The narrative of Wales's relationship with the rest of the world over the first two decades of the twenty-first century has many strands. They do not all tell the same story. The narrative, after all, must be more than a story of government policy and action, for the impulse to reach out is not confined to government. There are many other actors – businesses, universities, cultural organisations and the third sector. Their motivations and effectiveness often differ and all are impacted in different ways by events beyond Wales. It cannot, either, be a straightforward story of steady progress since the global backdrop across those first two decades of the century changed markedly and dramatically: the first a decade beginning with optimism and growth, the second a decade of economic austerity and often frustrated ambition, culminating in an apocalyptic combination of Brexit and a global pandemic.

Commentary on devolution in Wales during those first two decades tends to fall into one of two categories: patient understanding of the growth of a fragile new institution born out of the narrow and nervous public endorsement of the 1997 referendum, and less patient frustration that the institution's achievements have not been sufficiently impressive and radical, and have not realised the highest hopes that were placed in it by its proponents. Both commentary strands have more than a grain of truth in them, although the first view can tend to complacency and the second to excessive excoriation.

When considering Wales's relationship with the wider world the first thing to remember is that 1999 was not 'ground zero'. There is history to contend with: Welsh emigration to America and other parts of the world across four centuries, Welsh domination of the international coal trade,

Welsh involvement in empire, volunteer participation in the Spanish Civil War, the international connections of radicalism and pacifism and the cultural openness of working-class industrial Wales. Some of that is captured in buildings, some in institutions: Cardiff's Coal Exchange building and, in the city's monumental civic centre, the Temple of Peace, a legacy of the Welsh League of Nations Union set up as the First World War ended. (The unsung Welsh Centre for International Affairs is still housed there.) In more recent times the Welsh Development Agency (WDA) and the Wales Tourist Board, both important channels to the rest of the world, were established in the 1970s and had successful reputations before being absorbed into the Welsh Government (WG) apparatus in 2004. The WDA, in particular, 'recognised the value of culture to its work and positioned eminent companies in the ambassadorial roles'.[1]

Culture

It is appropriate, therefore, to begin not with government but with culture. Given the rough and tumble of a globalised world it is understandable that small countries are often impelled to shout loudly, 'We are here'. In part that can be a simple craving for recognition in a world where, for the most part, bigger players monopolise the stage. But in the cultural sphere, where all arts have an international dimension or context, there are many reasons to strive for international engagement: the *developmental* impulse – to explore wider horizons and different cultures, to make connections in terms of ideas and people, to test one's artistic output on a wider stage or to broaden the market for one's own work; and the *representational* impulse – to carry a flag for one's organisation or country, either as a simple matter of inner pride or in support of other governmental purposes, often economic. (In 2021, which flag, it seems, is now a matter of controversy.) Much international cultural activity by Welsh artists and organisations results from a mix of all these impulses and does not necessarily wait on government – and yet there is a consensus that even now the frequency and depth of international engagement is insufficient.

As already suggested, these impulses in the cultural field pre-date the advent of democratic devolution in 1999. The Llangollen International Eisteddfod was born in the immediate aftermath of the Second World War in 1946. The BBC's Cardiff Singer of the World competition was launched in 1983, as a biennial event, consequent on the opening of a much-needed modern concert hall in Cardiff – St David's Hall. The Hay Literature Festival was launched in 1988, quickly becoming the largest literary festival in the UK. The WDA often underpinned its overseas business campaigns in the 1980s and 1990s with cultural backup from Welsh National Opera or the BBC National Orchestra of Wales – whether in Amsterdam, Barcelona, Stuttgart, Tokyo or New York, where glitzy royal endorsement has sometimes ramped up the profile. Wales Arts International (WAI) – a partnership between the Arts Council of Wales (ACW) and the British Council – emerged formally in 1997 as the culmination of ad hoc collaboration between the two bodies, begun some years earlier at the behest of Welsh Office ministers anxious for some cultural underpinning for their new involvement with the 'four motor regions' of Europe.

As the last decade of the century progressed, culture undoubtedly benefitted from an extraordinary coincidence of events, including the political: the transformation of the Wales Committee of the Arts Council of Great Britain into ACW, by Royal Charter in 1994; the election of the Blair government and the devolution referendum (albeit narrowly won) in 1997; the creation of the British-Irish Council with direct Scottish and Welsh participation, the opening of Irish consulates in Cardiff and Edinburgh, and a European Summit meeting in Cardiff, all in 1998; the inauguration of the National Assembly in 1999, and the massive cultural investments made as part of the millennium celebrations.

This multi-faceted fillip to cultural policy and activity was sorely needed, not only because the arts were emerging very slowly from a prolonged period of financial austerity, but also because ACW was itself struggling to emerge from a period of internal turmoil. The Assembly's initial foray into the culture field came from its Post-16 Education and Training Committee that initially held the culture brief. This was chaired by Cynog Dafis AM and was much influenced by a paper from Professor Dai Smith that cited Raymond Williams's phrase 'Culture is ordinary', and also gave the Committee a title for its own report – *A Culture in Common*.

That report in 2000 laid great emphasis on the cultural role and obligations of the new Assembly, including an international cultural dimension. Under the heading 'National Ambition – International Reach', the Committee recommended the strengthening of WAI and that 'publicly funded arts and cultural organisations should be encouraged to make a contribution to realising its objectives year by year'. It urged that 'all the National Assembly's cultural agencies should work in tandem to create a thriving environment for international cultural and economic impact'.[2] The Committee tilled the ground and erected a valuable signpost, but action had to await the formation of the Labour-Liberal Democrat coalition the following year. The new Minister for Culture, Sport and the Welsh Language, the Liberal Democrat Jenny Randerson, set in train the creation of a much fuller cultural strategy that was published in 2002 under the title *Creative Future*.[3]

Creative Future opened by setting out a public policy context that referenced both the European Union and the cultural promotion objectives of UNESCO, while the international section of the strategy adopted the same title as the corresponding section of *A Culture in Common*: 'National Ambition – International Reach'. This laid stress on the importance of two-way traffic – not only the encouragement of a Welsh cultural presence overseas, but also the hosting of international events in Wales. For the latter it was able to point to the Rugby World Cup that had taken place in the new Millennium Stadium in autumn 1999. The Committee did not see all this as mere flag-waving. 'Our international engagement must also be more than opportunistic public relations,' it said. 'We recognise the important contribution people in Wales can make to European and international cultural networks and organisations – and the contribution they too can make to Wales. We must deepen that engagement.'[4]

It would be true to say that not all of this extensive agenda for international engagement was borne out in subsequent years, at least not in the systematic way envisaged in the *Creative Future* strategy. In part this was because the Labour-Liberal Democrat coalition came to an abrupt end at the 2003 Assembly elections, and Randerson was succeeded in the culture post in the new government by Labour's Alun Pugh. But whatever the priorities of successive culture ministers, there was no escaping the logic that international cultural aspirations would be part and parcel of an emboldened national mindset.

In 2003, within a year of the publication of *Creative Future*, Wales and Scotland were staging their first exhibitions at the Venice Biennale, despite the fevered objections of the British Council's senior visual arts officer responsible for the British pavilion. In official terms they were not allowed to have their own 'pavilions' as the Biennale authorities bizarrely deemed that they were not 'sentient nations'. In fact, the Biennale's decision had much more to do with Chinese objections to non-state participants (perhaps a harbinger of disturbing events two decades later). However, the objection was circumvented by creating a new category of 'extra' participants that eventually allowed sixteen 'non-state' actors to take part.

On the visual arts front, the artist William Wilkins – an indefatigable Welsh cultural entrepreneur – had, since early 1999, been piecing together support for another visual arts initiative, the Artes Mundi International Arts prize. The aim was 'to bring exceptional and challenging international art to Wales and to generate unique opportunities for individuals and local communities to engage creatively with the urgent issues of our time'. That last social purpose was deliberate, chiming with the Welsh political and cultural milieu and helpfully distinguishing it from the much hyped Turner Prize that many thought was going through a sterile phase. Partnering with National Museum Wales, the first award was made at a ceremony at the museum in Cardiff in 2004. It went to a Chinese-American, Xu Bing, with a poignantly simple artwork created from dust from the site of New York's Twin Towers, destroyed in the 9/11 attack. This first award was covered extensively in newspapers in New York, Paris and Tokyo, although comprehensively ignored by the London press.

It is worth noting that the Artes Mundi initiative – a biennial event – was avowedly internationalist not only in its title and the range of participating artists, but also in its curatorial direction and the peopling of the selection and judging processes. Its first director was Tessa Jackson, who had been the director of Bristol's Arnolfini gallery. The two selectors for the first event were drawn from Dublin and Tokyo, and the final judges from the USA, the Netherlands, Japan and Wales, together with the editor of the *Journal of Contemporary African Art*. The winners of the first eight prizes came from China, Finland, India, Israel, Mexico, USA, UK and Thailand.

Not to be outdone, in 2006 the Welsh literary world launched the Dylan Thomas Prize for writers under forty. This had been steered by the Swansea-based historian, Peter Stead. Unsurprisingly, this engaged primarily with the English-speaking world, with four of the eleven winners to date coming from the USA. Taken together with Artes Mundi and the

BBC's Cardiff Singer competition, this new initiative gave Wales three international events of quality in music, literature and the visual arts. Two other international events of similar significance were attracted to Wales in 2013: WOMEX, the world music expo regarded as 'the number one networking platform for the world music industry', had long been a target for WAI, while the third quadrennial World Stage Design exhibition was staged at the Royal Welsh College of Music and Drama whose stage design department had worked assiduously to bring it about. The two previous exhibitions had been staged in Toronto and Seoul.

The remarkable feature of this activity is how much of it has been driven primarily by individual cultural organisations rather than by government, although government often takes sensible advantage of it. The larger organisations – Welsh National Opera, the BBC National Orchestra of Wales, National Museum Wales, NoFitState Circus, National Dance Company of Wales, Hay Festival and its offshoots – operate in a historically internationalised context. Hay Festival founder, Peter Florence, another quintessential cultural entrepreneur, argues that this has to be driven by the artists. 'Listen to the entrepreneurs, take your hand off the brake, find where the energy is. It always comes from the bottom.'[5]

This is most apparent in the world of opera where artistic and financial imperatives intrinsic to the form have always driven a high degree of international co-production. Successive Welsh National Opera music directors have come from Italy, Germany and the Czech Republic – respectively Carlo Rizzi, Lothar Koenigs and Tomas Hanus. Of its artistic directors in the last two decades, Anthony Freud has since run Houston Grand Opera and is currently at Lyric Opera of Chicago; John Fisher came to the company from New York Metropolitan opera; David Pountney had directed at every major opera house in Europe; while the current incumbent, Aidan Lang, returned after five years as general director of Seattle opera. For many years the principal conductor of the BBC National Orchestra of Wales was Japanese – Tadaaki Otaka – and he remains its conductor laureate. Its principal guest conductor is a Chinese-American, Xian Zhang. Until Brexit intervened four of the six resident artistic collaborators at NoFitState Circus were from other European countries – Italy, Austria, Hungary and Ireland – while the company's business model up to the outbreak of COVID-19 was highly dependent on European touring. Again, pre-Brexit, four of the nine contracted dancers with the National Dance Company of Wales were from other EU countries – Italy, Spain, France and Belgium.

International work is not confined to the large companies. Hijinx Theatre, based at the Wales Millennium Centre, is a relatively small company dedicated to working with actors with learning disabilities, although it prefers to be judged as a theatre company rather than as an expression of disability arts. The company has been in existence since 1981, and in recent years its business plan has relied on an increasing volume of international work. A single production, *Meet Fred*, produced in association with Blind Summit, became a touring success, giving 235 performances in 117 cities in twenty countries and three continents, with the work translated into a dozen languages. These countries include the USA, China, Germany, Italy, Spain and Vietnam. Meanwhile its biennial Unity Festival brings some sixty artists working in the same field to Wales from around the world. It also increasingly engaged with the film and television industry, having become the UK's largest casting platform dedicated to neurodivergent actors.

Unlike the performing arts, and especially the large ensembles, the literary world inevitably operates at a more individual level, and yet its reach can be considerable and its influence perhaps even more pervasive in its field. The Hay Festival, having firmly established its credentials within the UK, has developed a considerable international outreach, with versions of the festival in Spain, Denmark, the Netherlands and Croatia within the EU, and the United Arab Emirates, Nigeria, Kenya, India, Bangladesh and almost every country in South America beyond. Funded via ACW, the annual Hay Festival-Creative Wales International Fellowship has enabled Welsh writers to attend 'festival editions' around the world. Among the ten recipients to date have been Mererid Hopwood, Owen Sheers, Jon Gower and Alys Conran. Hay has also been a principal collaborator in UNESCO's publishing project, World Book Capital. The festival's founder, Peter Florence, claims three principal benefits: exchange and fellowship between writers, the experiences brought back to Wales and thirdly, and most importantly, a recognition that Welsh culture can be global – and in either of our languages. If anything, he claims, the Welsh language has gained more benefit because 'a minority language finds community in so many places'.

That experience is surely familiar to the less well-known Mercator Institute at Aberystwyth University that was created in 1988, following an initiative of the European Parliament to recognise regional and minority languages. It has hosted the Literature Across Frontiers programme ever since and was awarded successive competitive contracts under EU culture programmes that spread across the two decades of devolution, the latest being from 2014 until 2020. Literature Across Frontiers, operating under Mercator's umbrella, was designed to promote literary exchange and translation and has operated across seventy-six countries, including all the EU countries. One of its projects, Literary Europe Live, worked across sixteen European literary festivals and venues to develop writers, translators and literary curators. At the time of writing its future hangs in the balance.

The creation of the National Poet of Wales role by Literature Wales in 2005 was another initiative that had both a domestic purpose and an increasingly international one. The first post-holder, Gwyneth Lewis, was followed by Gwyn Thomas, Gillian Clarke and the current holder, Ifor ap Glyn. All had been deeply engaged with developments in Welsh society. Ifor ap Glyn has been a particularly active cultural ambassador, writing two poems for the UEFA Champions League Final held in Cardiff in 2017, as well as taking his work to festival stages in Poland, China, Lithuania, Germany, Ireland, Cameroon and the USA.

There is little doubt that the 2016 referendum was the prelude to a dark night of the soul for Welsh cultural organisations. The sector had long been the loudest supporter of our continued membership of the EU, sharing with the education sector a profound belief in a world where ideas and innovation, good practice and people could travel without let or hindrance. This belief was never confined to the relationship with Europe, but Europe was central to it on grounds of proximity and history, with common roots in Christian, Jewish and even Muslim traditions and transcending any linguistic or political differences. In June 2016, at the height of the referendum campaign, one hundred representatives of the cultural community in Wales – authors, poets, actors, musicians, curators and film-makers – were signatories to a declaration in support of the Remain cause.

In the days immediately after the referendum, every artist and organisation had to reassess assumptions that had been unquestioned for five decades, many holding onto the hope that the eventual break would be a soft one involving retained membership of the EU's Creative Europe programmes. That was not to be, with the eventual EU-UK agreement at the end of 2020 breaking with all these programmes, save for the Horizon higher education research programme. The sectoral angst was genuine and principled rather than only a cry of woe at the loss of funding, since the arts in Wales had actually made less use of EU funding streams than either England or Scotland. This may have been because, on average, arts organisations in Wales tend to be much smaller than equivalent organisations in the other two countries and thus more likely to find the EU's admittedly heavy bureaucratic processes, as well as the requirement in many instances to find 50 per cent match funding, more daunting. Neither did we help ourselves in Wales by locating our Creative Europe Desk within the creative industries section of WG's European Funding Office, rather than – as in Scotland and Northern Ireland – within their respective arts councils. One result, surely unintended, was that the European Commission's own Creative Europe website did not list a culture desk for Wales. Sometimes, these apparently minor administrative details matter. Of greater significance at home was the use of the European Regional Development Fund (ERDF) to support the development of Wales's arts infrastructure, with major EU capital contributions towards, for instance, the development of Galeri at Caernarfon, Theatr Mwldan at Cardigan and two university arts centres at Aberystwyth and Bangor.

However, immediately after the UK referendum a survey of Welsh arts organisations by ACW and WAI identified three key concerns: first, that there would be a general perception in the rest of Europe that we would be less open to collaboration; secondly, that there would be new obstacles to operating across borders and, thirdly, that restrictions on freedom of movement would impose prohibitive costs and burdensome administration. By now it is clear that it is the last of these that poses the most formidable obstacle to continued engagement. It affects both small and large organisations.

Rhian Davies, director of the Gregynog Festival in mid Wales, who has always pursued a determinedly international approach to programming, has seen the 'evaporation of pitches' from EU countries. Alison Woods, executive director at NoFitState Circus, says all-important European bookings are down by 30 per cent and that she is 'still looking for a sustainable business model'. The task ahead is to avoid the combination of two events, COVID-19 and Brexit – either of which could have posed existential challenges on their own – from being cataclysmic.

Artists and arts organisation need time and resources to recover their financial, artistic and psychological equilibrium – a task that will not be accomplished overnight.

The roll-call of international cultural activity by Welsh organisations across the two decades is substantial, impressive even for a country that does not have the size, profile or budget of Scotland or the autonomous clout of an independent country like Ireland. Yet it is still possible to raise questions about whether more could have been done by our own cultural actors, and with greater collective impact, had government been readier to acknowledge this scale of activity and more active in promoting synergies and coordination. Some naturally look to the collaboration between the British Council and WAI. This would seem to be a natural fit: ACW being fully aware and connected to all sectors on the ground in Wales, and the British Council providing what ACW's own director, Nick Capaldi, readily praises as 'the unqualified success of the British Council's in-country staff and specialists'.[6] Nevertheless, it seems that the partnership between the two bodies is currently a looser collaboration than the joint venture that was envisaged at the outset. In its early years WAI was housed in the British Council's Cardiff office, whereas by now it is fully ensconced in ACW's offices. Since the arts specialisation at the Welsh level lies more within ACW than with the British Council, this seems an appropriate arrangement. The director of WAI sits on the British Council's Wales advisory committee, but there is no jointly managed budget. On the plus side, despite years of financial austerity WAI's total staffing level has been sustained and it currently has two senior officers – one for Europe and the other for the rest of the world. However, its limited resources mean that it is primarily focused on delivery, often having to respond to WG priorities but with insufficient time and capacity to ponder future strategies.

On the British Council side, although strategic intent inevitably derives from its central board and officers, the arrangements for accommodating the interests of Scotland, Wales and Northern Ireland are less than adequate – out-dated even a quarter of a century ago. The chairs of the advisory committees for each of the three countries take it in turns to sit on the council's main board, with rotating two-year terms. Quite apart from the fact that this musical-chairs arrangement misunderstands comprehensively the nature of the devolution settlement, as well as implying an indifference to the cultural distinctiveness of each country, it also stands in marked contrast to the permanent representation of the three countries on the boards of the BBC, Ofcom, Visit Britain and many other public bodies. It remains to be seen whether what should be a straightforward internal reform will fall foul of any post-Brexit centralising pressures. The decentralisation of some core functions to its offices outside London is an answer to a different question.

That said, in recent years British Council Wales can take credit for commissioning two substantial reports on Wales's international presence in the fields of the arts and sport, and a third dealing more generally with its 'soft power'.[7] In many ways that on sport had the easiest task, since sport is the most high-profile civilian flag carrier that we have. That is true in many senses. First, unlike the arts, it is an area of human activity in which, for historical reasons, the British 'sub-state actors' have preserved a national status in an international context. This has given Wales, as well as Scotland and Northern Ireland, an unusual degree of international exposure that has been jealously guarded, to the extent of resisting participation in a British football team at the Olympic Games. Secondly, sport is a field where there is an infrastructure, or rather super-structure, of autonomous international organisations in many of which Wales can participate in its own right – such as UEFA, FIFA and World Rugby. Thirdly, the global reach of sporting contests in almost all sports, whether in terms of real spectators or global television viewing, creates a degree of visibility that is unmatched in any other field.

In her foreword to the report on sport, Professor Laura McAllister, a former chair of Sport Wales and a Welsh women's football international, called for 'more muscular sports diplomacy initiatives', regretting that 'for too long matching sporting objectives with Welsh social, trade or foreign policy objectives has been a story of missed opportunities and under-investment in time, effort and resource'. The report urged Wales to become 'the first sub-state government in the world to have a specific sports diplomacy strategy'.

The earlier report on the Welsh international presence in the arts was undertaken by Yvette Vaughan-Jones, the first director of WAI and, at that time, the director of Visiting Arts, a UK-wide organisation. Her report argued that while ambitious international cultural events gave Wales the benefit of increased profile and provided much needed continuity, more could be achieved, particularly at the more granular level. While acknowledging that culturally Wales could mount a 'first class offer', the report called for more investment in showcasing expertise and skills, nurturing curators and creative producers and networking them into the global ecosystem. It argued that a proliferation of international agencies in Wales caused confusion and duplication, and called for a 'cross-agency sharing of strategies and investment into a sustained Welsh presence at international showcasing events' to counteract 'the perceived invisibility of Wales'.[8] It also called for the development of showcasing platforms in Wales by building on current successes such as Artes Mundi and the Hay Festival in collaboration with the wider cultural sector.

Given the meatiness of these three reports, it is surprising that there is no evidence that their recommendations have been considered jointly and systematically by all the parties that need to be involved – including WG – although their broad thrust was echoed in ACW's own response to WG's consultation on a new international strategy during 2019. In particular, ACW sought 'a menu of developmental services' to build the cultural sector's capacity to engage and participate internationally.[9] This would have included a funding pot to assist people to travel, business support to ensure individual and organisations are prepared and equipped to exploit established markets, and support for involvement in trade fairs, showcases, festivals and biennales, including showcase events here in Wales. For instance, Wales still lacks an annual multi-dimensional international showcase such as the Edinburgh Festival, although the Wales Millennium Centre's embryonic Festival of the Voice has the potential to develop in that direction.

Surprisingly, neither the British Council report nor ACW's response – two well-informed reports representing the two lead organisations in the field – were referenced in WG's final published international strategy, published just before the first COVID-19 lockdown began. It acknowledged that cultural diplomacy 'would be key to raising our international profile' and that 'we must continue to use our cultural relations and diplomacy to full effect; from showcasing our world-class cultural organisations overseas to welcoming international organisations to Wales' – but it did not set out any specific actions to reflect that key importance.[10] All in all the place of culture in the document was disappointing – especially the lack of specificity – given the scale of cultural assets that Wales can deploy, their track record and the scope for improvement in those areas that might not be deemed market ready.

The subsequent WG action plan[11] – one of a suite of five[12] – was sensitive enough to admit reservations about the use of the words 'soft power' in the cultural context, expressing a preference for the phrase 'public diplomacy', because 'relationships are built on trust and mutual benefit for the purposes of contributing towards local and global good, not power dynamics'.[13] The short-term actions listed for 2020–1 – including the development of a 'global virtual St David's Day' – must have been in train when the action plan was being assembled, with a further eight actions listed for the medium term, 2022–5. Those listed medium-term actions are worthy objectives, although few match the request of the Senedd's External Affairs Committee, during the consultation, for 'a detailed suite of measurable targets and action points'.[14]

One of the actions planned for 2022–5 raises an important point about governmental process. It says that WG will 'undertake a mapping exercise over the next five years to better align and amplify Wales' presence internationally with our partners'.[15] Mapping exercises can mean many things, but since this is raised in the context of a document on cultural diplomacy, one has to ask whether the proposed mapping will be confined to that sector. Much greater value would be gained from also mapping the crossovers between culture, business and the environment, etc. Forward mapping also raises the delicate issue of the lack of comprehensive auditing of past activity, so that we know whether we are raising or lowering the benchmarks.

In short, on the cultural front, over the last two decades and more, the cultural sector in Wales has demonstrated time and again its capacity to deliver at the highest international quality level. Many parts of the sector accomplish that overseas in as many places as they can afford, both for their own artistic development, profile and commercial reasons, but, when asked, also as willing players in 'Team Wales'. The current gaps are in past auditing, forward planning and coordination, and in identifying synergies between cultural and economic objectives early enough to ensure the biggest bang for the Welsh buck, although conscious that the two do not always align. There is also the issue of broader institutional connections through participation in a range of cultural networks in Europe under the auspices of both the EU, where continuing observer status can be negotiated, and the Council of Europe, of which we are still members. There is a job of work to be done in identifying and prioritising the most appropriate European and wider international networks with which to engage as there are, in fact, rather too many, given our own scarce human resources.

Addressing these issues is going to be especially pertinent in the coming years if the scale of international activity by Welsh artists and organisations is not to decline, for the threats at home and abroad are many and profound: the consequences of the COVID-19 pandemic in terms of both travel constraints and the finances of arts organisations and governments everywhere, and other travel restrictions and increased costs resulting from the UK's departure from the EU, not to mention increased international instability.

Higher education

Education is another expression of culture, and one that has played a substantial part in Welsh history and, not infrequently, in Welsh myth-making. The travelling schools of Griffith Jones, Llanddowror, the image of the University of Wales built on the pennies of the poor or that of the bright scholarship boy escaping poverty in Emlyn Williams's 1938 play *The Corn is Green*, burnish our self-image as a people with an exceptionally high regard for learning. The record in the last half century has been more sobering, as we face a world that is ever more competitive and where measures and rankings have become increasingly international. There is no other sector in our institutional life that is now more subject to comparative measures than higher education, with lists of UK and world rankings published and heavily publicised regularly. Some of the more astute institutions even claim to have learnt how to game the system. These are the uncomfortable signs of the marketisation of higher education. And it is a global market – increasingly so as the constraints of a COVID-19 pandemic have accelerated online delivery, raising questions about current practice and obliterating familiar parish boundaries in ways that also have fundamental financial implications.

These developments are bound to present particular challenges to Welsh universities, in part because of their relatively small size. In terms of income in 2018–19 Wales's largest university, Cardiff, was only eighteenth amongst the top twenty UK universities. It was also the only Welsh university to be ranked in the top 200 in the 2021 world university rankings. It came in at 191.[16] I hasten to add that this is not a full measure of the manifold achievements of Cardiff or of the other Welsh universities, or of their value to society at large, be that Wales or the UK or, indeed, the world. But it does underscore the scale of the challenges that they all face, redoubling the imperative for collaboration, both domestic and international.

As if the combination of COVID-19 lockdowns and online technology were not challenge enough, the coincidence of both with our departure from the EU is destabilising in other ways: disrupting the habit and depth of collaboration and connections built up over half a century, a wholly beneficial development that I have described elsewhere as an evolving single market of the mind that had deeper implications than simple transactional arrangements.[17] Brexit's potential for harm lay not only in the disruption of income streams but also in disrupting the free flow of people – in this case both staff and students.

Money issues tend to take priority. The sector had been much relieved when it became clear that the Trade and Cooperation Agreement between the UK and EU would retain UK access to the EU's Horizon Research Programme, but was then greatly alarmed when, in the March budget, it appeared that the Treasury had made no provision for funding the costs of that participation. Twelve days after the budget, Professor Julia Buckingham, President of Universities UK, wrote to the prime minister, on behalf of a sector deeply concerned that this would amount to 'an effective cut of something in excess of £1bn … equivalent to cutting 18,000 full-time academic research posts'.[18] This, she argued, would also lead to a further reduction of £1.6bn in private research and development investment. She was also concerned at a further £120m shortfall as a result of cuts to the Overseas Development Assistance budget.

In short order the government appeared to rectify the problem, promising an additional £250m for 2021–2, but there was no clarity as regards the long term, a dimension that is so basic to fundamental research. It was also silent on the Overseas Development Assistance cut. Although Universities UK welcomed the announcement, others feared budgetary sleight of hand. The government repeated its budget pledge to raise total research and development (R&D) spending to 2.4 per cent of GDP by 2027. Universities UK expressed gratitude.

However, evaluation of that last government commitment requires some context. In 2016 Digital Science recorded that the last time UK R&D spending stood at 2.4 per cent of GDP was in 1981. By 2016 it had dropped to 1.3 per cent, considerably less than Germany's 2.85 per cent.[19] But even this had to be seen alongside the very poor performance of British business which, Digital Science claimed, was investing a massive 80 per cent less in R&D than German businesses, putting UK private sector investment at below the averages for the EU-15 and EU-28 nations.

These doubts about the true scale of the UK Government's commitment to the Horizon programme must be deeply concerning for both WG and our higher education institutions, because Welsh universities have been disproportionately dependent on EU research funding. In 2016, across the UK, EU funding represented roughly one-third of the competitive funding distributed by the UK's Research Councils and Innovate UK. For Welsh universities it was two-thirds. This is a mirror image of the relationship with the private sector which accounts for 45 per cent of total R&D across the UK, but only 10 per cent in Wales – reflecting the structural shape of Welsh business with its preponderance of small firms.

That said, there was a real gain in international involvement across the first two decades of the century. For example, between 2000 and 2006 Cardiff University won eighty-four awards from the EU valued at c.£18m, but between 2007 and 2013 this rose to 168 awards valued at €71.7m. Of those 168 awards, 120 involved consortia of a minimum of three partners from at least three member states in areas such as health, physics and astronomy, ICT and energy. At Aberystwyth, between 2008–9 and 2013–14 the percentage of its research funding derived from the EU rose from 5.6 per cent to 16.5 per cent. But not all EU funding to universities came from the Horizon programme. For instance, up to 2017 Swansea University had received £113m from EU structural funds – £79m from the ERDF, £31m from the ESF and £3m from Interreg[20] – three funds from which the UK is now excluded.

Important though the funding quantum is, its real significance has always lain in the qualitative gains of international collaboration, the recruitment and exchange of research staff and the research itself. Although EU funding has represented only a minority share of total research funding for Welsh universities – around 16 per cent – it has been significant in sharpening the leading edge of research, aiding improvement in quality ratings during research assessment exercises, and establishing international benchmarks of success. What is yet to be seen is whether one little-noticed price of our continued involvement in the Horizon programme will be the relinquishing of a leadership role in many research projects because we are not fully within the EU fold.[21]

The availability of these international yardsticks also prompted initiatives to raise our game, albeit after a slow start. WG was slower to develop a science policy than the Scottish Government, Scotland appointing its first chief scientific officer in 2006, but Wales not doing so until 2010. In 2015 the Learned Society of Wales – another devolution by-product, that had been established only as late as 2010 – and the Leadership Foundation for Higher Education undertook a study of Wales's comparatively low research performance and concluded that the issue was not so much the quality of personnel but rather the sector's lack of overall capacity, insufficient scale and a concentration in less expensive areas of study.[22] The conclusion was that Wales was short of 621 staff, especially in key STEMM disciplines.[23]

This resulted in the creation of the Sêr Cymru programme in 2016, jointly funded by WG, the EU and the Welsh higher-education sector. By 2020 it had led to the creation of 150 posts, including twelve Sêr Cymru chairs who came from a wide range of disciplines – including nuclear engineering, advanced materials, solar energy, systems medicine and earth observation – and from a variety of places – universities in USA, Australia, Switzerland, Edinburgh, London and Sussex, and a number of independent research institutes. It is a cruel irony that our departure from the EU, a significant part-funder, may threaten the programme at a point when it is still too early to assess whether these appointments can bring about a sea change in the research performance of Welsh universities.

Whatever details remain to be discovered about the UK Government's true financial commitment to research in general (which, overall, seems considerable) and to the Horizon programme in particular (which seems more questionable), participation in the EU's Horizon programme is, at least, written into the Trade and Cooperation Agreement. The same cannot be said of the Erasmus programme that has long been the most imaginative mechanism for the internationalisation of educational opportunity, not only for those in higher education but also for young people in further education and in work. The Erasmus scheme was launched in 1987 following six years of piloting. It had been shaped by a Welshman, Hywel Ceri Jones, then a senior official with the European Commission, and by the turn of the century was a firmly embedded plank of EU policy and practice. A major expansion took place during the 2007–13 period, with a further increase during 2014–20, by which time it had expanded its scope to include vocational education and youth exchange schemes. By 2020 the cumulative total of participants had passed the 4 million mark, including 2 million students, 800,000 lecturers, teachers, trainers and youth workers, 650,000 in vocational education and training, and more than 500,000 young people. For the 2021–7 period the Erasmus budget was increased again to €26 billion, envisaging an increase in participation from 10 million to 14 million young people. In addition a sister strand – the European Solidarity Corps – was to command another €1 billion to enable 350,000 youth volunteers to take part in humanitarian and social projects.

The story of our participation in the Erasmus scheme, across the UK and in Wales, has been mixed, with numbers declining from a 10,133 high in 1997–8 to nearer 7,000 in 2005–6, then recovering steadily to nearer the 10,000 figure by 2017–18.[24] A further 8,172 students participated through work placements, while 29,797 students and work placements came to the UK from the other EU countries. By 2018 the UK was the sixth highest country in terms of participation by outward-going higher education students, with 9,993 students on study placements. But this was well behind Spain (34,276), Germany (33,282), Italy (30,876) and France (30,505). Even Turkey (13,131), not a member state, exceeded the UK figure. Student participation from Wales, too, had been well below its UK population share, but reached that 5 per cent benchmark in 2018, as did Northern Ireland with 3 per cent. England, at 73 per cent, was well below its 84 per cent population share, leaving Scotland, as the only UK country to massively outperform its 8 per cent population share, achieving a full 20 per cent of UK participations. In contrast, Wales appeared to be doing well in bids for Erasmus+ projects, achieving the highest success rate – 60.6 per cent – from its applications. But all was not as it seemed as Wales accounted for only 4 per cent of total UK bids, against Northern Ireland's 6.3 per cent and Scotland's 16.4 per cent.

Earlier discouraging data had prompted three 'EU funding ambassadors', in a report to WG, to urge greater involvement in Erasmus+ from the Welsh universities, recommending that the sector, including further education, should carry out a stocktake of its participation to provide 'a clearer all-Wales view of the strategic value of investment in internationalisation so as to enhance the attractiveness of Wales and Welsh universities on the world stage'.[25] The report was written in March 2016, only three months before the referendum on our membership of the EU, whose result threatened a dangerous hiatus in international engagement for both the university sector and other parts of Welsh society.

Despite much campaigning on the issue from civil society organisations and strong representation from the devolved administrations in Edinburgh and Cardiff, the UK Government chose to prioritise the Horizon research programme over other involvements, such as the Erasmus and Creative Europe programmes, in its negotiations with the EU. It could have chosen otherwise. It could have chosen participation in Erasmus as an 'associated third country'. It did not. We will, instead, hover outside as a 'non-associated third country', although this does, at least, preserve a future opportunity for a government of a different persuasion.

The UK's abandonment of the tried and tested Erasmus programme in favour of the rapidly cobbled 'Turing' alternative turns an old proverb on its head – not the abandonment of the bird in the hand for two in the bush, but the abandonment of the two in the hand for the one in the bush. The announcement of the Turing scheme on Christmas Eve 2020 had all the hallmarks of haste, taking some days to gain fuller definition and with its £100m funding in place only for its first year. It referred to the involvement of 'the best universities in the world', raising a question about the lack of a vocational element. It envisaged 35,000 placements ranging from two weeks to twelve months anywhere in the world. It was some weeks later that a 35,000 target figure was broken down into 20,000 for higher education, 10,000 for further education and 5,000 for schools. It also became clear that, unlike Erasmus, Turing would not involve any reciprocity. We would be sending students out from the UK, and not welcoming students and volunteers from other countries to experience this country and study here – a loss both to individuals and to our own institutions. Neither would there be an equivalent of Erasmus's funding strand for partnerships or collaborative projects.

The response from the universities was muted, caught between their enthusiasm for Erasmus and their concern, particularly in England, not to alienate the UK Government at a point when the COVID-19/Brexit combination was threatening their finances. The reaction from the Welsh and Scottish governments, on the other hand, had been unambiguous and a joint plea was made to the EU Commission for special arrangements. In part their hopes rested on the fact that, in the interest of eliminating the north-south border on the island of Ireland, Northern Ireland had been granted continued access to Erasmus under the UK-EU agreement. However, the EU Commission made it clear that membership of the Erasmus scheme for Wales and Scotland could be only on the basis of a UK commitment, leaving both countries with no option but to seek bilateral arrangements.

In March 2021 it was WG that stole a march on Edinburgh – at the time much distracted by the Alex Salmond/Nicola Sturgeon feud – by announcing its own Erasmus replacement scheme, specifically aimed at filling the gaps left by the Turing proposal. The contrast with Turing was stark. The new International Learning Exchange – that would be run by Cardiff University in partnership with the rest of the sector – would be a 6-year programme rather than Turing's single-year commitment, and a reciprocal arrangement rather than one-way traffic and with a strong emphasis on youth. The allocation of £65m over the 6-year period for the Welsh scheme compared favourably with the first-year allocation of £100m for Turing for the whole of the UK.

This Welsh initiative also chimed with Global Wales, a partnership between WG, the Higher Education Funding Council for Wales, Universities Wales and British Council Wales. This had been piloted between 2015 and 2018 and followed by Global Wales II with support from WG's EU transition fund. Its aim was to increase Wales's market share of international student recruitment, increase the number of international research partnerships and boost Wale's profile in key international markets. Initially, it identified three priority markets: the USA, India and Vietnam. Again reinforcing the two-way traffic principle, in 2021 Global Wales also offered twenty-four postgraduate scholarships, each worth £10,000, to study a masters programme in Wales. Importantly, this was on offer not only to applicants in the three priority countries but also to applicants from the EU. Taken together, the Erasmus replacement scheme and the Global Wales initiative present a case par excellence of a devolved administration pushing its way further into the international arena from the base of its devolved powers.

International strategy

The fortunes of the culture and education sectors over the last two decades as well as their current situation give ample proof that until the arrival of COVID-19 it was Brexit that was destined to end up as 'the great disruption'. In 2020 a much bigger rival for that accolade arrived. The coronavirus changed the world context utterly. Whereas at the beginning of 2020 one could, arguably, have had a debate as to whether other world markets offered a realistic alternative to the European market we were due to exit, now we faced life outside the EU knowing that the world was facing the biggest depression in a century. This would have massive consequences for the whole of the UK but especially for its poorer parts, in which we must, sadly but predictably, include Wales.

It was the rupture with the EU that made the development of a more robust international strategy for Wales a pressing priority. The task fell to Baroness Eluned Morgan in 2018, upon her appointment as Minister for International Relations and the Welsh Language in Mark Drakeford's new administration. A year of consultation saw the publication of that strategy in December 2019. It was an embryonic Welsh foreign policy. But then the world changed. A month later the COVID-19 pandemic was upon us all. One had to feel for Baroness Morgan. Not only did the pandemic descend swiftly after publication of the strategy, but by October 2020 Drakeford felt obliged, as a result of pandemic pressures, to switch Morgan to another post to assist the Minister for Health, Vaughan Gething, by taking responsibility for mental health. Responsibility for international relations reverted to the office of the First Minister. Given the pressures, this sudden switch seemed understandable, but one hopes it is only a temporary change for the international brief is too important to have to fight for the attention of a first minister already juggling so many balls.

A little history is necessary. We had to wait twenty years for the creation of the external affairs post (although Mike German, first deputy minister in the Labour-Liberal Democrat coalition, briefly held the post of Minister for Rural Affairs and Wales Abroad in 2002–3). The delay has always been difficult to explain, especially since the Scottish Government had a minister for external affairs within a year of the inception of the Scottish Parliament in 1999. It may have been that our previous First Ministers, Rhodri Morgan and Carwyn Jones, relished the international ambassador role, the latter perhaps even more so than the former. After all, Carwyn Jones had been instrumental in pushing for the abolition of the WDA, penning a 'Gregynog paper' on the issue in 2003 for the Institute of Welsh Affairs (IWA).[26] But neither can be said to have published a detailed international strategy, although a 2015 document during Carwyn Jones's tenure claimed to provide 'a framework'.[27]

In 2018 Mark Drakeford, as well as facing the prospect of Brexit, also had to find a role for Eluned Morgan whose credentials for the post must have seemed tailor-made for an international brief: two years at the international Atlantic College at St Donats, a degree in European studies and fifteen years as a Member of the European Parliament, where she was the Labour Party's spokesperson on energy, industry and science. Comparisons with the comparable Scottish post were instructive. There, for the most part, the international brief (designated external affairs) was paired with responsibility for culture, one of the lighter ministerial briefs. Drakeford's original intention was to do something similar in Wales – combining international relations with responsibility for the Welsh language, culture, tourism and sport. In both countries the load was shared with deputy ministers. But there was a difference. At the time in Scotland's Cabinet, Michael Russell, had responsibility not only for external affairs but also for the constitution and for Europe. His deputy was designated minister for Europe and international development, creating a strong European focus in the two posts. In Wales, in Drakeford's administration, it was a deputy minister, Lord Elis-Thomas, who led on tourism, culture and sport until his retirement in May 2021.

Although the list of Eluned Morgan's responsibilities when holding the international relations brief included 'Wales in Europe', the person who led on this issue in the 2016–20 WG was the counsel general, Jeremy Miles, the designated Brexit minister, a role that took in issues relating to the EU structural funds as well as the UK Shared Prosperity Fund that was scheduled to replace them. He also chaired the Cabinet sub-committee on European transition. The difference between the external briefs in Scotland and Wales at that time may be accounted for by the fact that Wales's counsel general could not exercise powers conferred on Welsh Ministers. According to a public note, Jeremy Miles's role involved policy advice and coordination, but 'any matter requiring a formal decision of Welsh Ministers under a statutory power will be exercised by the First Minister or a nominated portfolio Minister'.[28]

There was no doubt that in her short period in the international role the task of shaping an international strategy lay squarely with Eluned Morgan. It would be easy at any time to dismiss an international strategy for Wales as a cork on an ocean wave, but this one was launched in a truly forbidding climate. First, there were the hard facts of the scale of change. For more than fifty years we had been inside a big tent – competing with our EU partners, yes, but also sharing values and common rules. We had operated within a secure framework, part of a continental entity that has massive commercial clout in the world. We were also witnessing the continuation of financial austerity, increased instability in several continents and, in 2021, increasing tension between China and the Western world. The fact that a formal WG international strategy now exists and that related action plans are being elaborated should be a cause for increased optimism, but they will need to be pursued with extraordinary tenacity, and more resources, if they are to prevail against the current clouds. UK Government ministers, especially those of more ideological bent – and there is no shortage – will tell us not to worry. After all, the UK is the sixth largest economy in the world. But numbers matter and however you look at it, whether from a doctrinaire neoliberal standpoint or through our prime minister's imperial nostalgia, 60 million is a lot less than 500 million – in fact, about one-eighth. Proximity also tells.

Secondly, this is a very competitive environment. The Scots and the Irish have always had more clout than Wales in the international field because of their relative size, history and budgetary headroom. In 2019–20 WG's budget for international relations and international development was £7m, set against the equivalent Scottish budget of £24m. Similarly, the tourism budget in Wales was £16m, against Scotland's tourism budget of £45m. In 2020–1, despite a very significant increase of £3m (40 per cent) for international relations and development, the gap closed only slightly, with the Scottish figure also rising by £2m. Strangely, none of the £3m increase in the Welsh spend was devoted to more boots on the ground as WG was operating a freeze on staff numbers. Even so, the disparity in overseas staff numbers between the two countries is likely to remain as stark as the budget differences. Comparisons with Scotland – that can be made in many fields – are usually dismissed by WG ministers who can justifiably point to Scotland's greater size and to the more generous treatment given to it under the Barnett formula. A parallel generosity has been shown to Northern Ireland in the interest of peace. Nevertheless, such examples of *force majeure* confer very considerable advantages on those two countries in the international marketplace.[29]

A third Brexit-related challenge will come from Ireland, a country that will now be a more effective competitor, enjoying continued protection from the EU over and above the continued benefits of single-market membership as well as the benefits of Ireland's controversial lower corporation tax. The Irish Government spends close on €800m on foreign affairs and was scheduled to add another €54m to that budget in 2020. The new Brexit-dictated border down the Irish sea will surely mean that Northern Ireland will enjoy further spin-off from its southern neighbour's spend. Add to these factors the UK Government's new concentration on helping the north of England, as well as that region's increasing efforts to shape its own destiny, and one can see that Wales has an awful lot to do to be an effective competitor even with its UK and Irish rivals.

So, putting aside the budgetary constraints (which will almost certainly intensify given the effects of the pandemic on the public finances) how does Wales's new international strategy stand up to these challenges? The first plus must be the fact that we have a strategy at all. But that would be to damn it with faint praise. Apart from the 40 per cent increase in budget, the strategy has a strong values base – centred on Welsh creativity, technology and commitment to sustainability – set in the context of Wales's pioneering Well-being of Future Generations (Wales) Act 2015. The document's main focus is, of course, economic but, thankfully, it does not ignore the role of culture and sport in flying the flag for Wales internationally, although its treatment of both is cursory.

Its three overall aims are to raise the profile of Wales, to grow the economy through increased exports and inward investment, and to establish Wales as a globally responsible nation – citing the Future Generations Act and commitments to sustainable development and Wales in Africa. On the business and research front it wants to focus on three areas in particular: cyber security, compound semi-conductors and the creative industries. Some business people would have liked that list to be longer, but those who in the past have criticised the government for failing to prioritise can hardly complain. Where the document shares a common failing with some other WG strategy documents is in the relative absence of numbers and, I would argue, an excessively rhetorical style – as if we first have to convince ourselves.

Although there is a fair amount of data about current performance in its forty pages, there are only three numeric targets: an aim, over the next five years, to increase exports by 5 per cent from the current level of

£17.2bn (implying an increase of £860m); an aim to increase contacts amongst the worldwide Welsh diaspora to 500,000 (although it does not state the current level of contacts); and thirdly, an aim to plant 15 million trees in Uganda as part of its Wales in Africa programme. In the days before coronavirus the targeted 5 per cent increase in exports over the next five years would surely have seemed low given that, over the last three years, there had been a 29.7 per cent increase in exports from Wales: 2016 +10.4 per cent, 2017 +12.8 per cent, and in 2018 +4.3 per cent. These three years did follow two years of decline (2014 –4.9 per cent and 2015 –6.2 per cent) so that taking the five years together the overall increase was only 3.5 per cent.

Given the scale of increase in more recent years, targeting a 5 per cent increase over the next five seems unduly modest unless it assumes either a massive hit from Brexit, continuing volatility in export performance or, now, a new global depression. Interestingly, the export data does not suggest any difference in trends as between export performance in EU and non-EU markets, nor any shift from the former to the latter.

Table 9.1: Welsh exports 2013–2018 [30]

	EU		Non-EU		Total	
	£m	%	£m	%	£m	%
2013	9,836		6,774		16,610	
2014	8,314	–15.5	5,821	–14.1	14,135	–14.9
2015	7,997	–3.8	5,256	–9.7	13,253	–6.2
2016	8,852	10.7	5,778	9.9	14,630	10.4
2017	9,963	12.5	6,516	12.8	16,479	12.6
2018	10,534	5.8	6,656	2.1	17,190	4.3

Source: Welsh Government Statistics for Wales, *Statistical bulletin*, October 2018, p. 2.

If one compares 2013 with 2018 there was a 7.1 per cent increase in Welsh exports to the EU and a 1.7 per cent decline in our exports to non-EU countries. Interestingly, the biggest percentage increase over that five years was in exports to west European countries outside the EU (48 per cent), reinforcing the argument for the importance of proximity. Another striking feature is that when you combine exports to the EU with those to other European countries outside the EU, the European share of total exports has risen marginally but consistently in each of the last four years. In 2013 it stood at 62.5 per cent of the total, rising to 65.2 per cent in 2018.

Where the document could have been bolder on exports, it promised a new approach to the diaspora – a concept that too often invokes heady unrealism. Much depends on how the diaspora is defined. If we are talking about the descendants of people who emigrated from Wales in the nineteenth and twentieth centuries, Wales cannot claim a diaspora on anything like the scale of Ireland or Scotland. When, in the nineteenth century, the Irish fled their famine and the Scots their highland clearances, Welsh people congregated instead at home in the coal-mining valleys. It is the resulting disparity in emigration numbers that meant that, in the USA, the Welsh never developed the powerful and coherent political lobby that the Irish, and to a lesser extent the Scots, can mount even today.

On the other hand, the notion of a global Wales network of active connections and influence is one that has long needed more systematic organisation. (It was first proposed in the late 1990s by the IWA, which carried out a scoping study funded by the WDA.) It can build not only on past migration but also on the experience of post-war decades of foreign direct investment in Wales, existing trade, international academic research and cultural connections. WG has commissioned the Alacrity Foundation – an offshoot of Sir Terry Matthews's empire – to find a method of harnessing the diaspora. In a field often dripping with sentiment a hard-headed approach will be welcome.

Conclusion

Taking an old-fashioned view it might appear as if, by dint of both Wales's small size and the top-down nature of British Parliamentary sovereignty, an international dimension will never play a huge part in Welsh life or government. This could not be further from the truth. No generation in history has been more interconnected and interdependent than our own. That is true whether you look at business or science, the environment, education or art. Government, at whatever level, has to reflect and respond to the nature and conduct of a society that, in its daily living, is both local and international. Arguably, in

Wales government has been a follower not a leader in this respect. By now it is clearer than ever that the engagement of WG and Welsh organisations – be they businesses, arts organisations, universities or any other kind of civil society organisations – with those who labour in like vineyards in other countries is essential to sustain and improve our own performance. This is not about aggrandisement but about our real interests. It is for all these reasons that the devolved governments need their place at the table in many wider discussions, as of right not by grace and favour.

This is why an international strategy for WG is more central to our future than ever. And it needs to start closer to home. Working outwards, that should start by according the external affairs function full ministerial status within WG. It should then drop the idea of a 6-monthly meeting of stakeholders – a more probable platform for grandstanding – in favour of an external affairs stakeholders' group, working through sub-sets on particular policy fields: for instance, an environmental group, a trade group, a culture group, etc. In the cultural field there is a need to bring WG, ACW and the British Council into a more formal, action-focused partnership to coordinate mutually supportive activities. On a broader front, one can also imagine the harnessing of wider civic society through a Wales European, or civic forum. Such steps, taken together, rather than being a means of top-down direction, would be a way of harnessing and augmenting more effectively the energies from below.

The dimension that cannot be ignored in all this is the UK dimension, a currently fraught arena as a result of the Brexit aftermath and renewed centralising impulses. This is an arena from which Wales and the other devolved administrations are too often excluded by the UK Government, whether by intent or culpable neglect. It is clearly a problem at the highest level of heads of government, where it even threatens the stability of the whole of the UK. Neither is this a problem only for unionists. Whatever future is envisaged for these islands – unitary, federal or confederal – mechanisms for policy engagement across borders will be essential.

The issue persists at other levels too. It is not only the board of the British Council that lacks permanent representation from Wales, Scotland and Northern Ireland, but also crucial organisations such as UK Research and Innovation and the research councils. Many years ago the same could have been said of the board of Visit Britain, but there the gap was remedied, and the roof has not fallen in. The issue has its European dimension, too, where the Trade and Cooperation Act is totally silent on any role for the devolved administrations. Questions are bound to emerge about the possible input of Welsh and Scottish Governments into the envisaged UK-EU Partnership Council, paralleling their previous input within EU structures via UKREP.

But what of the global dimension? One of the conclusions of the British Council Wales 2018 report into the deployment of soft power is that in the current climate there is an increasing role for sub-state or non-state actors.[31] This, it argued, is the result of several global megatrends. They include geo-political instability, the digital revolution and, most importantly, the diffusion of power which, it says, has encouraged a host on non-state actors to join the global fray, giving regional governments a changing role in global affairs. Among these actors it included multi-lateral organisations, NGOs, philanthropies, multi-national corporations, civil society groups and trade unions. It regarded sub-state governments as perhaps the most important. In its own Well-being of Future Generations (Wales) Act 2015, Wales has a significant calling card that is, deservedly, attracting increasing world-wide attention. It is a powerful expression of values, and values matter. All these factors should be encouragement for us not to be cowed by those who wish to see relations between central and devolved governments as a zero-sum game, and devolved governments cabined and confined. That is also why we must insist on seeing the current agreement between the EU and the UK as a floor not as a ceiling, and to resist allowing our European continental focus to atrophy, even as we continue to engage with the rest of the world.

Despite the recent steps forward, there is yet room for sharpening our international strategy, for resourcing it better in terms of money and people, and for improving delivery by engaging non-governmental players more consistently and effectively. That work has begun, yet it is still a work in progress. Neither is it a strand of work that stands in isolation from all others. In the end the real foundation of a successful international strategy, and the factor most likely to get the world knocking at our door, will be the quality and flair of what we achieve here in Wales. The world starts at home.

Notes

1. Elin Royles, 'Substate Diplomacy, Culture and Wales', *The Journal of Federalism*, 46/2 (2016), 232.
2. NAW, *A Culture in Common*, para. 3.48 (Cardiff: NAW, 2000).
3. NAW, *Creative Future – Cymru Creadigol, A Culture Strategy for Wales* (Cardiff: NAW, 2002).
4. NAW, *A Culture in Common*, p. 57.
5. Interview with the author, 2020.
6. Interview with the author, 2020.
7. Yvette Vaughan-Jones, *International Showcasing Strategy for the Arts in Wales* (Cardiff: British Council Wales, 2018); Stuart Murray and Gavin Price, *Towards a Welsh Sports Diplomacy Strategy* (Cardiff: British Council Wales, 2020); Jonathan McClory et al., *Wales Soft Power Barometer 2018; measuring soft power beyond the nation state* (Cardiff: British Council Wales, 2018).
8. Vaughan-Jones, *International Showcasing Strategy for the Arts in Wales*, p. 5.
9. WG International Strategy, 'Notes towards a Culture chapter', ACW (2019), 10.
10. WG, *International Strategy* (Cardiff: WG, 2020), p. 25.
11. WG, *Action Plan: International Relations through Public Diplomacy and Soft Power 2020–25* (Cardiff: WG, 2020).
12. The others were: WG, *Priority Regional Relationships and Networks, Diaspora Engagement, Wales and Africa* and *Export Action plan* (Cardiff: WG, 2020).
13. WG, *Action Plan*, p. 3.
14. External Affairs and Additional Legislation Committee, NAW, *Report on the Welsh Government's Draft International Strategy* (Cardiff: NAW, 2019).
15. WG, *Action Plan*, p. 10.
16. *Times Higher Education World University Rankings*, 2021.
17. Geraint Talfan Davies, *The Single Market of the Mind – Education and Culture in Wales after the Europe Referendum* (Cardiff: IWA, 2017).
18. Universities UK, media release, September 2021.
19. Jonathan Adams and Karen Gurney, 'The Implications of International Research Collaboration for UK Universities', Digital Science and Universities UK (2016).
20. ESF – European Social Fund; Interreg – EU programme supporting interregional cooperation.
21. Davies, *The Single Market of the Mind*, p. 25.
22. Peter W. Halligan and Louise Bright, 'The case for growing STEMM research capacity in Wales', Leadership Foundation for Higher Education and the Learned Society of Wales (May 2015).
23. STEMM – Science, Technology, Engineering, Mathematics and Medicine.
24. House of Commons, 'The Erasmus Programme', Briefing Paper (2021).
25. Grahame Guilford, Hywel Ceri Jones and Gaynor Richards, 'Europe Matters to Wales: EU policy and funding opportunities for Wales 2014–2020' (November 2015).
26. Carwyn Jones, 'The Future of Labour', *The Gregynog Papers*, 3/4 (2004).

27. WG, *The Welsh Government's International Agenda* (Cardiff: WG, 2015).
28. WG website, May 2016–April 2021.
29. Stephen Orme, 'The Executive's International Relations and comparisons with Scotland and Wales', Northern Ireland Assembly Briefing Paper (2020).
30. Welsh Government Statistics for Wales, *Statistical bulletin* (October 2018), 2.
31. WG, *Action Plan*, pp. 4–5.

Select bibliography

Adams, Jonathan and Karen Gurney, 'The implications of International Research Collaboration for UK Universities', Digital Science and Universities UK (2016).

Davies, Geraint Talfan, *The Single Market of the Mind – Education and Culture in Wales after the Europe Referendum* (Cardiff: IWA, 2017).

Guilford, Grahame, Hywel Ceri Jones and Gaynor Richards, 'Europe Matters to Wales: EU policy and funding opportunities for Wales 2014–2020', November 2015.

Halligan, Peter W. and Louise Bright, 'The case for growing STEMM research capacity in Wales', Leadership Foundation for Higher Education and the Learned Society of Wales (May 2015).

Jones, Carwyn, 'The Future of Labour', *The Gregynog Papers*, 3/4 (2004).

McClory, Jonathan et al., *Wales Soft Power Barometer 2018; measuring soft power beyond the nation state* (Cardiff: British Council Wales, 2018).

Murray, Stuart and Gavin Price, *Towards a Welsh Sports Diplomacy Strategy* (Cardiff: British Council Wales, 2020).

NAW, *Creative Future-Cymru Creadigol, A Culture Strategy for Wales* (Cardiff: NAW, 2020).

Vaughan-Jones, Yvette, *International Showcasing Strategy for the Arts in Wales* (Cardiff: British Council Wales, 2018).

WG, *Action Plan: International Relations through Public Diplomacy and Soft Power 2020–25* (Cardiff: WG, 2020).

INDEX

A

A Culture in Common 237
A Living Language: A Language for Living 210
A Winning Wales 98
Aberystwyth University 186, 241, 243
Action for Children 186
Additional Learning Needs and Education Tribunal (Wales) Act (2018) 164
Advancing Gender Equality in Wales Plan 161
Agriculture Act 133, 134
Airbus 108
Alacrity Foundation 260
All Wales Convention 167
All Wales Ethnic Minority Association 154
Amsterdam Treaty 159
An Economic Renewal (2010) 103
Andrews, Leighton 48, 67, 77, 189, 193
Anglesey Aluminium 105, 106, 112
Air link Cardiff-Ynys Môn 101
Artes Mundi prize 239, 246
Arts Council for Wales 17, 237, 243, 244, 246, 261
Auditor General for Wales 43

B

Ban on smoking in Scotland and England 47

Bangor University 192, 243
Barcud 102
Barnardo's Cymru 185, 186
Barnett Formula 103, 110, 130, 135, 257
BBC (board of) 245
BBC National Orchestra of Wales 237, 240
Betsi Cadwaladr Health Board 46
Better Government for Older People Cymru 164
Bevan, Aneurin (Nye) 37
Bevan Commission 40, 50, 52
Bing, Xu 239
Black Voluntary Sector Network Wales 154
Blaenau Gwent 68
Blair, Tony (and Blairism/Blairite) 3, 6, 7, 8, 31, 120, 123, 124, 185, 237
Blyth 111
Bourne, Nick 17
Brennan, Kevin 1, 11, 15
Brexit 95, 108, 109, 121, 123, 125, 126, 127, 128, 129, 130, 131, 132, 133, 134, 135, 137, 139, 142, 143, 198, 225, 240, 243, 245, 248, 249, 253, 255, 257, 259
Brexit and our Land 137
British Council 237, 238, 244, 245, 246, 254, 261, 262
British Gigafactory 111

British-Irish Council 237
Brooks, Lord Jack, 4, 5
Brown, Gordon 43
BSC Port Talbot steelworks 112
Buckingham, Julia 249
*Building a Strategy for Children and
    Young People* 185
Burns, Angela 47
Butler, Rosemary 13
Buxton, Dorothy 181

C
Cameron, David 17, 18, 45, 124
Capaldi, Nick 244
Cardiff 102
Cardiff Airport 105
Cardiff Bay Barrage 3
Cardiff Singer of the World 236, 240
Cardiff University 186, 248, 250,
    254
Carlile, Alex, 18
Catalonia 220
Ceredigion death rates 42
Chapman, Christine 185
Children Act 2004 186, 191
Children and Families (Wales)
    Measure (2010) 184, 197
Children in Wales 186
Children, Young People and
    Education Committee 188,
    193, 214
Children's Commissioner for Wales
    162, 183, 186, 187, 188, 193,
    194, 197
China 97, 257
Chwarae Teg 185
City and Growth Deals 95, 98,
    107–9
Clapham Common 6
Clarke, Gillian 242
Climbié, Victoria 186

Clwyd, Ann MP 45
Coal Exchange, Cardiff 236
Coleg Cymraeg Cenedlaethol 213,
    222
Common Agricultural Policy (CAP)
    123, 130, 133, 135, 139, 142
Companies House 96
Conran, Alys 241
Conservative party 51
Conway, Lawrence 3, 18, 20, 37
Cornwall 110
Council of Europe 247
COVID/Coronavirus 31, 54, 56, 78,
    80, 84, 109, 110, 125, 129,
    143, 195, 198, 240, 243, 246,
    248, 249, 253, 255
Countryside Council for Wales 120
Creative Europe programme 242,
    243, 253
Creative Future 238
Crosland, Anthony 182
Cwmni Da 102
Cymdeithas yr Iaith Gymraeg 211
Cymraeg 2050 210, 211, 213, 214,
    215, 217, 218, 221, 223, 224,
    225, 226
Cymraeg i Blant 223
Cymraeg Byd Busnes 223
Cymru Yfory 168

D
Dafis, Cynog 237
Davidson, Jane 12, 21, 67, 120, 122,
    124, 185, 192
Davies, Alun 217
Davies, Andrew 4, 11, 24, 25, 27, 30
Davies, Jocelyn 19
Davies, Rhian 243
Davies, Ron 3, 6, 99, 119, 121, 153,
    155
Designed for Life 44, 45, 49

Department for the Environment, Food and Rural Affairs (DEFRA) 129, 133, 134, 139

Department of Trade and Industry 2, 97

Development Bank of Wales 106

Disability Wales 154

Donaldson, Graham 72

Dragon Studios 102

Drakeford, Mark 1, 4, 10, 15, 21, 22, 23, 28, 30, 31, 37, 39, 48, 55, 179, 184, 255, 256

Driver and Vehicle Licensing Centre 96

Dylan Thomas prize 239

E

Economic Resilience Scheme 138

Edinburgh Festival 246

Education Reform Act (1988) 65

Education and Learning Wales (ELWa) 66, 69, 99

Education and Training Action Group 66

Education Workforce Council 70

Edwards, Nicholas 38, 99

Elis-Thomas, Dafydd 182, 194, 256

English Nature 121

Entrepreneurship Action Plan 98

Environment Act (2016) 120, 129, 137, 140, 143

Environmental Agency 120

Equalities and Human Rights Commission 186

Erasmus EU exchange programme 109, 123, 251, 252, 253, 254

Essex, Sue 4, 12, 30, 122

Estonia 85, 86

Estyn 68, 72, 74, 75, 77, 78, 214

European Commission 131, 197

European Commission Regional Office 2–3

European Development Bank 123

European Environment Agency 127

European Food Safety Authority 127

European Parliament 242

European Regional Development Fund/Regional Funds 123, 127, 135, 243

European Union Aid (Objective One) 96, 98, 250

Evans, Sir Chris 104

Every child matters 186

External Affairs Committee 247

F

Florence, Peter 240, 241

Finance Wales 105

Finland 7, 86, 87

Fisher, John 240

Food, Farming and Countryside Commission 136, 142

Food Policy Alliance Cymru 142

Foot and mouth outbreak 11, 31

Ford engine plant 102

Forestry Commission 120

Foundation phase 27

Francis Report into Mid Staffordshire NHS Trust 45

Franco regime (language policy) 220

Freud, Anthony 240

Funky Dragon 184, 185, 186, 187, 188

Future Generations Commissioner 193, 194

G

Galeri, Caernarfon 243

General Teaching Council for Wales 70, 73

Geneva Declaration on the Rights of
     the Child 181
German, Mike 17, 18, 255
Gething, Vaughan 49, 255
Gibbons, Brian 43, 48
Glamorgan council 62, 63, 105
Global Wales 254
Glyn, Ifor ap 242
Goodway, Russell 4, 5
Gove, Michael 133
Government of Wales Act (1998) 95,
     154, 157, 167, 207
Government of Wales Act (2006) 14,
     154, 156, 172, 187
Gower, Jon 241
Grammar schools 63, 64
Gregynog Festival 243
Gregynog Paper 255
Griffiths, Lesley 48
Griffiths, Paul 5, 6, 14, 23, 28,
     30
Gwent 68
Gwyther, Christine 27

H

Hague, William 39
Hain, Peter 19
Hanus, Tomas 240
Hart, Edwina 4, 12, 23, 24, 25, 30,
     36, 37, 44, 48, 51
Hart, Julian Tudor 43
Harvard University 2
Hattersley, Roy 6
Hay Literature Festival 237, 240,
     241, 246
Health boards and trusts 49
Health and Harmony 133
Health and social care 36
Health Challenge Wales 45
Health Foundation report, *The Path
     to sustainability* 49

*Healthier Wales: Our Plan for Health
     and Social Care* 50, 55
'Heartbeat Wales' 37
Hijinx Theatre 241
Hitachi 106
Holyhead 63
Hopwood, Mererid 241
Horizon 106, 243, 249, 250, 251,
     253
Human Transplantation (Wales)
     Act 53
Hunt, David 38, 39
Hutt, Jane 4, 12, 19, 21, 30, 40, 43,
     122, 165, 185
Hywel Dda Health Board 47

I

Iaith Pawb 208, 209, 210, 226, 227
*Improving Health in Wales: A Plan for
     the NHS with its partners* 41
India 97
Industrial Revolution 96
Ineos Grenadier 111
Innovate UK 250
Institute of Welsh Affairs 255, 260
Intergovernmental Panel on Climate
     Change (IPCC) 128
Internal Market Act (2020) 111
Irish language policy 221
Islwyn 8, 9, 27

J

Jackson, Tessa 239
Jebb, Eglantyne 181
Johnson, Boris 124, 132
Jones, Carwyn 31, 48, 123, 161,
     187, 188, 189, 255, 256
Jones, Elin 19
Jones, Griffith 248
Jones, Harry 11
Jones, Helen Mary 8, 18, 27, 185

Jones, Hywel Ceri 251
Jones, Ieuan Wyn 16, 18, 19, 101,
    106

K
Kinnock, Neil 20, 21
Koenigs, Lothar 240
Korczak, Janusz 181

L
Labour 1, 2, 153, 169, 170, 256
    in Scotland 7
    New Labour 22, 31, 40, 66,
        185
    Welsh Labour 26, 120, 123,
        131, 141, 161, 168, 170,
        172, 182, 189, 190, 192,
        208, 213, 238
Labour Government 76
Lang, Aidan 240
Law, Peter 16, 17
League of Nations 181
'Learning Pathways' 71
LEADER initiatives 123
Learned Society of Wales 251
Learning to Live Differently 122
Lewis, Gwyneth 242
Lewis, Huw 68, 72, 189
LG factory 97
LGB Forum Cymru/Stonewall
    Cymru 154
Liberal Party 62, 169
Liberal Democrats 15, 16, 185,
    238
Life Sciences Hub Wales 104
Literature Wales 242
Llanddowror 248
Llanelli 8, 9, 27, 102
Llangollen International Eisteddfod
    236
Llwybr Newydd: New Path 141

Local authorities 63
Local Enterprise Partnerships
    (England) 107
Localism Act (2010) 107

M
Major, John 38
Mainstreaming Equality Strategy
    159
*Making the Connections: Delivering
    Better Services for Wales* 100
Marek, John 16, 17
Matthews, Sir Terry 260
May, Theresa 124
McAllister, Laura 245
Melding, David 10, 16, 17, 29, 30,
    185
Mercator Institute 241, 242
Merthyr Tydfil 42, 68
Michael, Alun 3, 4, 6, , 9, 12, 15,16,
    24, 31, 99, 184
Miles, Jeremy 256
Miliband, David 40
Miners' strike 64
Minority Ethnic Women's Network
    154
Montessori, Maria 181
Morgan, Eluned 217, 255
Morgan, Gillian (Dame) 13
Morgan, Huana 30
Morgan, Julie 4, 9, 30, 185
Morgan, Prys 2 , 25
Morgan, Kenneth O. 2
Morgan, Rhodri 1, 2, 3, 5, 6, 9, 162,
    185, 187, 188, 255
    MP for Cardiff West (1987) 3
    Select Committee on Public
        Administration 3
    NAW 3
    leadership campaign 7
    Liberal Democrat coalition 11

Morgan, Rhodri (continued)
  House of Commons 12
  Assembly coalitions 15
  Quangos 17
  Plaid coalition 18, 19, 20
  'clear red water' 23, 120, 121,
      164, 182
  and Welsh nationalism 25–6
  and Welsh Labour 123
  and Whitehall/Westminster 123,
      140
  legacy 29–31, 172, 184, 198
  influence of women 30
  and health 37, 38, 40, 43, 47,
      51, 52
  education 67, 79
  economy 99, 112, 123
Mudiad Ysgolion Meithrin 223

N
Nacro Cymru 186
National Academy for Educational
      Leadership 70
*National Approach to Professional
      Learning, The* 74
National Assembly Advisory Group
      (NAAG) 153, 155
National Assembly for Wales (also
      Welsh Assembly, Senedd) 1,
      122, 135, 141, 152, 153,
      156, 157, 158, 159, 164,
      167, 183, 185, 187, 188,
      189, 193, 197, 207, 208,
      209, 237, 238
  1999 Election 8
  2007 Election 17, 46, 61, 110
  2021 Election 31, 88, 141
National Academy for Educational
      Leadership 75
National College for School
      Leadership 74

National Curriculum 65
National Dance Company of Wales
      240, 241
National Farmers Union 133
NHS Directorate 37
NHS Wales 39, 41, 47, 101
*NHS Escalation and Intervention
      Arrangements* 46
National Museum Wales 239,
      240
National Partnership Forum for
      Older People 164
National Poet of Wales 242
Natural Resources Wales 120
National Survey for Wales 50
Neath Port Talbot 68
Network to Promote Linguistic
      Diversity 225
NoFitState Circus 240, 243
North American Free Trade
      Agreement (NAFTA) 126
NSPCC Wales 186

O
Ofcom 245
Office of National Statistics 96
Older People's Commissioner for
      Wales 162
One Wales coalition agreement/One
      Wales government 101, 102,
      189, 213, 215
One Wales: One Planet 122, 192
Optoelectronics 97
Organisation for Economic
      Cooperation and
      Development (OECD) 67,
      110
Osborne, George 123, 132
Otaka 240
Oxford University 2
Owen, John Wyn 37

P

Parliamentary Review of Health and Social Care in Wales, The 49
Plaid Cymru 1, 2, 15, 106, 182, 185, 208, 209, 213
Play Wales 186
Price, Adam 21, 26
Programme for International Student Assessment (PISA) 67, 79, 80
Project Skyline 136
Prosiect 2050 217, 220
Prudent Healthcare 39, 50, 52
Public Finance Initiatives 24
Public Goods Scheme 138
Public Health Wales 49
Pugh, Alun 238

Q

Qualifications, Curriculum and Assessment Authority (ACCAC) 69
Qualifications Wales 69
Quangos 17, 100
Qatar Airlines 105

R

Randerson, Jenny 12, 238
Redwood, John 39, 41, 99
Regulation and Inspection of Social Care (Wales) Act (2015) 191
Review of Maternity Services at Cwm Taf 46
Rhondda 8, 9, 27
Richard, Sir Ivor 13
Richard Commission 14, 167
Rights of Children and Young Persons (Wales) Measure (2011) 162, 164, 183, 184, 190, 193, 197
Rights to Action 183
Rizzi, Carlo 240

Royal College of Physicians 47
Royal Glamorgan Hospital 48
Royal Welsh College of Music and Drama 240
Rural Development Commission 121
Russell, Michael 256

S

Salmond, Alex 254
Save the Children 181, 186
School Effectiveness Framework 77
School Standards and Organisation (Wales) Act (2013) 214
Schools
    Welsh medium 63, 81
    Roman Catholic schools 81
    Church in Wales 81
Secretary of State for Wales 153
Sêr Cymru programme 251
Seth, Nikhil 122
Severn Barrage 106, 108
Shared Prosperity Fund 109, 110, 135
Sheers, Owen 241
Silk Commission 167
Singapore 85,
Smith, Dai 237
Social Services and Well-being (Wales) Act (2014) 53, 163, 164, 191
South Glamorgan County Council 2
South Korea 97
Spanish Civil War 236
SPECIFIC 104
Sport Wales 245
St David's Day 247
Starting to Live Differently 122
Stead, Peter 239
Striking the Right Balance 216
Sturgeon, Nicola 254

Swansea Bay Tidal lagoon 106, 107,
    111
Swansea University 186, 250
Swansea University Centre for Public
    Policy 22
Successful Futures 72
Sullivan, Mike 1, 5, 22, 23, 30, 40
Sustainable development 120–44
Sustainable Development
    Commission 121

T
Tanker drivers dispute 11
Techniums 99, 101
Temple of Peace 236
Thatcher, Margaret 38, 131
Theatr Mwldan, Cardigan 243
Third Sector Scheme 159
Thomas, Gwyn 242
Tinopolis 102
*Together for Health: A Five Year Vision
    for the NHS in Wales* 48
Tomos, Rhodri Glyn 19
Thomas, Gwenda 14, 15
Transgender Wales 153
Trusted to Care inquiry 46
Turing scheme 253, 254

U
UK Government 66, 105, 106, 127,
    156, 166, 186, 191, 206, 251,
    253, 256, 261
UN Special Rapporteur 196
UNCRC (Incorporation) (Scotland)
    Bill (2021) 193
UNESCO 180, 241
UNICEF 185
Universal Declaration of Human
    Rights 180, 181
United Nations Beijing Declaration
    and Platform for Action 159

United Nations Convention on
    the Rights of Persons with
    Disabilities 164
United Nations Convention on the
    Rights of the Child 162, 163,
    179, 180, 181, 182, 183, 185,
    186, 187, 190, 191, 193, 194,
    198
United Nations Development
    Programme 122
United Nations Framework
    Convention on Climate
    Change 143
United Nations Principles for Older
    Persons 164
United Nations Sustainable
    Development Goals 121, 192,
    198
Unity Festival 241
Universities UK 249
University of Wales 62, 248

V
Vaughan-Jones, Yvette 245
Velindre NHS Trust 49
Venice Biennale 238, 239
Violence against Women, Domestic
    Abuse and Sexual Violence
    (Wales) Act (2015) 162
Visit Britain 245, 262
Visiting Arts 245
Voluntary (also Third) Sector
    Partnership Council 157

W
Wales Act (2017) 156
Wales Arts International 237, 240,
    243, 244
Wales Centre for Health 41
Wales in Africa 258, 259
Wales Millennium Centre 241, 246

Wales Tourist Board 17, 100, 236
Wales Women's National Coalition 153
Wales UNCRC Monitoring Group 163, 186
Walker, Peter 37, 38, 99
Wanless Report, The, *The Review of Health and Social Care in Wales* 44, 48, 49
Wellbeing of Future Generations (Wales) Act (2015) 21, 53, 108, 120, 121, 124, 125, 134, 137, 140, 141, 143, 164, 192, 258, 262
Welsh Ambulance Services Trust 49
Welsh Baccalaureate 70
Welsh Conservatives 185
Welsh Constitutional Convention 153
Welsh Development Agency 3, 17, 96, 98, 99, 100, 101, 103, 236, 237, 260
Welsh Government (also Wales Assembly Government) 1, 11, 13, 14, 17, 22, 31,35, 40, 61, 69, 88, 97, 98, 101, 103, 104, 106, 107, 121, 151, 158, 159, 160, 161, 163, 164, 165, 168, 169, 170, 179, 182, 186, 187, 193, 194, 196, 197, 208, 210, 213, 214, 215, 216, 217, 218, 219, 220, 221, 223, 224, 225, 226, 227, 228, 236, 244, 246, 247, 256, 261
Welsh Health Planning Forum 37, 38, 39
Welsh Health Survey 42, 50
Welsh in Education Strategic Plan 213
Welsh Language Act (1993) 206, 207, 215

Welsh Language Board 215, 216, 218, 219
Welsh Language Commissioner/ Commission 216, 217, 219
Welsh Language Partnership Council 223
Welsh Language Promotion Grant 223
Welsh Language (Wales) Measure (2011) 209, 215, 216, 225
Welsh League of Nations Union 236
Welsh Local Government Association 187
Welsh National Opera 237, 240
Welsh Office 2, 65, 66, 96, 124, 155, 165, 172, 206, 220, 237
Welsh Technology Board 223
Welsh Youth Parliament 188, 193, 197
Wilkins, Williams 239
Williams, Emlyn 248
Williams, Kirsty 18, 68, 185
Williams, Raymond 237
Withybush Hospital, Haverfordwest 47
WOMEX 240
Wood, Leanne 18,
Woods, Alison 243
Worker Educational Association 2
WWF Cymru 142
Wylfa nuclear power plant 105, 107, 111

Y

Youth Matters 186

Z

Zhang, Xian 240